D1388356

THE CORPORATE TAKEOV

This book is

The Corporate Takeover of Ireland

KIERAN ALLEN
University College Dublin

IRISH ACADEMIC PRESS
DUBLIN • PORTLAND, OR

First published in 2007 by
IRISH ACADEMIC PRESS
44 Northumberland Road, Dublin 4, Ireland

and in the United States of America by
IRISH ACADEMIC PRESS
ISBS, Suite 300, 920 NE 58th Avenue
Portland, Oregon 97213-3786

7 by Kieran Allen
printed 2007
2007

www.iap.ie

British Library Cataloguing in Publication Data
An entry can be found on request

ISBN 978 0 7165 3411 2 (cloth)
ISBN 978 0 7165 3412 9 (paper)

Library of Congress Cataloging-in-Publication Data
An entry can be found on request

Printed by Biddles Ltd, King's Lynn, Norfolk

Contents

List of Tables

Table 1.1: Adjusted Wage Share of total economy – Compensation per employees as percentage of GDP at factor cost per person employed.

Table 4.1: The Rise of Tax Havens, 1999 and 2002

Table 4.2: Tax Written Off by Revenue Commissioners

Table 4.3: Major Components of Total Taxation in Ireland and EU Averages, 2002

Table 4.4: Inspection and Prosecutions carried out by Labour Inspectors

Table 5.1: Ranking of EU 15 according to how supportive their childcare system is to a dual earner model

Table 7.1: Beds by Categories of Long Stay Accommodation: Various Years

Table 8.1: EPA Audits, Compliance Record and Prosecutions

Table 8.2: Greenstar's Prices for Household Waste in Northeast Wicklow

Table 9.1: Rate of Return on Capital Employed by Vodafone and O2

List of Abbreviations

AIB	Allied Irish Banks
ASTI	Association of Secondary Teachers of Ireland
BCI	Broadcasting Commission of Ireland
CEO	Chief Executive Officer
CIE	Coras Iompair Eireann
CIF	Construction Industry Federation
CORI	Conference of Religious of Ireland
CPI	Centre for Public Inquiry
CRADA	Cooperative Research and Developments Agreements
CRH	Cement Roadstone Holdings
CWU	Communication Workers Union
DCU	Dublin City University
DETE	Department of Enterprise, Trade and Employment
EGFSN	Expert Group on Future Skills Needs.
EPA	Environmental Protection Agency
ERT	European Roundtable of Industrialists
ESB	Electricity Supply Board
FARC	Revolutionary Armed Forces of Colombia
FIRE	Finance, Insurance and Real Estate Sector
G-7	Group of seven richest nations
GAA	Gaelic Athletic Association
GATS	General Agreement on Trade in Services
GDP	Gross Domestic Product
GM	Genetically Modified
GNP	Gross National Product
GRTI	Georgia Tech Research Institute
HEA	Higher Education Authority

HSE	Health Services Executive
IBEC	Irish Business and Employers Confederation
ICT	Information and Communication Technology
ICTU	Irish Congress of Trade Unions
IDA	Industrial Development Authority
IEA	Institute for Economic Affairs
IFSC	Irish Financial Services Centre
IFSRA	Irish Financial Services Regulatory Authority.
IMF	International Monetary Fund
INM	Independent News and Media Plc
IPHA	Irish Pharmaceutical Healthcare Association
MRSA	Methicillin Resistant Staphylococcus Aureus
NIB	National Irish Bank
NRA	National Roads Authority
NTPF	National Treatment Purchase Fund
NUIM	National University of Ireland Maynooth
ODCE	Office of Director of Corporate Enforcement
OECD	Organisation of Economic Cooperation and Development
PAYE	Pay As You Earn tax
PPARS	Personnel Payroll And Related Systems
PPP	Public Private Partnership
PRSA	Personal Retirement Savings Account
R&D	Research and Development
RAE	Research Assessment Exercise
RTE	Radio Telefis Eireann
SFI	Science Foundation of Ireland
SIPTU	Services, Industrial, Professional and Technical Union
TASC	Think Tank for Action on Social Change
TRIPS	Trade Related aspects of Intellectual Property
UCC	University College Cork
UCD	University College Dublin
TCD	Trinity College Dublin
VAT	Value Added Tax
WTO	World Trade Organisation

Acknowledgements

Pierre Bourdieu once argued that sociology can only claim to be a science if it can unearth the hidden. He was referring to dense networks of power which are often invisible but which deeply affect the lives of many. Uncovering these power structures brings one into conflict with the privileged. Genuine sociology, Bourdieu argued, must therefore be subversive.

This study of corporate power in Ireland has tried to reveal a structure of corporate privilege which is immensely damaging for society. But, in all honesty, there was not much to uncover because the data is already out there. In fact, it is all over the newspapers, in government reports, in the annual statements of companies themselves. It is necessary only to connect the dots and to stand back and ask how we have allowed it to become so normal.

The vast bulk of research on Irish society is focused on the powerless. Sociologists study migrants, the homeless, drug addicts, women in the home, but rarely do they look inside the boardrooms of large corporations. This approach is sometimes undertaken for laudable reasons. Researchers want to 'give voice' to the underprivileged or they want to influence state policy so that some reforms are granted. The effect, however, has been to leave a great gap in the study of Irish society. Despite overwhelming evidence of links between the political and economic elites, the activities of business people and the networks they form is largely under-studied.

Much of the material for this book is, therefore, drawn from non-academic contemporary documentary sources. It rests on the hard investigative work undertaken by others and it is my sincere hope that I have acknowledged this through the references I have provided in each chapter.

It is, however, impossible for any academic to interpret this data alone. Over the past two years I have interviewed many people who have very concrete understandings on how corporations affect their areas of work. Many would prefer to remain nameless for a variety of reasons but I would particularly like to thank Maura Harrington, Michael O'Seighin, Joe Fogarty, Deirdre de Burca, Fergus O'Dowd TD, Joe Moore, Dr Peader O'Grady, Niall Smyth, Bob Quinn, Brian Trench and Dr Joe Barry and Louise O'Reilly for setting aside time for interviews. I would also like to express sincere gratitude to those public officials who still regard it as their duty to provide citizens with information as their right. This is in remarkable contrast to the ethos of the private sector.

A number of people have read over the various chapters and made helpful comments. They include Willie Cumming, Mary Kelly, Marnie Holborow, Paula Brudell, Peadar O'Grady, Joe Moore, Charles Allen, Dave Palcic, Mike Milotte and Bryan Fanning.

Finally, I was always delighted to see a shining light ahead and express my particular appreciation to its holder, Kulwant Gill.

Introduction

The air does not come any cleaner than in North Mayo as gusts from the Atlantic bring wind and rain over a landscape, covered in miles of blanket bog. New houses built by returned migrants are dotted all around as many seek a lifestyle that is slower and a little different to New York or London. Many fled with bitter memories, but returned to a place which can still give glimpses of a rare communion between people and nature. An announcement, however, in 1996 that a major gas field had been discovered seventy kilometres off the coast ruptured the rural peace. What followed was a titanic struggle that split neighbour from neighbour but then united them in opposition to Shell, one of the largest corporations in the world.

Shell committed five local Rossport men to prison for defying a court injunction to allow them to lay a massive pipeline through their lands. Willie Corduff, Micháel O'Seighin, Brendan Philibin, Phillip and Vincent McGrath wanted to defend their area's beautiful heritage and made only the most modest of demands. They asked Shell to process the gas at sea rather than run a pipeline inland. After their imprisonment a tremendous crowd of 5,000 people assembled in Belmullet to shout 'Shell go to hell'. Many believed that a battle that Michael Davitt had fought a hundred years ago was being re-run – but this time it was not against landlords but global corporations. 'We are Irish citizens not corporate subjects', proclaimed one placard. It caught a mood that went very far beyond the beautiful landscape of North Mayo.

Gas is often found as part of a complex of hydrocarbons,

which contain other trace elements. These elements have to be separated out and the gas dried so that it can be transported for long distances. In Ireland, it travels on a national grid and can then go, via an inter connector, to power stations in Britain and beyond. Typically, the processing of gas is carried out at sea either on huge floating or fixed platforms. Alternatively, the gas could be pumped for some distance and then processed in a shallow water fixed steel jacket off the main shore. Both these options limit the damage to the immediate environment because emissions and discharges can be dispersed far out to sea.

However, large corporations show little concern for local environments and Shell was certainly no exception. In 1995, it tried to sink the redundant Brent Spar platform into the depths of the North Sea, and was only stopped by a public outcry. It has destroyed much of the Niger Delta with oil spills that have poisoned local water sources. It forged a bloody alliance with the Nigerian dictatorship to protect its plunder, and was implicated in the hanging of Ken Saro Wiwa. So when it took over the original company that discovered the gas off North Mayo, alarm began to spread.

The original company was Enterprise Energy Ireland, and it proposed to build an onshore refining terminal at Bellanaboy, which is eight kilometres inland. A certain gloss was put on this by referring to an 'offshore landline' going to a refinery in a 'coastal area'. The company probably thought that the natives would not get too restless as long as there was a little PR spin and some familiar exercises in 'consultation with stakeholders'. It calculated that it could then override any residual opposition and have a pipeline complex travel across a deep, unstable bog to reach the Bellanaboy terminal. In places, the pipeline would come within seventy metres of houses, and this was particularly worrying because of the high pressures that would be used. Pressure in gas pipelines is measured in bars – a bar being the equivalent to fifteen pounds per square inch. The tyres of an average car contain about two bars while the national gas grid that connects Cork to Dublin can run at around eighty bars. The pipeline from the Corrib gas field to the refinery in Bellinaboy was, however, originally designed to take pressures of up to 345 bars. This was exceptionally high and was, according to the Minister for Marine and Natural Resources, 'unique both in Ireland and Europe'.[1]

When Shell took over the lead role in the project, it had its own reasons for taking risks. By processing the gas inshore, it could save €360 million in capital costs and reduce its operating costs by 40 per cent a year.[2] Moreover, if this experiment in using high pressure pipelines to refine the gas 'inshore' worked in North Mayo, it could be spread elsewhere. That possibility was singularly attractive for a company that was facing some very big problems. More than a decade previously, the markets discovered that its annual rate of return on investment averaged just 7.9 per cent when the industry average at the time was 9.3 per cent.[3] Fearing a run on its shares, Shell imposed high targets on its global divisions to build up their reserves. The move, however, backfired because, like the Siberian commissars who got orders from Moscow in the old Soviet regime, the local managers learnt to inflate the figures for headquarters. Suddenly matters went from bad to worse when huge 'losses' were discovered in Shell's oil and gas reserves in Nigeria and Australia, and nearly five billion barrels of oil were supposed to have gone missing from its proven reserves.[4] The pressure was on Shell to cut costs, and if that meant a dangerous pipeline in Mayo, so be it.

Shell, however, took no account of the power of grassroots mobilization. Environmentalism as a wider philosophy may have had little purchase in north Mayo, but activists soon emerged who became amateur experts on pipelines. 'That bloody company has forced me to learn more about pipe line safety than I ever wanted to know', said Micháel O'Seighin.[5] Although long retired as a schoolteacher and looking forward to gardening and music, he found himself devoting hours to internet research. He learnt that pipeline accidents are uncommon – but, unfortunately, they do occur. In 2004, for example, eighteen people died in a gas pipeline explosion in Ghislenghien in Belgium, and in August 2000, eighteen died in New Mexico when an underground natural gas pipeline ruptured. Others, such as Maura Harrington, had a long experience of activism that stretched from H Block campaigns to women's rights to fighting the union bureaucracy in the Irish National Teachers Organization. They were joined by Mark Garavan, a local sociology lecturer who had learnt carefully how to articulate an argument to a mass media. Together they formed the local Shell to Sea campaign that also included Jerry Cowley, the independent TD for the area. It met every Sunday night to plan the opposition.

The political establishment, however, were firmly behind Enterprise Energy Ireland and later the Shell-led consortium. Frank Fahey, the Minister for Communications, Marine and Natural Resources, hosted a public meeting in Geesala to mobilize support for the project.[6] Within the cabinet, the Taoiseach, Bertie Ahern and Frank Fahey worked assiduously to promote the company's interests. They introduced a Gas (Amendment) Act of 2000 to allow a person other than Bord Gais to build a pipeline. They brought in a statutory instrument to give the Minister power to grant Compulsory Purchase Orders to acquire land for the pipeline.[7] Normally these orders are reserved for state projects but this was the first time ever that a Compulsory Acquisition Order was to be used for the benefit of a private company. Fahey's department also convened a special Marine Licence Vetting Committee that rejected the idea of processing the gas offshore.[8] Coillte, the state-owned forestry company, sold over 400 acres to the consortium as a site for the refinery but would not reveal the exact price, claiming privilege under the laws of 'commercial secrecy'.[9] Bord Gais, the state-owned gas company, agreed to build a special extension to the national grid to receive gas from the Corrib field, even before planning permission was granted.[10]

The protestors received only one positive official response when Kevin Moore, a senior planning inspector of Bord Pleanala, recommended that Shell should not receive planning permission for the project. He argued that, 'it was difficult to move away from a now informed opinion that the choice of preferred option is primarily based upon the cost difference between it and other offshore options ... rather than on environmental or technical constraints'.[11]

However, neither Shell nor the political elite was deterred. After An Bord Pleanala initially turned down the planning application, the Taoiseach, Bertie Ahern and Frank Fahey held a special meeting with Shell executives to assure them that an appeal would be dealt with as speedily as possible. Four days after the meeting, top officials from An Bord Pleanala, including its chairperson and deputy chairperson, met with a delegation from Shell and the Irish Offshore Operators Association, the industry body for the oil and gas moguls. The delegation made a twenty-minute presentation on 'The Case for Indigenous Gas' and asked the board for general guidance on how a large complex planning application might be approached by the developer.[12] Shell duly re-submitted their application and one year later it was granted.

When people face threats to their bodily security, they naturally turn to the state for justice. The state, after all, is supposed to protect the constitution and guarantee rights for all its citizens. Where there is conflict between 'the environment' and 'development' the state, it is believed, should mediate to promote the common good. Yet the story of this book is precisely about how this legitimate desire has become utopian. Far from receiving support from their state, local people have been baton charged by the Gardai for daring to protest at the building of Shell's refinery. The political state that was supposed to serve the people as a whole has been replaced by a corporate state.

The Irish state has long adopted a subservient role to the oil corporations. In the late 1960s, Marathon Oil was granted a licence that effectively gave it control of the south coast of Ireland for a nominal sum of just €635.[13] It then went on to discover large quantities of natural gas off the Kinsale Head and signed an agreement with An Bord Gais to supply 125 million cubic feet of gas per day for twenty years. After this debacle, Justin Keating, Minister for Industry and Commerce in 1975, introduced more stringent exploration terms, including a tax rate of 50 per cent; a maximum 50 per cent stake for the state in any commercial wells; production royalties of between 8 per cent and 16 per cent; obligations to drill at least one well within three years within the licence field and more limited ownership rights for the oil and gas corporations.

Due to a slowdown in worldwide exploration and production, this was modified in 1985 to allow for a sliding scale of royalties and state participation. However in 1987, a fundamental change occurred when Ray Burke became Minister for Energy. Burke entered into direct and private negotiations with Marathon executives against the advice of his top officials. He told a senior official to give the company 'whatever they are looking for' in discussions about the price of gas from the Kinsale head.[14] He abolished the requirement that the state have a 50 per cent stake in any commercial project and that royalties be taken. He also introduced a clause facility whereby exploration, development and production expenses extending back 25 years could be written off against tax.

Subsequently, the Flood Tribunal branded Ray Burke as the recipient of corrupt payments after it was discovered that he had received €200,000 in political donations. The tribunal noted that money that he received from Century Radio

> ensured that he was available to serve the interests of Century's promoter, as is evidenced by his willingness to meet with their bankers and to give them assurances that he would take steps, including, if necessary, the introduction of legislation which would be to Century's benefit.[15]

With a Minister with this appalling record, the Irish people had little defence against the oil companies.

Burke rejected a proposal to reduce the 50 per cent tax rate on profits, claiming that it would be 'over-generous'.[16] Five years afterwards, however, Bertie Ahern showed his generous side when he became Minister for Finance and introduced new terms for oil and gas exploration. Tax rates were cut to 25 per cent and the companies were given full ownership of the fields. Future governments, it appears, were bound into a tax regime that could not be changed during the lifetime of an authorization. The corporations were not required to sell oil or gas to the Irish state at 'bulk discount' prices but could benefit from full market prices. The 1992 terms also granted generous frontier licences that effectively gave corporations full control over vast areas for up to twenty-one years. The terms were so good for business that the World Bank rated Ireland as one of the top seven countries that offered 'very favourable' terms for exploration. By contrast, George Bush's home state of Texas was rated 'tough'.[17]

Since the 1992 terms were announced, large tracts of the sea have been handed over to global corporations. Some were even able to purchase reports about their chosen fields, which contained seismic and geological data that had been drawn up by the Irish state. For the princely sum of €10,157 this data was made available to those who were considering drilling in the Porcupine Basin and elsewhere. Not surprisingly, they have managed to find oil and gas comparatively quickly. Enterprise Oil, for example, drilled only three wells offshore in Ireland between 1984 and 1996 and all three produced an oil show – including the largest struck in the Corrib field.[18]

The hand-over of natural resources has not only benefited foreign multinationals but also some very wealthy Irish business people. Providence Resources, whose main shareholder is Tony O'Reilly, won a licence for the Dunquinn Prospect in the Porcupine Basin. The licence cost €11,000 plus an annual rental of €27 per square kilometre to enjoy the bountiful terms introduced by Bertie Ahern. Less than two years after winning the licence, Providence Resources did a deal with Exxon-Mobil, a company that O Reilly had previously close connections with. Under the terms of the agreement, the giant US corporation will spend up to €100 million developing the prospective area while Tony or Sir Anthony O'Reilly is set to make more than €1.4 billion as the oil and gas flows. The Irish state will gain almost nothing.

In a world where oil and gas supplies are becoming more scarce and many warn that it has already reached 'peak oil', these are extraordinary arrangements. Other countries have decided to put social interests over the apparent 'rights' of ownership claimed by large corporations. Hugo Chavez's Venezuela has not only nationalized the oil but has offered to sell some at subsidized prices to the poor in North America. In Bolivia, the government of Eva Morales sent in troops to occupy the gas fields and retake them for the country. It may be argued that these poorer countries desperately needed to control their resources – and undoubtedly they do. But Ireland is hardly known for its quality public services and lavish budgets devoted to public facilities. Might not some of the natural resources that have so generously been bestowed on global corporations and their wealthy Irish allies been better spent on cutting waiting lists in public hospitals?

When asked in an interview with *Forbes* magazine in September 1983, how he managed to secure potentially lucrative blocks for exploration, Tony O'Reilly gave an unusually candid answer. He told the magazine that his geologist had chosen six blocks of the seabed for exploration and added, 'Since I own 35 per cent of the newspapers in Ireland, I have close contact with the politicians. I got the block he (the geologist) wanted.'[19] It was a comment that revealed more about how the political system really works than any number of worthy, official explanations. In modern society all are supposed to have an equal say in the running of their countries – but some get to be heard much quicker.

The oil and gas companies make no secret of the fact that they devote considerable resources to lobbying politicians. Shell, the principal company involved in the Corrib field, spent $27 million and employed 120 lobbyists between 1998 and 2004 just to promote its interests with the US federal government. Marathon, who are also involved in the Corrib consortium, spent €29 million.[20] At least in the US one can track these activities, whereas in Ireland lobbying takes a far less open form. Marathon Oil, however, has contributed to Fianna Fail and Enterprise Oil has hosted a table at Fianna Fail's fund raising event at the Galway races.[21] Yet even without these direct donations, it is clear that oil companies exercise a considerable influence over the Irish government. Their control of vast resources, of technology and expertise and, crucially, their close ties to the power of the US state means that they have leverage over Irish politicians. Perhaps that is the only plausible interpretation as to why the Irish state has gone to extraordinary lengths to look after their interests in Mayo.

Against such formidable opponents, a small activist campaign has taken on the global corporations. Instead of looking to their own state for protection, they look to other communities around the world for ideas on how to confront Shell. It is a striking case of how corporate globalization is being matched by a globalization of resistance. The Annual General Meeting of Shell has become a meeting point where opponents from around the world sometimes gather to strategize. Activists from County Mayo in Ireland travel to meet others from Port Arthur Texas who complain that 80 per cent of their neighbours who reside near a Shell refinery suffer from respiratory and heart conditions. They, in turn, liaise with Nigerian activists who have never forgiven Shell for their complicity in the murder of the Ogoni leader, Ken Saro Wiwa in 1995. Or they may link up with activists from Durban, South Africa who protest that a jointly-owned refinery of Shell and BP dumps nineteen tons of sulphur dioxides a day into the air that their poor community breathes. Or with campaigners from Vila Caricoca in Sao Paola in Brazil where Shell has operated large fuel-holding tanks without a valid permit.[22]

From across the globe, these activists despise the banality of a corporate language, which talks of partnership while worsening the lives of many of their neighbours. They are tired of the endless dialogues, the projects and pilot projects – the 'greenwash' that pretends a concern for the environment while carrying on in the usual way. They want action – and sometimes will take direct action to achieve their goals. Welcome to the world of grassroots activism and the fight against the corporate takeover of the world.

To understand what is at stake, we need to move from the local to the global to see how large corporations are taking over our world.

NOTES

1. 'Shell seeking injunctions against seven opposed to gas pipeline', *Irish Times*, 7 March 2005.
2. An Bord Pleanala, Inspector's Report Development of Gas Terminal at Bellagelly South, Bellanaboy, Belmullet Co Mayo, Register Reference 01/900, p.197.
3. 'Shareholders want to know where Shell's reserves went', *Observer*, 18 January 2004.
4. I. Cummins and J. Beasant, *Shell Shock: The Secrets and Spin of an Oil Giant* (London: Mainstream Publishing, 2005), p.25.
5. Interview with author.
6. 'Corrib Gas Seminar in Geesala', *Western People*, 20 July 2001.
7. Centre for Public Inquiry, *The Great Corrib Gas Controversy* (Dublin: CPI, 2005), p.31.
8. Ibid., p.32.
9. In a phone call to author.
10. 'The Corrib Diary: Never Ending Saga', *Western People*, 8 July 2005.
11. An Bord Pleanala, Inspectors Report Development of Gas Terminal, p.69.
12. CPI, *The Great Corrib Gas Controversy*, p.42.
13. S. Mara, Gas Lads, *Magill* 2002 http://www.corribsos.com/index.php?id=54.
14. F. Connolly, 'Burke insisted on price concessions for Marathon Oil', *Sunday Business Post*, 27 May 2001.
15. *The Second Interim Report of the Tribunal of Inquiry into Certain planning Matters and Payments* (Dublin: Stationery Office, 2002), p.139.
16. CPI, *The Great Corrib Gas Controversy*, p.59.
17. Ibid., p.65.
18. Ibid., p.66.
19. F. Connolly, 'O'Reilly: More Mega Millions', *Village*, 11 May 2006.
20. Lobby Watch, Centre for Public Integrity, www. publicintegrity.org/lobby/search.
21. CPI, *The Great Corrib Gas Controversary*, p.68.
22. Friends of the Earth, *Behind the Shine: The Other Shell Report 2003* (London: Friends of Earth, 2003).

Chapter One

The Rise of the Mega-Corporation

There is no escape from corporations in the modern world as their logos and advertising jingles are everywhere. They enter our subconscious and we are invited to construct our very identities around their products. We have become so used to them that we barely notice how they function. They are the background and the foreground of everything we do in late capitalism.

Historically, however, corporations are a comparatively recent phenomenon and their vast power would astonish a time traveller from the not-so-distant past. A corporation can be defined as an entity of indefinite duration, which has all the legal rights of a person.[1] This may seem a rather vague definition but it conveys at least one unusual legal feature – the equation of a business organization with a living, feeling human being. Unlike humans, however, a corporation is protected by the laws of limited liability. This means that whatever debts it incurs are not the property of the individuals who own the company. This is quite a privilege and so corporations were originally only allowed to operate under a special charter granted by the king or queen. These charters were handed out to particular favourites who, presumably, had their own ways of doing a good turn for their monarch.

The most famous early corporation was the East India Company that was formed in 1600 from a charter granted by Queen Elizabeth I to a group of London merchants. It grew into a colossus that robbed the treasures of India and established its own private army to run the sub-continent. Its activities became legendary because of the ruthless way it plundered the country.

On one occasion, it manipulated the local grain market in Bengal by buying up rice when the dry season foretold a shortage, contributing to a famine that killed 10 million people. At the height of the famine in 1770 it even increased the land tax on the peasantry. India's first Prime Minister, Jawaharlal Nehru noted that, the word 'loot' was originally a Hindu word that made its way into the English language through the activities of the East India Company.[2] Edmund Burke, the Irish writer who became the founding intellectual of modern conservatism, was so shocked by its activities that he tried to have Warren Hastings, the Chief Executive Officer of the company, impeached in the House of Lords. Unfortunately, Hastings was acquitted.

The savage history of the East India Company established a link in the popular mind between corporations and colonialism. When the American revolution overthrew the rule of King George III, charters to establish corporations came to be controlled by an elected parliament. Individual states such as Maryland decreed that depending on their line of business, companies could only be formed for twenty, forty or fifty years as a safety measure. An early American pamphleteer, Thomas Earle, explained that, 'chartered privileges are a burden, under which the people of Britain and other European nations groan in misery'.[3] The American states limited the number of charters that were issued and by 1800 only some 200 charters were granted. Often the legislators also stipulated clauses limiting the capital that might be accumulated or, in the case of Pennsylvania, established a fund so that a share of their income had to be put back into public utilities. During the American Civil War, however, corporations became more powerful as they accumulated huge profits from the conflict. With increased financial muscle they were able to send 'borers' – company agents – into the House of Congress to argue for their charters to be liberalized.[4] So by the end of the nineteenth century, US corporations acquired the same legal rights as citizens and the registration of companies became a mere formality.

Since those early days, corporations have grown into enormous networks of economic power. Contrary to their own mythology, they did not normally grow as lone wolves who thrived in the wilds of the market place. Often they forged close

networks with political elites who sheltered them from competition and carved out special profitable niches for them.
Sometimes they grew to a critical mass and then created 'captive
markets' through government contracts or they manipulated
markets in their favour. Today this has become more common
because corporations are no longer dwarfed even by the global
market but rather dominate vast segments of it. They do not
pretend to be subservient to local states but use their formidable
strength to manipulate those states to serve their interests. Of
the top 100 economic entities in the world, fifty-two are now
corporations and only forty-eight are countries.[5] A company
such as General Motors or Shell controls more economic
resources than countries such as Denmark, Indonesia, Greece,
Finland, Portugal or Ireland. The top people of Goldman Sachs
share out more money than the entire income that is divided
between the people of Tanzania.[6]

Yet if there is a comparison in terms of size, there is none in
governance structures. General Motors or Shell is controlled by a
Board of Directors, which is elected by its shareholders. It is not
a democratic body as each shareholder votes according to the
amount of wealth he or she possesses. So a modest shareholder
may have one or two votes whereas a wealthy family may have a
million. Its internal structure is, therefore, based on a dictatorship
of money. Moreover, what may appear as one corporation at first
sight can in reality be a cluster or network of wealth as different
corporations hold shares in each other. It follows, therefore, that
the board of directors of one corporation is often controlled or
influenced by executives from others. So the board of General
Motors is composed of the Chief Executive Officer of Merrill
Lynch, plus the Vice Presidents of Pfizer and Du Pont and the
retired Chairpersons of Astra Zenica, Compaq computers,
Eastman Kodak, Sara Lee Jeans Corporation, Northrop
Grumman and Ernst and Young. What appears as a brand name
on cars, is, in fact, an image behind which shelters an extraordinary concentration of wealth

Most countries, by contrast, assign each citizen one vote and
they elect into governments citizens from different social backgrounds. Formally, the governing principle is democratic and
rulers claim legitimacy by adhering to the 'will of the people',
even if that will is only expressed in elections which occur every

three or four years. Laws may be biased in how they are drafted or how they are implemented but ultimately they demand obedience because they have been drafted by representatives of the people. Governments also acknowledge certain equality between human beings at a formal legal level and the citizenry is officially composed of people with equal human rights. All are supposed to be equal before the law and no one can claim to be 'above the law'. From this it follows that governments are also supposed to pursue the common good or to advance the interests of the nation rather than the purely selfish interest of the wealthy – or at least that is their formal position.

None of these principles of democracy, however, are accepted even at a formal level in corporations. A corporation can unashamedly reward its directors with performance bonuses, special pension schemes, inordinate salaries or golden parachutes on retirement – and need answer to only a tiny number of shareholders. It can sack employees who had linked their careers and hopes to its fortunes for decades – with no explanation. It can engage in rule-breaking and illicit trading and, if caught, sacrifice only a few figureheads. Not only can it do these things, but it is almost required to act like a collective psychopath to succeed.[7] Companies who do not behave as asocial entities, who show any feeling towards rivals or become sentimental about employees will be driven out of business. So when most of the economic resources of the planet fall into the control of corporations rather than governments, something profound has happened.

BIG PHARMA

The changes are sometimes difficult to comprehend and may best be illustrated by the way one product is organized and sold.

Most of us, at some point in our lives, will purchase drugs – or pharmaceuticals, the term used to denote legal substances. Ireland has become a major global centre for the industry that represents about 19 per cent of the country's exports. The Irish state has gone to enormous lengths to attract the pharmaceutical industry, allowing the corporations to enjoy low taxes and helping them find suitable locations. Since the early 1980s, Ringaskiddy has become one of the main locations because it gives the corporations access to vast amounts of fresh water and allows them to discharge their waste water easily. To facilitate their activities, Cork County Council created the largest capacity of processed water in the country while the Electricity Supply Board (ESB) installed the required power supply.[8] Many of the corporations were also given special pollution licences to incinerate waste material on site.

But who exactly are these corporations on which so much is bestowed?

Approximately ten pharmaceutical companies – Pfizer, Johnson and Johnson, GlaxoSmithKline, Sanofi-Aventis, Novartis, Hoffmann La Roche, Merck, Astra Zenica, Abbot Laboratories and Bristol-Myers Squibb, control more than half of all the legal drugs that are sold on the planet. Most have a manufacturing facility in Ireland. The largest corporation, Pfizer, now controls one eighth of the global drugs market. Twelve men and two women with an average age of 65 make the final decision on which drugs are produced by the corporation. It is doubtful if their principal motivation is the welfare of the sick as is evident when we ask a simple question: does the industry have an interest in developing drugs for which there is great need but from which one can derive little profit? The answer is, unfortunately, no. Tropical diseases are the main killers of the world's people but only sixteen of the 1,393 new drugs that reached the market between 1975 and 1997 were for tropical diseases and tuberculosis.[9] Pharmaceutical companies simply do not invest in what Médecins Sans Frontières have called the 'neglected diseases'.[10]

Instead the tiny number of people who sit on the boards of the pharmaceutical corporations decided to focus their products on the comparatively healthier Western world. About half of the €400 billion sales of pharmaceutical drugs go to the US where people pay high prices for the products. In 2002, the average price of the fifty drugs most used by US senior citizens was nearly $1,500 for a year's supply.[11] This strategy has made the industry by far the most profitable sector of modern capitalism – that is until very recently. In 2003, it lost its first place position and came in third place behind oil and banking.

Pharmaceutical corporations use their enormous economic resources to shape political decision-making around the world.

If they choose to, they could produce cheap generic drugs, but they prefer to sell 'branded' drugs that are far more expensive. To protect their brands, they influence states and get them to insist that no one copies their 'patents'. In other words, rivals are not allowed to use the chemical formulae to make cheaper generic versions of their drugs until patents have expired. The big corporations have especially targeted countries like India where companies such as Cipla can produce medicine for a fraction of the cost charged by 'Big Pharma'. Even if vast numbers of people suffer from a terrible illness such as HIV, the corporations use their political muscle to deny them access to generic drugs for as long as possible. In 2001, pharmaceutical companies that were led by GlaxoSmithKline took the South African government to court to stop them licensing cheaper generic drugs to fight HIV. The companies only backed down after an enormous global campaign that targeted their inhumane activities. Even after this case, they have worked closely with the Bush regime to attack the use of these generic drugs to treat HIV.[12]

The corporations claim that they must take this tough line because they need to devote colossal sums to research. Their research costs may certainly appear large but the top ten companies only spent 13 per cent of their sales on research in 2002 – compared to 31 per cent of sales revenue that went on 'marketing and administration'.[13] 'Marketing' is a general term that covers all sorts of activities. There are now 80,000 sales people in the US and their main role is to pester doctors to take their particular drugs. They do it because they think it works. Doctors who are exposed to visits from sales reps promoting anti-depressants, for example, are more likely to favour these drugs over non-drug therapy. They will also prescribe more expensive anti-depressants even when less costly alternatives are available.[14]

Pfizer alone has 38,000 foot soldiers in its global sales force team and they use a lavish expense account to wine and dine their medical quarry.[15] Some of their marketing techniques are seen as more than a little dubious. On one occasion it took sixty doctors on a trip to France to attend a Heineken Cup Munster rugby match.[16] Not to be outdone, Novartis also picked up the bill for allowing Irish psychiatrists to stay in the exclusive K Club in Kildare for two nights so that they could listen to lectures about hyperactivity. It transpired that Ritalin, which is manufactured by Novartis, was recommended as the drug to deal with the syndrome.[17]

A considerable proportion of the research activity of the pharmaceutical industry is concentrated on 'me too' drugs which are closely related to drugs whose patent is running out.[18] By producing these slightly newer drugs, the companies hope to maintain a share of lucrative markets. So there are now six statins on the market to reduce cholesterol (Mecavor, Lipitor, Zocor, Pravachol, Lescol and Crestor) which are all variations of the first. Dr Sharon Levin, a director of the Kaiser Permanente Medical Group put it like this:

> If I'm a manufacturer and I can change one molecule and get another twenty years of patent rights, and convince physicians to prescribe and consumers to demand the next form of Prilosec, or weekly Prozac instead of daily Prozac, just as my patent expires, then why should I be spending money on a lot less certain endeavour, which is looking for brand new drugs.[19]

Big Pharma often tries to persuade people of moderate income that they are sick and need drugs. The world's top selling prescription drug is Lipitor, marketed by Pfizer as a cure for high cholesterol levels. But how does one know what a high cholesterol level is? The official US National Institute of Health guidelines on what exactly constitutes high cholesterol were re-written in 2004 by nine experts – eight of whom had a direct financial relationship with the major corporations.[20] It is questionable how objective these experts are when there is such a conflict of interest. The new guidelines effectively raised the target market for high cholesterol sufferers from 13 million in 1990 to 40 million in 2004.

All of these issues illustrate a conflict between the welfare of the wider society and the motivation of corporations. Corporations make no secret of the fact that their bottom line is profit, not the welfare of human beings. In the past it was assumed that this conflict might be controlled through nation states restraining their acquisitive instincts. Today it is clear that the pharmaceutical industry is more likely to get states to become enforcers for their values. This pattern is set to widen as the concentration of economic power accelerates.

The 1990s are known as the decade of mergers and acquisitions in economic circles. Pfizer, for example, started a little later on this road but then merged with Warner-Lambert and Pharmacia, which was then the second largest pharmaceutical company in the world. By gobbling up their rivals, mergers have concentrated their power. Joseph Stiglitz, the former chief economist at the World Bank, describes the philosophy behind the mania,

> The merger mania of the nineties, like that of earlier decades, rest on a peculiar arithmetic: $2+2=5$. Add up two firms worth €2 billion each and come away with a firm worth $5 billion – enough money to pay the investment banker a nice $300 million fee, give the CEO a hefty bonus and ample stock options, hand a nice retirement package to the former CEO (after a brief stint as second fiddle, or an even briefer stint as co-head) and still give the shareholders plenty to be happy about.[21]

The total value of assets acquired through mergers and acquisitions grew fivefold, from a then record $500 billion in 1990 to a staggering $2.7 trillion (that is, $2,700,000,000,000) in 2000.[22] Where mergers did not occur, the big corporations entered into strategic alliances and partnerships. US corporations were at the fore in this activity, earning 58 per cent of all royalties and license fees in the 1990s.[23] Through such alliances, mergers and acquisitions, corporations can carve up the world market much like the old empires divided up the continent of Africa.

GLOBALIZATION

This is the real meaning behind the term 'globalization'. Sometimes, however, the concept is used in a vague way to describe a sort of inevitable 'growing of age' stage in human society. Writers such as Anthony Giddens see globalization as a 'time-space compression' that has a dramatic impact on human consciousness.[24] By this they mean that we receive 'real time' experiences of distant parts of the world and this leads to a reduction in national consciousness and a growth of 'individualization' and 'flexibility'. Others, such as Kenichi Ohmae, go even further and speak of a world where 'nation states have already lost their role as meaningful units of participation in the global economy of today's borderless world'.[25] These writers examine the phenomenon in an abstract way without reference to the control of economic resources. They see globalization as either the result of technological changes – such as the growth of information communications technology – or a sort of progress whereby humans move from tribes to nations and then to a stage of globalization. Looked at from this point of view, the claim that Ireland is one of the most globalized economies in the world is a cause of celebration.

The US magazine, *Business Week* is, however, far more realistic when it states that 'Globalization is the most powerful manifestation of capitalism ever seen'.[26] It allows the large corporations to develop new ways of facilitating further transfers of wealth – to themselves. The remarkable feature of the present era of globalization is that, everywhere, it has been accompanied by growing inequality. The share of national economies going to labour and the poor has declined while that of the wealthy has grown. This occurs no matter whether the local political elite speak a language of gung-ho capitalism or mild social democracy. In the US, for example, the share of GDP going to wages and salaries has fallen from 49.5 per cent in 2001 to 45.4 per cent in 2004. A drop of 4.1 per cent in three years is quite dramatic as each percentage point in GDP was the equivalent of $118 billion per year.[27] In the EU, the decline in the share going to wages has been slower but nevertheless has occurred. Significantly, the soft spoken Irish

TABLE 1.1
ADJUSTED WAGE SHARE OF TOTAL ECONOMY – COMPENSATION PER EMPLOYEES AS PERCENTAGE OF GDP AT FACTOR COST PER PERSON EMPLOYED.

	EU-15	Ireland
1980–1990	71.8	71.2
1991–2000	68.7	62.3
2001–2007	67.3	54.3

Source: European Commission Statistical Annex of European Economy, Spring 2006
Table 32.

version of social partnership brought a faster decline.

Globalization provides a new framework for class conflict because it allows the corporate elite to reverse past gains made by the majority of society. They have used their new economic strength in a number of key ways.

First, they have set up structures whereby workers in different countries are supposed to compete against each other. A major multi-national will source parts and supplies from diverse plants and will engage in 'management by stress' to demand that one group is more competitive than the other.[28] A regime of insecurity is created through constant 'benchmarking' where workers are rated against each other. Once the rhetoric is internalized by employees, a treadmill is created for continual improvements and higher targets. Managers constantly remind staff that they are only as good as their last customer and so ways have to be found to be even more competitive. In practice, this means new forms of flexibility and work intensity. Flexibility involves the erosion of job demarcation and the work-leisure divide. Techniques such as 'team working' and 'multi-tasking' erode traditional job descriptions and weaken a worker's ability to refuse managerial requests. 'Non-traditional' opening hours and calls for 'volunteers' to work unsocial hours become a means of ending overtime payments.

The strategy is to intensify work. Modern capitalism is based on an apparently equal exchange between wages and work. However, behind the formality is an interesting conundrum: a specific wage is exchanged for a more nebulous promise of work effort. The unspoken element of every employment contract is the *degree* of work or discretionary effort. Employees will not necessarily give maximum work effort in return for comparatively modest wages. Nor are they under any contractual obligation to do so. Modern managerial techniques, therefore, focus on removing the 'downtime' – time periods of less intensive effort. If the work day is like a piece of Swiss cheese, managers will attempt to plug every hole to get total 'commitment'. Or to put it differently, they seek to increase the rate of profit that can be made from each employee.

These pressures go some way to explaining work stress and dissatisfaction in modern societies. One survey in Britain found that 64 per cent of employees experienced an increase in the speed of work and that 61 per cent felt more effort was required in the last five years.[29] In Ireland, pressure for flexibility and work intensity comes directly through social partnership agreements. Whereas in the past workers were granted pay rises in response to rising rates of inflation, today they must first show 'verifiable' improvements in productivity to get a pay rise. The remarkable fact about social partnership is that there is little sharing between the partners. The Irish workforce is expected to show continual improvements in productivity as their unions effectively cede to management growing control over the organization of work. They are also supposed to accept some of the lowest number of holidays in the EU 15 with annual leave and public holidays amounting to just twenty-nine days a year compared to a poorer country like Greece where workers receive thirty-seven days.[30]

None of this is inevitable, and the image of corporate mobility is highly exaggerated. Contrary to what is often thought, production facilities cannot be moved at will. In some labour intensive industries, such as textiles, it is certainly easier but, even here, the corporations incur costs. The reason is that few production plants today are stand alone facilities – they are more likely to be surrounded by networks and contractors who supply materials, often on a just-in-time basis. Moving location, therefore, is not like lifting a pawn from a chessboard, but involves the development of complex relationships with local elites and suppliers. The Intel plant in County Kildare illustrates this. Alongside generous tax breaks and grants, the firm enjoys access to a plentiful supply of water, waste disposal facilities, friendly environmental agencies, relationships with local universities, a special road to facilitate access and numerous other hidden advantages. In other words, it is well embedded in local networks and would incur considerable costs if it were to move. Of course, it might eventually be able to do so – but only after considerable preparation and planning. All of this means that its workforce is hardly powerless should they choose to act collectively. The problem is not solely Intel's power – but rather the acceptance of its myth of invincibility.

Outside the world of work, the corporations want to hollow out what is left of social rights or the social wage. In the post-war, 'golden age' period of modern capitalism, a welfare state was conceded to most industrial populations. In a poorer country such as Ireland, the elite sheltered behind the Catholic concept of 'subsidiarity' and did not concede too much. Instead, the 'good family' was supposed to look after their elderly and not have them shamed into becoming a 'burden on the state'. Nevertheless, the population still expected a modicum of public services as a right. They were not to pay for education or hospital treatment; their dustbins were to be collected; and if they were poor, they expected to be eventually housed by local authorities. The resources for these services sometimes came from re-distributive taxes imposed on wealth. Today, however, corporations don't want to pay any tax and so demand that social rights are redefined as individual responsibilities.

The change is best illustrated through the writings of two intellectuals who offered a defence of the 'mixed economy'. In his collection of essays on *Citizenship and Social Class* which appeared in 1950, T.H. Marshall claimed that citizenship had evolved in modern society so that it no longer simply meant freedom under the law or the right to vote but included 'social rights'. These implied that every one had a right to share to the full in the heritage of society and needed to enjoy a certain standard of living to do so. 'Social rights' did not remove inequality, he argued, but they did imply the subordination of the market to social justice.[31] For Karl Polanyi whose *Great Transformation* originally appeared in 1944, it was axiomatic that if the market was the sole director of the fate of human beings, it would result in the demolition of society itself. This fact engendered a 'counter-movement' of state regulation to provide security for the mass of people and to protect capitalism from itself.[32] Both these writers hailed from a moderate social democratic tradition and could not imagine the removal of social restrictions on capital. Unfortunately, the modern corporate elite do not just imagine – they aim to make it happen.

The attack on social rights comes in the name of the customer and choice. The state is no longer seen as a guarantor of the welfare for its citizens but oversees the smooth functioning of the market. Citizens are re-defined as customers who must take responsibility for themselves. If pension coverage is dropping, for example, it is up to each individual to open their own Personal Retirement Savings Account (PRSA) and the state should not force their company to take any responsibility for them. Previous services provided by the state such as waste collection are turned into commodities and then privatized. Through these mechanisms the costs imposed by society on corporations is reduced and instead new forms of 'corporate welfare' are provided by society to business.

The assault on public services is helped by a new architecture of global governance that reduces democratic decision-making. Like the leaning tower of Pisa, it always leans one way – towards the demands of the corporations. The IMF and the World Bank focus on underdeveloped countries and have used their debt crisis to dismantle barriers that were erected against entering their markets. For developed countries, the key institution is the World Trade Organization (WTO).

This grew out of the General Agreement on Tariffs and Trade which was established in 1947, under American pressure, to open up the former colonies of Britain and France to free trade. In 1995, as the roller coaster of globalization sped up, it was renamed the World Trade Organization and adopted a different method of governance. Originally decisions were made on a consensus basis and the most important changes were made at regular rounds that occurred every few years. With the formation of the WTO, consensus decision making between states was replaced by a judicial and executive power, which is charged with removing barriers to free trade. A Disputes Settlement Body operates like the Supreme Court which adjudicates on barriers to free trade and has the strongest enforcement procedure of any international agreement. WTO panels are binding and if countries do not comply, they are automatically subject to sanctions. Disputes panels operate in secret and are composed of three or four unelected trade experts whose ruling is final.

Corporations employ vast armies of lobbyists to get states to take cases to the WTO. So agri-business corporations got the US to take the EU to the WTO because of its ban on hormone-treated beef. They won their case because the WTO is also entitled to adjudicate on scientific evidence in relation to food health. The biotechnology corporations have taken this one step further by getting the US, Canada and Argentina – the largest producers of Genetically Modified food – to take the EU to the WTO court over the moratorium it imposed on new GM crops. They also won their case and the moratorium was declared illegal. Most surveys show that the vast majority of the people of Europe are opposed to GM food and a number of countries – Austria, France, Greece and Germany – have banned some of these foods. Nevertheless for all the talk about 'market choice', the biotechnology industry is using an undemocratic mechanism to force GM products into the food chain.

The WTO is by no means the sole institution that imposes a corporate agenda. The EU has developed its own undemocratic structures to allow corporations to gain considerable influence behind closed doors, as the GM debate again indicates. The EU moratorium of GM food was lifted in 2004 and ever since the EU Commission has attempted to open a space for GM crops even though the overwhelming majority of the people of Europe are against them. It states openly that 'new biotechnology techniques have the potential to deliver improved food quality and environmental benefits through agronomically enhanced crops'.[33] In line with this position, the EU Commission has sought to overthrow national bans. It has approved the importing of a Monsanto animal feed that consists of living genetically modified organisms. The structures of the EU allow national governments to shelter from public scrutiny and endorse corporate interests.

Corporate lobbying is also extensively developed at the EU and one of the most influential groups is the European Roundtable of Industrialists (ERT) that brings together chairpersons and chief executives of the continent's largest corporations. There are two Irish members on the board – Michael Smurfit and Peter Sutherland – who support efforts to influence policy. One ERT member, Baron Daniel Janssen, described the ERT's influence as having produced a 'double revolution' in EU decision making. It had succeeded in 'reducing the power of the state and of the public sector in general through privatization and de-regulation' and 'transferring many of the nation states' powers to a more modern and internationally minded structure at European level'.[34] One set of writers noted approvingly that 'The ERT was the main driving force to urge the European Commission to create the Single Market, and saw to it that it did not result in a fortress Europe'.[35]

About 15,000 professional lobbyists work in Brussels and over 70 per cent work directly or indirectly for corporations. Their aim is to influence policy decisions that are rarely scrutinized by the wider public because few are aware of voting records in the

EU. This allows the EU to provide an important mechanism for national governments to promote policies to de-regulate their economies. They do this by issuing 'directives' which are incorporated into national law. The EU has issued directives to open up the electricity industry to private competition; to remove the state postal monopoly; to prevent state subsidies to a variety of industries. Corporations gain further influence in the higher institutions of the EU through the activist competition policy and 'independent' Central Bank that answers only to the financial markets.

This wider tendency to reduce the scope of democratic decision-making is embodied in two important global treaties which dramatically enhance corporate power. The first is the Trade Related aspects of Intellectual Property rights agreement (TRIPS), which was negotiated at the WTO in 1994. This aims to protect the interest of the giant pharmaceutical, software and biotechnology industries. It gives legal status to the notion that a corporation can possess knowledge and can profit from it for long periods of time. A wide variety of items ranging from the genetic structure of Basmati rice to school teaching materials can now be patented in order to be marketed and sold. The most bizarre case is, surely, the jingle 'Happy Birthday to you'. The patent for this hundred-year-old song is held by Time Warner, who can collect revenues every time it is used in television and films!

The second is GATS, the General Agreement on Trade in Services, which came into force in 1995. GATS is such a complex agreement that only corporations who can employ huge teams of lawyers gain greater advantage. Its aim is to open the services sector to the full wind of global competition and so create extra investment opportunities for corporations. Services are a very general term, but the WTO identifies eleven major categories, which cover virtually everything with the exception of military activity and prayer. They include education, water supply, waste collection, health, electricity, telecommunications and broadcasting. Governments can only make regulations, which are 'no more burdensome than necessary' for these sectors and cannot impede competition of global services providers. GATS works through various rounds, but there is 'a built-in commitment to continuous liberalisation'. Once commitments are made by governments to open up particular services to market competition, they become irreversible.[36]

David Hartridge, Director of the WTO Services Division, has conceded that 'without enormous pressure generated by the American financial services sector, particularly companies like American Express and Citicorp, there would be no services agreement'.[37] These companies worked through powerful lobby groups such as the US Coalition of Service Industries which established close ties with the US government. Its members are often included on official US trade delegations and the Coalition candidly boasts that its 'in-depth knowledge of how to effectively use services trade negotiations to advance the interests of its members ... are unmatched'.[38]

FINANCIALIZATION

There is one other important development that has paved the way for the domination of the big corporations. 'Financialization' refers to the pattern whereby the profits come through financial channels rather than through trade and commodity production. More specifically, it means a greater reliance on liquid rather than physical assets to gain profit from speculative activity.[39]

Up to the 1970s, financial speculation was regarded as a dangerous activity that might destabilize economies if left unchecked. John Maynard Keynes, the dominant figure in post-war economics, even called for the 'euthanasia of the rentiers'.[40] He argued that finance had to be tightly controlled and national central banks had to limit its mobility. Most national governments broadly agreed. In Ireland, for example, you had to receive written permission from the Central Bank to take more than a few hundred pounds out of the country and only authorized dealers were entitled to hold large reserves of foreign currency. These types of controls were linked to the Bretton Woods system which fixed the exchange rate between currencies for most of the post-war period.

The system of stable exchange between currencies, however, broke down when the dollar came under pressure with the defeat of the US in the Vietnam War. In a dramatic move, the US authorities trumped their rivals by suspending capital controls in 1974 so that money was free to move in and out of the United States. This made the US banks and money markets more attractive to the holders of the petrodollars – vast sums owned by oil producers which were not invested in the Arab world. Later, ceilings on loans were also scrapped so US banks could loan out as much as they pleased. The moves to 'liberalize' finance forced others to follow suit and soon the whole global financial system was opened up to any magnate who wanted to play at the casino.

Floating currencies and the removal of controls on financial capital dramatically increased risk but also created enormous scope for speculation. Let's assume that one was a commodity dealer, buying coffee beans in Brazil, and had built up long-term contracts with various trading companies and coffee houses. They depended on you to deliver a steady stream of beans and this, in turn, forced you to establish supply contracts with farmers and traders in Brazil. However, all your efforts might come to naught if you suddenly found that the currency you held had devalued against the Brazilian currency. Conversely, you might be able to make extra profits if your currency was re-valued. The answer was to quite literally 'hedge' your bets – to hold a basket of currencies, so that one was not caught out by sudden changes.

Yet the very act of holding such funds allowed you to speculate against the rise and fall of particular currencies. You no longer needed to just make money buying and selling coffee beans – you could also gain from buying and selling money. And once you learnt to speculate on money, you could also learn to speculate on the shares of other companies who might not be so good at managing risk. Alternatively, you could invest in a specialized 'hedge fund', the most famous being the Quantum Fund of George Soros, which pooled money together for speculative purposes. The players of this particular fund managed to pocket $1billion in 1992 by speculating against the British pound. In 1990, there were 200 hedge funds but by 2000 there were 4,000 such funds, controlling over $14 trillion.[41] Collectively, these developments gave rise to a huge expansion of the sector known as Finance, Insurance and Real Estate. In the US, FIRE surpassed manufacturing in 1991[42] and now employs 16 per cent of the private sector workforce and a quarter of the private sector's net fixed capital stock.[43]

It would be wrong, however, to regard finance as a parasitical sector of the modern economy, leeching off the healthy productive sectors. The two sectors merge together, often with the same major players involved. The level of risk and the scale of profits to be made from speculation mean that many non-financial companies have developed extensive arms to engage in financial engineering. General Electric, for example, began making light bulbs, computers and aerospace engines but has developed GE Capital as a huge finance house. General Motors Acceptance Corporation – the leasing and insurance wing of General Motors – has become highly profitable even as the car manufacturer makes big losses. The integration of production with speculation and financial activities helps to explain why modern corporations are obsessively concerned with share prices. The higher their share prices the more speculative capital they can attract to make more speculative gains. Money earned from shares is not necessarily invested in productive activity – but rather in further share price, derivative and currency speculation. During the 1990s boom, for example, the biggest block of shares was actually purchased by US corporations themselves. From 1994 to 2000, corporations re-purchased an average of $121 billion per year of their own shares![44]

Not every one wins in the casino and, as even a small dip on the bottom line can frighten the 'electronic herd', there is a huge temptation to manipulate the figures. So corporations have developed techniques for shifting debts 'off-balance' and for papering over a host of fake transactions. Huge accountancy firms who earn vast amounts from the same firms in consultancy fees have assisted them in this. The most notorious was Andersen – who pleaded guilty to helping Enron shred documents and cover up the robbery of its employees' pension funds – but is by no means unique. Ernst and Young had to make a $335 million settlement to the California public employees fund for misrepresenting the health of the Cendant Corporation. Price Waterhouse Coopers were the auditors when Lucent inflated their books by $679 million and came under investigation.[45] In the four years prior to Enron's collapse, 700 US firms were forced to re-state their accounts.

The growth of high finance is sometimes linked to the idea of a post-modern world where substances dissolve behind a myriad of images. There are no realities any more – just endless discourses that entrap us in their webs. This certainly may be the outlook of the trader in Merrill Lynch or Chase Manhattan who keeps rolling on their funds to ever new speculative heights – regarding the stock market index as the only true reality. If that were all, it might be regarded as an amusing game – harmful only to the casino players. Unfortunately, however, the coupons for playing have been bought with the accumulated labour of society as a whole.

WHOSE PROBLEMS?

The corporations face big problems, and this adds to the pressure they exert on society as a whole. The first major problem is the declining rate of profit in manufacturing industry. Robert Brenner has shown that between 1970 and 1990, the rate of profit in manufacturing for the G-7 economies was, on average, about 40 per cent lower than between 1950 and 1970.[46] Corporations can still make very high profits and indeed the absolute amount of profit has risen. However if this profit is measured as a return on the rate of investment, it can still show a decline. Lower returns often mean a decline in the rates of investment, and this has affected productivity growth. Paul Krugman sums up the problem:

> From World War II until 1973, the average growth was a brisker 2.8 per cent annually, enough to double living standards in twenty five years. Since 1973, productivity has risen on average less than 1 per cent annually, at a pace that would take eighty years to achieve the rise in living standards that took place in the generation after WWII.[47]

Declining rates of profit and productivity forces corporations to squeeze more out of their workforce and to make governments give them the most favourable environment to do so.

Second, the sheer chaos of the system has led to an over-accumulation of capital in certain industries. In the 1990s, for example, telecommunications was seen as a key industry for future profits and vast funds were located there. By 2000 the market capitalization of telecommunications companies stood at $2.7 trillion – or close to 15 per cent of the total for all US non-financial corporations. The huge surge of investment, which was stoked up by speculative money in search of super-profits, meant that enough fibre optic cable was laid to circle the globe 1,566 times.[48] One of those fibre optic cables was supposed to be laid across the Atlantic in a special partnership deal between the Irish government and the US firm, Global Crossing. Yet the huge level of over-investment meant that profit rates sank dramatically. Initially firms such as Global Crossing and more dramatically, Worldcom, engaged in 'creative accounting' to over-state their earnings, but eventually could not stave off bankrupt-cy. It was a classic example of how the anarchy of the market leads to phenomenal waste.

Globalization and financialization give corporations extra leverage to attempt to deal with declining rates of profit and the over-accumulation of capital. Their sheer size and the implicit threats to relocate production abroad allow them to pressurize governments. Financialization means that governments who do not conform find that the money they raise on bond markets disappears as ratings agencies such as Moody and Standards and Poor's mark them down for giving too many concessions to the poor. (The New York Times once ran the aptly titled headline 'The man from Moody's Rules the World'.)[49] Financialization is also linked to new cries for 'shareholder value' which refers to the demand for extra dividends payments to keep up the price of shares. Through these mechanisms growing pressure is placed on workers and society as a whole to conform to corporate interests. A Goldman Sachs study of the US and Europe was quite candid in noting that

> The share of gross value added going to wages and salaries has declined [like a similar] trend in the US since the early 1980s. In fact for the US, this appears to be an extension of a trend that has been in place since the early 1970s ... We believe that pressures ... for returns on capital ... have forced US industry to produce higher returns on equity capital and their response to this has been to reserve an increasingly large share of output for the owners of capital.[50]

'Reserving a larger share for the owners of capital' – it could hardly be any clearer! Yet there is no reason why the rest of soci-ety needs to oblige.

Sometimes little boys and girls can get to look behind all the pomp and mystique to shout 'the emperor has no clothes'. That shout may start in tiny villages like Rossport or in whole countries like Venezuela or Bolivia where they see no reason to facilitate the robbery of natural resources. Or it can come from the streets of Dublin when thousands protested at the reduction of wages in Irish Ferries. But to spread further, it will have to challenge the ideology of neo-liberalism.

NOTES

1. C. Perrow, *Organizing America* (Princeton: Princeton University Press, 2002), p.33.
2. Quoted in N. Robins, 'The World's First Multi-National', *New Statesman*, 13 December 2004.
3. Quoted in R. Grossman and F. Adams, *Taking Care of Business: Citizenship and the Charter of Incorporation* (Yarmouth, MA: Charter Ink, 1993), p.6.
4. Ibid., p.8.
5. S. Anderson and J. Cavanagh, *Field Guide to the Global Economy* (New York: Norton, 2005), p.6.
6. L. Elliot and D. Atkinson, *The Age of Insecurity* (London: Verso, 1998), p.102.
7. J. Bakan, *The Corporation: The Pathological Pursuit of Profit and Power* (London: Constable, 2004).
8. C. van Egeraat, 'The Pharmaceutical Industry in Ireland: Agglomeration, Localisation or Simply Spatial Concentration?' National Institute for Regional and Spatial Analysis, Working paper No.28, February 2006, p.13.
9. P. Trouiller, O. Piero, E. Torreele, J. Orbinski, R. Laing and N. Ford 'Drug Development for Neglected Diseases: A Deficient Market and a Public Health Failure'. *The Lancet*, 359, 9324 (22 June 2002), pp.2188–94.
10. 'An Epidemic of Neglect: Neglected Diseases and the Health Burden of Poor Countries', *Multinational Monitor*, June 2002.
11. M. Angell, 'The Truth about Drug Companies'. *New York Review of Books*, 51, 12 (15 July 2004), pp.52–58.
12. R. Gross, 'Bush and Big Pharma Team up to Discredit WHO and Generic Medicine' at. www.ipjustice.org.
13. M. Angell, *The Truth about Drug Companies* (New York: Random House, 2004), p.48.
14. J. Lexchin, 'Doctors and Dealers: Therapeutic Education or Pharmaceutical Promotion?'. *International Journal of Health Services*, 19 (4) (1989), pp.663–79.
15. 'Pfizer's Funk', *Business Week*, 28 February 2005.
16. 'What does sponsorship really cost', *Irish Times*, 7 October 2004.
17. P. O Grady, *Why is the Irish Health Service in Crisis* (Dublin: Bookmarks, 2005), p.21.
18. See M. Goozner, *The $800 million Pill* (Berkeley, CA: University of California Press, 2004), Chap.8.
19. Angell, 'The Truth about Drug Companies'. *New York Review of Books*, 51, 12 (15 July 2004), p.56.
20. R. Moynihan and A. Cassels, *Selling Sickness: How Drug Companies are Turning us all into Patients* (Crows Nest, New South Wales: Allen and Unwin, 2005), p.4.
21. J. Stiglitz, *The Roaring Nineties: A New History of the World's Most Prosperous Decade* (New York: Norton, 2003), p.162.
22. J. Gelinas, *Juggernaut Politics: Understanding Predatory Globalisation* (London: Zed, 2003), p.37.

23. J. Kleinert, *The Role of Multinational Enterprises in Globalization* (Kiel: Springer, 2004), p.16.
24. A. Giddens, *Beyond Left and Right* (Cambridge: Polity, 1994).
25. K. Ohmae, 'The End of the Nation State', in F. Lechner and J. Boli (Eds), *The Globalization Reader* (Oxford: Blackwell, 2003), p.207.
26. Editorial in *Business Week*, 6 November 2000.
27. I. Shapiro and D. Kamin, 'Share of Economy Going to Wages and Salaries Drops for Unprecedented 14th Straight Quarter'. Briefing Paper from Center on Budget and Policy Priorities, 29 October 2004
28. K. Moody, *Workers in a Lean World* (London: Verso, 1997), p.87.
29. M. Bunting, *Willing Slaves: How Overwork Culture is Ruining our Lives* (London: Harper Collins, 2004), p.30.
30. Income Data Services, 'Wide Variations in EU Holiday Entitlements – UK amongst the lowest'. London: IDS, 11 August 2003.
31. T.H. Marshall, *Citizenship and Social Class* (Cambridge: Cambridge University Press, 1950).
32. K. Polyanyi, *The Great Transformation* (Boston: Beacon Hill, 1957).
33. Quoted in Corporate Europe Observatory, *Power Struggle over Biotech in Brussels* (Brussels, CEO, 2004), p.3.
34. 'The Naked Lobbyist', *New Internationalist*, No.347, July 2002.
35. Quoted in A. Storey, 'The European Project: Dismantling Social Democracy, Globalising Neoliberalism'. Paper presented at 'Is Ireland a Democracy', Sociology Department, National University of Ireland Maynooth, 2/3 April 2004, p.5.
36. E. Gould and C. Joy, *'In Whose Service'* (London: World Development Movement, 2000).
37. Ibid., p.5.
38. Ibid., p.6.
39. See G. Krippner, 'The Financialization of the American Economy'. *Socio-Economic Review*, 3 (2005) pp.173–208.
40. J.M. Keynes, *The General Theory of Employment, Interest and Money* (London: Macmillan, 1973), p.376
41. Gelinas, *Juggernaut Politics*, p.43.
41. Gelinas, *Juggernaut Politics*, p.43.
42. D. Henwood, *Wall St* (London: Verso, 1999), p.76.
43. R. Brenner, *The Economics of Global Turbulence*. Special issue of *New Left Review*, No.229 (1998), p.211.
44. R. Pollin, *Contours of Descent* (London: Verso, 2003), p.62.
45. V. Prashad, *Fat Cats and Running Dogs: The Enron Stage of Capitalism* (London: Zed Books, 2002), p.20.
46. Brenner, *The Economics of Global Turbulence*, p.7.
47. P. Krugman, *Peddling Prosperity* (New York: Norton, 1994), p. 57–8.
48. R. Brenner, 'Towards the Precipice' *London Review of Books*, Vol 25, No. 6, 6 February 2003, pp. 18–22.
49. *New York Times*, 27 February 1995.
50. Quoted in R. Dore, *Stock Market Capitalism: Welfare Capitalism* (Oxford: Oxford University Press, 2000), p.9.

Chapter Two

Wrecking your Head

When Irish Ferries got rid of their Irish workforce and tried to recruit Latvian migrants on €3.50 an hour, they met with huge public opprobrium. However, one well-known economist came to their rescue. Maynooth lecturer and *Irish Times* columnist, Jim O'Leary, claimed that both the Latvian workers and the Irish workers were in fact benefiting from the reduction of wage rates. The Latvians were 'stepping up the economic ladder' while the Irish workers could use their redundancy payments to acquire new qualifications or set up small businesses. Overall, Irish Ferries was a signal to 'Irish people who might otherwise choose a low-skill track to raise their levels of educational attainment' and so 'the long run effect will be to raise living standards'.[1] It was a textbook case of globalization, but only economists, it was implied, could cut through the fog of emotion and reveal the real benefits.

Jim O'Leary is a non-executive director of Allied Irish Banks (AIB) and prior to taking up his academic post he was the chief economist with Davy Stockbrokers. On this occasion, however, he was speaking not as a private sector executive but as an academic economist. Conventional economists carry a certain aura because they appear to be scientific and purport to explain mystical processes to the layperson. In his article, O'Leary adopted the patient tone of an expert who wanted to enlighten his readers and take them beyond the realms of simplistic understandings. He appeared to stand above sectional interests and speak in rational, objective terms about 'realities'.

Economists have assumed a role that is akin to a new priesthood and speak with all the certainty once used about the spiritual realm. Their very own special language about 'flexibility', 'competitiveness' and 'controls on public spending' have infiltrated into everyday speech in much the same way as people in the past spoke about 'occasions of sin' or 'indulgences'. Their pulpits are newspaper columns and television sound-bites. O'Leary appears regularly in the *Irish Times*, while Jim Power and Moore McDowell read their lessons in the *Irish Independent* and Dan McLaughlin manages to straddle most news media. Every morning RTE News puts out a special Business News slot where economists offer their diagnosis of government policy or the health of corporations. Interestingly, there is no equivalent Union News slot where shop stewards discourse on corporate labour practices.

Underneath the aura of science and objectivity, however, a right wing view of the world is normally promoted. A simple way to test this hypothesis is to ask when have you heard an economist talk of giving workers higher wages or calling on companies to restrain their growth in profits? Yet there could be no scientific law that states that higher wages and lower profits must be wrong in all places for all time. Such propositions could only be ruled out because of dogma rather than science. Nor could a science operate on the implicit assumption that higher profits must always be a good thing. Once again, only a pre-scientific dogma could assert that large corporations must always be allowed to accumulate more wealth.

The particular dogma to which most conventional economists adhere assumes that markets are the only efficient way to allocate scarce resources. Left to themselves, it is claimed, prices will adjust so that the supply and demand for goods achieves an 'equilibrium'. When this does not happen, it is assumed that extraneous factors, such as union action to prevent wage cuts or the imposition of taxes by the government, must be to blame. Hence, the hostility displayed by conventional economists to both these practices. When the Irish Congress of Trade Unions (ICTU) and Conference of Religious of Ireland (CORI) looked for extra money for the health service, Jim Power, chief economist with Friends First, illustrated the workings of this dogma. He warned that this 'left wing begrudgery ... will create the environment of the eighties where our brightest and best were forced to emigrate to get properly rewarded for hard work'.[2] But how could this possibly be? How could extra hospital beds or more infection control specialists lead to mass emigration? Only a dogmatic belief that interference in the market leads to economic ruin could give rise to this assertion.

Such accounts of the workings of the economy do not arise from a scientific understanding but from a neo-liberal outlook. Neo-liberalism is a viewpoint that assigns business the historic role of solving society's problems. It asserts that business is the embodiment of efficiency and that its methods and peculiar language must be infused into virtually every area of social life. Business has, apparently, won this position because it has been shaped in the 'cut and thrust' of the free market. The market demands risk-taking, innovation and competitiveness in contrast to the weaker elements in society who fear these features and seek the protection of a 'nanny state'. Neo-liberals must therefore remain in a constant state of watchfulness – exposing and challenging efforts by public officials or unions to curb the vital energies of business and the market. The neo-liberal believes that his or her mission is to stand up for the real instinct of humanity itself – a selfish desire to choose what is best for us as individuals. Clothed in the language of economic realities, the new priesthood promulgate this doctrine daily.

WHERE DID NEO-LIBERALISM COME FROM?

Uniformity among economists about the magical power of free markets is a relatively recent phenomenon and forty years ago a different orthodoxy prevailed. In 1962, when one of the intellectual fathers of neo-liberalism, Milton Friedman, published his classic *Capitalism and Freedom*, he felt that he was part 'of a small beleagured minority regarded as eccentrics by the great majority of our fellow intellectuals'.[3] The vast majority of economists believed in greater government intervention and supported the welfare state. They looked to the writings of John Maynard Keynes who viewed the market as a profoundly imperfect mechanism that sometimes failed because supply and demand did not always come into equilibrium. He argued that the state should manage the economy by, for example, increasing spending when there was a danger of a recession and withdrawing funds when there was a prospect of overheating. Keynes had been a conventional liberal who speculated on commodity markets and despised Marxist ideas. An elitist to his fingertips, he once attacked socialist ideas by rhetorically asking, 'How can I adopt a creed which, preferring the mud to the fish, exalts the boorish proletariat above the bourgeois and intelligentsia who, with whatever their faults, are the quality of life and surely the seeds of all human development'.[4] Yet under the shadow of the Wall Street crash, he came to believe that state intervention was necessary to save capitalism from itself.

The modern doctrine of market fundamentalism was born with Friedrich Hayek, who began his intellectual career working with Ludwig von Mises, the Austrian economist who polemicized against the idea of socialist planning. Moving on from these debates, Hayek focused on the manner in which economic knowledge and information could be disseminated in society. Could any central authority, he asked, possibly accumulate all the fragmented bits of knowledge possessed by individuals? The answer to this rhetorical question was, of course, no. Hayek then conceived of the market 'as a system for the utilization of knowledge, which no one can posses as a whole'.[5] Only the market could overcome the fragmentation of knowledge by sending out price signals that indicated where investment was needed or where there was an abundance or scarcity of goods. Once this premise was accepted, there was little room for any political authority to intervene in the economy. He wrote,

> It reduces the possible task of authority very much if you realize that the market has in that sense a superiority, because the amount of information the authorities can use is always very limited, and the market always uses an infinitely greater amount of information than the authorities can ever do.[6]

Hayek moved to the London School of Economics in 1931 and engaged in vigorous debates with Keynes. In 1944, he published his classic text, *The Road to Serfdom*, which argued that Nazism was not a reaction to socialism but rather an outgrowth of 'collectivism'. By that he meant a tendency towards greater state control, which both Keynes and the left had advocated. The alternative to both was individualism and the rule of law. Laws needed to be fixed and announced beforehand in order to effect the necessary constraints on government, and create the ensuing space for individual liberty. At the heart of Hayek's philosophy was a deep suspicion of democratic rule. He wrote:

> We have no intention, however, of making a fetish of democracy. It may well be that our generation talks and thinks too much of democracy and too little of the values it serves ... Democracy is essentially a means, a utilitarian device, for safeguarding internal peace and individual freedom. As such it is by no means infallible or certain.[7]

There was no intrinsic value in people coming together discussing, debating and making decisions for a common good. Hayek's suspicion of democracy harked back to fears raised by the French aristocrat, de Tocqueville, in the nineteenth century: if the poor have the vote and if they are more numerous, might they not decide to limit the wealth of the few? Later in *Law, Legislation and Liberty*, Hayek was even more explicit in arguing that,

> The predominant model of liberal democratic institution, in which the same representative body lays down the rules of just conduct and directs government, necessarily leads to a gradual transformation of the spontaneous order of a free society into a totalitarian system conducted in the service of some coalition of organised interests.[8]

His aim, therefore, was to reduce the 'politicization' of society in order to keep public action to a minimum. In this way, the 'spontaneous order' of the market could be given a free reign. These anti-democratic instincts, which have remained at the heart of neo-liberalism ever since, were expressed most clearly in Hayek's *The Constitution of Liberty* where he argued that while universal suffrage seemed to be the best arrangement in Western society. 'this does not prove that it is required by some basic principle'.[9] He claimed that the limits on suffrage are largely determined by matters of expediency, and he seemed to have little difficulty with suggestions that only people over 40 or income earners might have a vote. He explicitly argued that 'it is also possible for a reasonable person to argue that the ideals of democracy would be better served if, say, all servants of government or all recipients of public charity were excluded from the vote'.[10] His key concern was to limit the scope of decision-making though a constitution which hemmed in the areas on which a democratic government could decide matters.[11]

Hayek's ideas were marginal but he enjoyed two key advantages – he was backed by big money and a right-wing press. As Susan George put it, 'if some ideas are to become more fashionable than others, they must be financed: it takes money to build intellectual infrastructures and to promote a worldview'.[12] The *Readers Digest* produced a condensed version of *The Road to Serfdom* for their Book of the Month Club in 1945. The economics editor of the *New York Times* then gave it a blockbuster review, declaring it 'the most important book of our generation'.[13] In 1947, with the help of a Swiss businessman, Albert Hunold, Hayek and his associates founded the Mont Pelerin Society to promote right-wing ideas.[14] The society took its name from the resort where a handful of participants gathered to halt the decline in beliefs about private property and the 'free' market. US participants, who included the young Milton Friedman in their numbers, were sponsored by the Volker Fund, which was set up by the family of a Missouri businessman.[15] The Volker Fund sponsored university meetings, financed publishing houses, and distributed library books to promote market fundamentalist ideas. Hayek also established close links with the Foundation for Economic Education, a think tank formed by Leonard Read, the head of the Los Angeles Chamber of Commerce. The board and trustees of the Chamber included directors and former directors from General Motors, Du Pont, Chrysler and Goodrich Tyres. One of its first acts was to distribute a pamphlet by the young Milton Friedman and George Gilder advocating a case against rent controls.[16]

Hayek formed a close connection with the University of Chicago, which eventually became the intellectual powerhouse for the market fundamentalists. His appointment as professor was underwritten by the Volker Fund, which also helped to fund the university's School of Economics.[17] By the 1960s, the leadership of the school had fallen into the hands of Milton Friedman and George Stigler, two members of the Mont Pelerin society. The school established its intellectual credibility through the use of highly abstract mathematical models but some of its academics were also able to convey their ideas in more popular form. One of the clearest expositions of Friedman's views was contained in an interview with Playboy magazine![18]

Increasingly, the Chicago School, as the economics department came to be known, began to scrutinize many areas of human activity from a market perspective. One of the more bizarre examples was an article by Gary Becker and Jose Elias on 'Introducing Incentives in the market for Live and Cadaveric Organ donations' that claimed that a free market could help solve the problem of a scarcity in organ transplants. Their economic modelling was so precise that they were able to calculate the most appropriate price tag for human kidneys ($15,000) and human livers ($32,000).[19] Their enthusiasm for commodification of human organs was not, however, matched by a concomitant willingness to part with their own livers or kidneys for the going market price. This particular market would be sourced from among the poor of the developing world.

Within the inner circles, the Chicago School was seen as 'the artillery' of the market fundamentalist movement. It provided broad general ideas that could later be popularized in the right-wing press. Key figures included Robert Lucas, who developed the idea of 'rational expectations' as a model for the way in which market actors function. This is best characterized as an assumption that humans are egoistical calculating machines whose actions can be modelled in advance by economists. Another key figure, Ronald Coase, argued that 'property rights' had to be established to give individuals an incentive to conserve the environment. George Stigler developed an argument about the inevitable failure of government regulation that would follow on the capture of the regulatory agencies by vested interests.

The Chicago School were given a unique opportunity to implement their theories after the Pinochet coup in Chile in 1973.[20] From the mid 1950s, about 150 graduate students from the Catholic University of Santiago had received fellowships to study at Chicago under a US sponsored programme. When the Chilean military overthrew the elected government of the socialist

President, Salvador Allende, Pinochet turned to these graduates for an economic strategy. They duly obliged and became known as the 'Chicago boys' on the basis of their close working relationship with their 'spiritual father', Arnold Harberger, one of the key academics in the Chicago economics department. In 1975, Milton Friedman made a high profile visit to his protégés in Chile, telling them that the economy needed 'shock treatment' and deep spending cuts. He counselled Pinochet to ignore his poor image abroad and focus on curing the 'disease' of statism.[21] Ideas that had been germinating in a Swiss villa and in the halls of the North American university were finally rolled out in Chile, which became the first laboratory for new experiment.

The country was subject to whole scale privatization as thousands of public sector workers were let go. Tariff barriers were removed and the economy was opened up to financial speculators. The aim was to remove as many restrictions on the market as possible. The policies were deeply unpopular and could only have been implemented with the backing of a military dictator. Sergio de Castro, one of the main architects of the Chicago plan, later acknowledged this when he noted that 'public pressure was very much against us ... It was our luck that President Pinochet understood and had the character to withstand criticism.'[22]

After 1979, a second phase of the neo-liberal plan was put into operation when Jose Pinera took over as Minister of Labour. Social security was privatized and workers were told to pay into individual accounts managed by private financial firms. The experiment conducted on Chile was to become a blueprint for neo-liberal schemes all around the world. George Bush, for example, later proposed privatizing the whole of the US social security system along Chilean lines. To this day, key figures in the Chicago School defend the Chilean experiment. Gary Becker has written that the Chicago boys' work for Pinochet 'was one of the best things that happened to Chile'.[23]

The Chilean experiment ended in failure when the economy hit the rocks in the early 1980s and the state had to seize control of banks and large industrial concerns. But this did not stop the growth of the Chicago School's influence in elite circles. The school gained intellectual credibility because its staff won eight Nobel prizes in economics. An important sleight of hand was at work here, however, as the prize is not one of the original ones devised by Alfred Nobel but one created by the Bank of Sweden as a publicity stunt. The chair of the selection committee since 1980, Assar Lindbeck has advocated drastic cutbacks in Sweden's welfare state and has attacked Sweden's attempt to have 'capitalism without capitalists'. He follows Milton Friedman in favouring the introduction of a voucher system for schooling, claiming that, 'they are a brilliant way to combine collective financing with freedom of choice and competition among service providers'.[24] He has also worked with Michael Walker, founder of the rightwing Fraser Institute in Canada, and Gary Becker and Milton Friedman in constructing an 'Economic Freedom Index'.

One of Hayek's legacies has been the creation of think tanks. In the Hayekian world there are 'first hand dealers in ideas', comprised of scholars such as those found in the Chicago School, and there are 'second hand dealers', compromised of journalists, teachers, publicists and radio commentators who are expert at conveying ideas. Intellectuals are seen as key figures that help shape the direction of society – figures that the neoliberal movement seeks to recruit systematically. It organizes for the dissemination of their arguments through think tanks that can draw on vast sums of money to popularize neatly packaged arguments. One of Hayek's key associates was Anthony Fisher, owner of Britain's first battery chicken farm, who founded the Institute for Economic Affairs (IEA) For thirty years the Institute produced a steady stream of policy papers advocating privatization and deregulation. It adopted a particular focus on targeting 'opinion leaders' in order to shift policy making. On the anniversary of its foundation, Margaret Thatcher made a speech saluting the IEA, claiming with some exaggeration that 'they saved Britain'.[25] It was, however, one indication of the importance that neo-liberals assigned to their think tanks.

It took the revolt of the 1960s to win the big corporations over to the idea of think tanks. Business people are normally only interested in money making and are more than happy if they can do so without engaging in public controversy. The growth in radical ideas in the 1960s, as millions joined protests over the Vietnam War and demanded civil rights at home, obliged the corporations to adopt an altogether different attitude to the public arena. Faced with this anti-capitalist sentiment in the colleges and in society at large, the corporations responded by funding right-wing think tanks, pet university scholars and selected media gurus. The impetus for this strategy came from one of the highest figures in the US elite.

Just before he became a Supreme Court judge in the US in 1971, Lewis Powell, a board member of eleven major corporations, sent a memo to his friend, Eugene B. Sydnor, a key figure in the US Chamber of Commerce. He noted that the New Left were winning the battle of ideas, with nearly half of students favouring the socialization of basic US industries and 'perfectly respectable elements' joining in criticism of business. Businessmen, he argued, were not trained to 'conduct guerrilla warfare' in opposition to those who propagandized against the system. The US Chamber of Commerce needed, instead, to establish 'a staff of highly qualified scholars in the social sciences who believed in the system' who would do 'the thinking, the analysis, the writing and the speaking for them'.[26] It was a clear cry for the creation of right-wing think tanks.

One of the first to answer the call was William Simon, a former Wall Street bond trader and Secretary to the Treasury under Nixon. He wrote

> Funds generated by business ... must rush by multi-millions to the aid of liberty ... to funnel desperately needed funds to scholars, writers and journalists who understand the relationship between political and economic liberty. [Business must] cease the mindless subsidizing of colleges and universities whose departments of economy, government and history are hostile to capitalism.[27]

Soon, substantial contributions flowed in from Coca Cola, Dow Chemical, Ford Motor Co, General Electric, K Mart and Nestle corporations to help Simon found the Institute for Educational Affairs. Its purpose was to seek out and recruit promising PhD students for a right-wing ideas factory. The aim was to form a 'counter-intelligentsia' to take on leftist ideas.[28]

Since then a number of major foundations have emerged as sponsors for hundreds of neo-liberal think tanks. Nine of the largest, including Olin, Smith Richardson, Bradley, Coors, Koch and the Scaife foundation, control over €2 billion in assets.[29] They distribute funds to a vast network of inter-linked think tanks in many different countries. At the top of the hierarchy are those that employ hundreds of writers and researchers. The best known are the Heritage Foundation which produces a regular 'freedom index' that is frequently quoted in Irish newspapers; the Cato Institute, which campaigns for the privatization of social security; the American Enterprise Institute and the Hoover Institute. They are often quoted in the press as neutral academic institutions. They are, in fact, ideas brokers for big business.

Underneath these major think tanks, is an octopus-like network which has been described as 'perhaps the most potent, independent institutionalized apparatus ever assembled in a democracy to promote one belief system'.[30] The network creates its own intellectual heroes and turns them into household names by subsidizing their publications and choreographing their appearances in diverse media outlets. Milton Friedman's *Free to Choose*, Samuel Huntington's *The Clash of Civilisations*, Charles Murray's *Losing Ground*, Francis Fukuyama's *The End of History* became famous books through their author's association with these think tanks. These neo-liberal networks have infiltrated some US universities as funds flow into favoured programmes and visiting professorships are sponsored to preach the gospel of market fundamentalism. Harvard, Yale, Stanford and Chicago are among the universities which have benefited from these foundations with law and economics programmes alone receiving $45 million from right-wing think tanks.[31] The neo-liberals build for the future by recruiting thousands of graduate students who they hope will become the future right-wing intellectuals. Michael Joyce, from the Bradley Foundation, has rather cynically described it as 'like building a wine collection'.[32]

Where the US has gone, Europe and, more recently, Ireland, is following. The Atlas Economic Research Foundation, founded by Anthony Fisher, has been described as a 'think tank breeder' because of its role in developing new think tanks across the globe. Funded by Phillip Morris and Exxon Mobil, it runs regular conferences to teach budding intellectual entrepreneurs how to get their message across. In Europe, the giant pharmaceutical company Pfizer has played a lead role in helping to establish the Stockholm Network which functions like a mother ship for European think tanks attacking regulation, particularly environmental regulation.[33] Ireland's first right-wing think tank is called the Open Republic and lists among its Board of Directors Moore McDowell, Constantin Gurdgiev and Paul McDonnell. It is connected to the Fraser Institute in Canada and the Cato Institute in the US and, although relatively marginal in terms of Irish policy formation, it seeks to win an enlarged space for market fundamentalism. Rather ominously, it invited over Jose Pinera, the former Chilean labour minister under the Pinochet administration, to speak on social security privatization.[34]

Neo-liberal ideas, therefore, did not emerge spontaneously or simply through free and open intellectual discussion, but were backed by large corporations. They would not, however, have received the hearing they did had it not been the crisis that undermined previous economic orthodoxies. The first major recession to hit the Western world in 1971–73, commonly known as the oil crisis, undermined Keynesian planning. The failure of states to prevent the recession posed a problem in itself. But as the recession was also accompanied by high rates of inflation, many looked for new explanations of this 'stagflation'. Milton Friedman's work on the manner in which tighter controls over the money supply could eliminate inflation and prevent recessions seemed to offer an attractive alternative to the political elite. It became even more attractive when it was implied that a dose of unemployment might be just what was needed to put manners on bolshie trade unionists.

Friedman's victory was short-lived because it transpired that his monetarist policies – as neo-liberal doctrines used to be called – also failed to prevent recessions. Moreover, the idea of reducing state spending to tiny proportions in a modern industrial economy proved to be a pipe dream. Despite Reagan's endorsement of 'supply side economics' and Thatcher's virtual canonization of Hayek, the state did not significantly retreat within industrial economies. Friedman's ambition to cut state spending to about 15 per cent of Gross National Product (GNP) was never regarded as feasible. Although still dominant within the discipline of economics, neo-liberal ideas came under more sustained attack by economists such as Stiglitz and Krugman.[35] As doubts grew, the more academic economists began to either retreat further into mathematical modelling or to embrace new ideas that stressed the role of institutions in framing economic decisions.[36] All of which points to a paradox at the heart of the economic-speak that is churned out daily in our news media: why the public certainty when the intellectual foundations of the dogma are cracking?

The answer lies in the fact that neo-liberal economics is not a description about how actually existing capitalism works but is, rather, a utopia. It does not describe how corporations function but presents a model of how they should work. It combines descriptive and prescriptive elements to generate a fanatical zeal for an ideal world. The utopia is drawn from the late eighteenth century world of Adam Smith where no corporation or group of corporations could dominate the market and where each had to accept the price determined by that market. In a world of perfect competition where people have perfect information on prices and only enter mutually beneficial market transactions, there is a realm of freedom and efficiency. This idealized image was not true then – and it certainly is not true today. But by winning over a new class of hired intellectuals to this utopia, the neo-liberals hope to offer an endless programme of reform. This utopian element explains how Milton Friedman can claim to have won the intellectual argument – but not yet the practical argument. Rather bizarrely he has said that 'the world is more socialist today than it was in 1947'.[37]

To persuade the world to live up to the new utopia, neo-liberals typically employ two forms of rhetoric. They don the mantle of 'inevitability' by the endless repetition of phrases about 'the realities of globalization' and how 'you cannot buck the market'. The term globalization is used like the word 'the Republic' was used in Irish politics in the past. It is a utopian idea that has already materialized in some sphere of reality not immediately accessible to ordinary people whose minds have been distracted from 'the cause'. In a similar way, 'globalization' refers to a perfect neo-classical model to which each body of citizens will eventually have to conform. Resistance is said to be futile and economic fatalism has become the order of the day. However, as the Irish Ferries case illustrated, 'people power' is always possible – and even when it does not secure outright victories, it at least means that Latvian migrants get paid more than €3.50 an hour.

The neo-liberals also portray themselves as 'outsiders' who are fighting the elite. In the US, they have forged an alliance with the Evangelical movement to try to pit blue-collar workers and businessmen against a 'liberal-left' establishment. Magically, the class pyramid had been inverted to place college graduates at the top and businessmen and the poor at the bottom. True believers in the fundamentalist movement refer to the Director's Law, named after Aaron Director, one of the earliest participants of the Mont Pelerin Society. This purports to show that public expenditure is carried out for the benefit of the middle class and is financed by taxes that penalise both the rich and the poor.[38] So rich people like Bill Gates become the philanthropists who care for Africa's poor while, as the *Wall Street Journal* put it, anti-capitalist protestors are standing 'atop the prone bodies of people who hunger for the fruits of the earth'.[39] In a similar fashion, columnists in the *Sunday Independent* rant against the 'politically correct', 'pinkos' and the 'egg-heads' who trample on the consumerist instincts of ordinary folk.

This anti-establishment chic of the neo-liberals is, of course, a fraud. Unlike the radical activist movements that they sometimes mimic, neo-liberals work hand in glove with the wealthiest and most powerful elements in society. Far from growing from below, neo-liberalism is imposed through command and control models. Each year, for example, some 60,000 senior civil servants from all over the world file into the offices of the Organisation of Economic Cooperation and Development (OECD) to retrain themselves in neo-liberal policies. The mission of the OECD is to promote 'labour market flexibility' and 'economic liberalization' and some of its training methods include 'consensus through peer pressure'[40] – which sounds just a little bit like Maoist style group teaching. Once initiated into the mysteries of neo-liberalism, decision makers disseminate its dogma throughout society through a new business speak. Everything from nursing care to teaching has to be measured as 'outputs' and are then 'benchmarked' against other 'service providers' who also deal with 'customers'. Rather oddly, the Irish Office of Refugee Commissioners has now taken to calling asylum seekers its 'customers' – without noting the apparent irony that it regularly throws them out of its 'shop'.[41] While most people find this business speak mildly amusing, its advocates can live with irony. The real purpose is to normalize the outlook so that it becomes part of the fabric of the modern world.

Neo-liberalism, therefore, is the concentrated expression of the interests of the big corporations. Its agenda is none other than a rolling back of all barriers to profit making and its aim is nothing less than the full liberation for capital by the removal of social restraints. The utopian message at its heart means there is never a resting point. The sad fact is that there is no bottom at the end of 'race to the bottom'. Instead, three articles of faith are repeated tirelessly as if they were the answer to all human misery.

THE NEO-LIBERAL ARTICLES OF FAITH

1. The Market delivers free choice and most efficient use of scarce resources

According to Milton Friedman there are only two ways to allocate resources in modern society. The state can use coercion to ration resources according to a plan or, alternatively, prices can be established through voluntary exchange in a market and goods distributed according to consumer choice.[42] The market is the superior method because it allows producers and consumers to shop around and force a lowering of prices until equilibrium is established between supply and demand. Workers can also shop around between employers to get the best wage levels the market can bear. If they consider wages are too low, they can look elsewhere and force firms to raise wages to attract others. If wages are too high, companies will not hire workers and unemployment will force them to reduce their wage demands. In this way, the market turns the 'whole world into a parliamentary system' where people vote every minute, every hour, every day with their money.[43] This makes it the guarantor of individual freedom and choice.

Many economists from Adam Smith to Milton Friedman have developed this classic argument. Today, however, it is repeated endlessly as if it were a self-evident truth. There are, however, many flaws in the argument.

In the first place, Friedman implies that freedom is defined as the absence of state control. People, however, can also be controlled by impersonal market forces as well as a political power. Workers can be forced to stay with a particular employer because they do not have the resources to shop around without wages. Farmers can be forced to sell food at rock bottom prices because supermarkets such as Dunnes or Tesco have such a dominant position. People can be forced to sell their labour or even their bodies from fear of starvation or desire for survival. Yet in none of these cases have they been ordered to do so directly by a political authority.

Moreover, negative freedom, in the sense of freedom *from* external authority, is not the same as the positive freedom *to* carry out desires. Rich and poor people may both be free from state control but only the rich can 'choose' to live in better houses while the poor can only 'choose' tiny bedsits. The use of the term 'choice' is a travesty in this context because it compares two very different experiences. The rich have a genuine level of choice because they have the resources to select from many options. The poor are confined and forced to select from such a range so limited that the use of the term 'choice' is almost inappropriate. They have few positive freedoms because they are restricted by the impersonal power of the market.

Friedman's theory also rests on an implicit model of human nature. It assumes that people are 'rational egoists' who seek to maximize selfish interests and so constantly 'shop around'. But as even the financial speculator George Soros has pointed out, only 'the values that guided me in my money making activities (speculating on hedge funds) did resemble the values postulated by economic theory'.[44] In other aspects of his life he was guided by social responsibilities or the affections of his private life. In other words, Friedman's 'economic man' only describes a narrow, asocial range of the human experience. Most people do not in fact spend their time 'shopping around' but go to the same local shop out of habit, loyalty or even neighbourliness. They donate blood to the blood bank, help organize community games, look in on the elderly and receive nothing in return. If egotism was the sole motivating factor in human behaviour, the economy would not function because people would rarely go 'beyond the contract' and show enthusiasm for their work. The very idea that individuals only look out for themselves is a myth, created by a society that idealizes entrepreneurs and speculators. Throughout most of human history, the individual was subordinated to the social group and even today people do not behave from purely selfish motives most of the time.

Sometimes it is accepted that Fried\
philosophical concepts about freedom and\
hard-nosed economics still makes sense. Th\
tionable on many levels.

Let us take the idea of perfect information wh\
need for free exchange. As economists will explai\
mation is not intended to be a description of the r\
only part of a model that allows them to make predic   ̲ut
the world. But even if it is not intended to be an actu̲ ̲escrip-
tion, it still needs to bear some relationship to the workings of
actually existing capitalism. The problem is that, in the main, it
does not. In the real world, companies pitch advertisements at a
subliminal level or entrap people with their products before they
are of an age to assess the calibre of the information being impart-
ed to them. The tobacco industry, for example, spends $170,300
every day the US Congress is in session, lobbying its members to
prevent them from banning cigarette sales to minors.[45] The Irish
banking industry systematically overcharged because they knew
that individual consumers suffer from an 'information disadvan-
tage'. This has become a common practice for large financial
companies who 'clip' their customers with extra charges, knowing
that they find it difficult to unbundle the various services offered
through pension or insurance schemes.[46] Others, like Microsoft,
go to great lengths to create captive customers through an
'embrace, extend, extinguish' strategy. New software inventions
are embraced and integrated into its Windows operating system;
its properties are then extended into bloated packages; the competition is extinguished as customers only buy products that are
compatible with Windows.[47] The customer is so enveloped in the
Microsoft world that they are barely aware of the existence of
rival software – let alone having access to the 'perfect' information
on how rival software might be used.

Friedman also equates efficiency in the allocation of scare
resources with equilibrium between supply and demand in the
market. But the two are not one and the same. Clearly, it takes
time for the market to reach equilibrium –at which time consumer needs may have changed. Let's imagine that there is a
famine in a developed country where people have more money.
The scarcity of food will drive up prices dramatically and this
will send a signal to investors to switch extra resources into food

...ction. But the re-structuring in response to price signals will take time and in this period many people will have died. This is one of the reasons why most developed economies have not left food production to the market but subsidize food production to guarantee supply. The subsidy creates its own absurdity and is discriminatory against products from the developing world but it nonetheless provides an interesting example of the inconsistencies of governments who espouse neo-liberalism.

Market equilibrium may also be based on what Keynes called the phenomenon of 'beauty contests'.[48] In Keynes's day, newspapers held sexist beauty contests by publishing pictures of young women and asking their male readership to nominate the five prettiest. A naive entrant would use their own concept of beauty to make nominations; the cleverer would try to anticipate what the average opinion on the prettiest would be; the really clever would try to work out what the average opinion thought the average opinion to be. In a similar way, people often use third degree expectations to set prices in the market place. The stock market is a classic example of this because share prices are often based on dealers' expectations of what other dealers think expectations will be of share prices in the future. Sometimes an irrational exuberance sets in as occurred during the stock market boom in dot.com companies. The Irish housing market is another example of Keynes' beauty contests because prices are based not just on the value of a house but on hopes of what others will think 'a good investment'. Paying €300,000 for a two-bed apartment, however, can hardy be regarded as the most efficient use of resources!

The argument about how the market must lead to efficient use of scarce resource also fails to address the problem of 'externalities'. These are some costs that are not borne by the producer or their buyers but are, rather, imposed onto society at large. What appears as an 'efficient' allocation of resources can, therefore, look very 'inefficient' when looked at from a wider social perspective. The price of cars, for example, does not include the cost of treatment for asthma sufferers or spending on injuries caused by road accidents. Modern food can appear very cheap but that is only because corporations offload the costs of obesity or illness onto the wider society. Airline transport may appear cheap but that is because it takes no account of the damage fuel emissions cause to the atmosphere. As the market does not automatically measure these 'external' costs, it cannot claim to be the only way to generate efficiency.

A dogma typically works by endless repetition – as is evident from the ubiquitous claims about the 'free market' from which there is no escape. But no matter how powerful its advocates, a dogma offers only a partial, one-sided view of the world. The market is a human creation, which grew to dominate society in a particular historic period. Assigning it near-magical powers is an unusual form of fetishism that could only be performed by fanatical believers.

2. Free public services are wasteful – establish property rights and user fees

Neo-liberals abhor the idea of a free public domain and hark back repeatedly to a famous essay by Garrett Hardin on 'the tragedy of the commons'.[49] Hardin was an environmentalist who was concerned about over-population and took as an example the image of common land where herdsmen had grazing rights. He argued that it was rational for each herdsman to add extra cattle to common land since the cost incurred by overgrazing was carried by everyone rather than the individual herdsman. The holding of land in common led to environmental degradation because people did not have the incentives to make the sacrifices necessary to protect the land. The tragedy of the commons is that 'each man is locked into a system that compels him to increase his herd without limit ... in a world that is limited'.[50] While Hardin did not write explicitly about economic arrangements, his essay has been used by neo-liberals to suggest that any resource held in common will be degraded.

Neo-liberals also attack the idea that public officials could manage common resources without putting their own interests first. A 'public choice' school treats actors in the 'political' market as being motivated by the same self interest as those in the economic market. Voters, according to this view, do not have the incentive to monitor the political process effectively as too much information is required. This means that public officials can get away with 'rent seeking' – using state agencies to maximize their own interest by forming close relationships with organized interest groups.[51] The solution, according to the neo-liberals, is to break up the public domain, establish firm property rights and charge user fees to enforce efficiency.

These rather obtuse arguments are frequently used to turn free public services into commodities that have to be paid for. Throughout most of the EU water is now provided by private firms as a commodity for which people must pay. Major multinationals like Vivendi and Suez Lyonnaise claim that only privatization can conserve this valuable resource and use 'tragedy of the commons' style arguments to advance their case. They promise that private ownership and market mechanisms will divert supplies of water to areas of scarcity by sending it by pipelines, tankers or even floating plastic bags - provided a profit can be made.

The concept of intellectual property equally rests on the argument against the commons. It is claimed that inventors need financial rewards in order to 'incentivise' them to make new discoveries. In the absence of such incentives, it is suggested that scientists will make little effort for the collective good. Instead of universities putting knowledge into the public domain as before, neo-liberals argue that a patent should be taken out on every invention and the inventor rewarded each time it is used. Property rights are also being established in areas previously regarded as 'inalienable' such as the genetic code of plants or animals. If these are no longer part of the common heritage of the planet, but are privately owned, it is claimed that advances can then be made by the new science of bioengineering. More broadly, the argument for property rights is being extended to public services, natural resources and items held in government trust such as airwaves on the electro-magnetic spectrum or public lands.

The argument against the commons can be disputed, however, on the grounds both of efficiency and its inherent assumptions about human nature. Hardin's original argument confused the idea of a commons with unlimited public access where there are no rules. It did not allow for common ownership within which people would draw up regulations to restrict their individual interests. No argument is advanced for why social groups cannot develop rules to sustain their collective interests. Most herdsmen would understand the danger of overgrazing and would, presumably, want to prevent it. Hardin never explained why they could not discuss this possibility together and devise rules to stop it occurring. The most elementary point about social groups is that they develop a 'moral order' that enforces norms on the individual. Have fishermen not developed codes about catching within seasons? Do people not refrain from cutting down trees in public forests? Are there not readily accepted public health rules to sustain our cities? These socially accepted codes are only breached when a private, for profit motive intrudes into the wider culture.

Nor should we assume, as the public choice theorists suggest, that benefits deriving from proper public services extend only to public officials and special interest groups and not to the wider community. The fact that most cities have a street lighting system is not attributable to the self-interest or manipulative activities of clever public officials intent on retaining their cushy jobs. People understand that they do not have the individual capacity to keep their streets lit. Everybody, neo-liberals included, gains from seeing at night or from going to school in the light. Similarly, in the case of education. Some very wealthy people may have the capacity to hire private tutors, run their own private laboratories and undertake their own scientific research. But the vast majority do not and, as in the case of street lighting, need to have education organized in common. The demand for quality public services does not arise, therefore, from 'rent seeking' public officials but from interests of the vast majority. Neo-liberals, however, must deny the inherent rationality of providing these services because they fear that a wealthy minority may be forced to pay more in taxes.

The assumption that public sector workers who campaign for better services are 'rent seeking' is also fallacious. Many of us go to work to get a wage but we survive by developing an interest in what we did. If we did not already know it, we soon recognize that 'dossing' or 'swinging the lead' is the hardest way to get through the day. It is, therefore, hardly surprising that nurses should develop concerns about how their patients are being treated. A teacher who does not care about whether there are computers in their classroom, or science labs to conduct experiments, is hardly the sort of person whom we would entrust children to. Not surprisingly, then, they are among the first to warn society at large about the need for investment in these services. Of course, they may advocate the hiring of more nurses or teachers on better pay but this is perfectly legitimate because benefits conferred on individual workers can also extend to the wider public in the form of a well staffed and resourced service.

The wider claim that private ownership over natural resources leads to better stewardship is not supported by empirical evidence. In a market economy, corporations are driven by the immediate competitive needs rather than by long-term planning. If share price movements drop, they need to show quicker returns on investment and may have to cut back on projects. This explains why private companies often abuse their ownership of natural resources. Far from water companies being the champion of conservation, they have been shown to frequently cut corners to make quicker profits. The British Environmental Agency, for example, has cited water companies as being among the worst environmental offenders. Five major companies have been repeatedly prosecuted for violations ranging from water leakages to illegal disposals.[52] Stewardship over water is more likely to be guaranteed by extensive public investment in a common piping network to reduce leakages and other water conservation measures.

Equity in supply is similarly more likely to be guaranteed by public ownership. Private companies do not treat people as citizens but as customers with varying degrees of spending power. They ration access according to credit card balances rather than human need. They have no interest in redistributing a relatively scarce resource from one 'customer' to another and so pay little attention to different human needs. Older people who suffer from hypothermia need more heating in winter but will often tend to be poorer. If there is public control over gas and electricity, such needs can be recognized and tariffs reduced or free heating supplied accordingly. Private companies will subscribe to the social norm that older people should not be left to die if they are regulated by the state and receive a subsidy. But this only begs the question: how could they be more 'efficient' if the public has to spend extra resources on regulating them?

The argument for property rights over common ownership of knowledge is truly absurd. The market may encourage calculation, impersonal relations and monetary gain – but these are hardly the qualities that stimulate inventions and creativity. Other qualities such as sharing, collaboration and sociability are more likely to generate new ideas and discoveries. But these characteristics will tend to develop in a 'gift economy' where people give freely in the hope that all will benefit. The best-known modern example of common ownership operating for the greater good is the Open Software movement, which gave rise to the Linux/GNU operating system. In the 1960s, it was assumed that the proprietary codes of software should be available to all but when this was closed down by the patenting system, Richard Stallman, Linus Torvalds and a host of other 'hackers' created their open software movement within which participants are motivated by fun or intellectual puzzles to create a community that both supports and critiques each other's work.[53] Because the software is open, anyone can look 'under the hood' and check the codes and the result is better software. By contrast, when the research is taken over by a company like Microsoft and one organizational culture comes to dominate, more rigid thought patterns often ensue. Glitches are regularly found because the software is not subject to the same level of public scrutiny.

A similar problem emerged with claims to property rights during the Human Genome Project. John Sulston, one of the chief scientists involved, has pointed out that the project worked because it was the result of open collaboration. However once the human genetic structure was discovered, corporations started taking out patents on individual genes and charging licences to use their property. When scientists at a public university discovered that a defect in a particular gene produced resistance to HIV, they also, unfortunately, found that they had to pay a private company a licence fee to work on this gene.[54] This type of financial cost restricts the sharing of information. The advancement of scientific findings that arose though public collaboration is thereafter hindered by private appropriation.

The attack on the commons in the name of property rights is, thus, not motivated by 'efficiency' or a desire to conserve natural resources. It is instead driven by the desire to assist large corporations to invade ever-newer areas of our lives.

3. Cut Taxes and Privatise!

This simple injunction is where all neo-liberal thinking leads. Privatization means the transfer of public assets into private hands and it began in earnest with Margaret Thatcher. By the 1990s there was little left to sell off and a second phase developed through Public Private Partnerships. Under these schemes, private companies get long-term tenders to provide services such as waste management, water supply or to run hospitals. Instead of a 'design-build' contract for a school, they get a 'design-build-finance and operate' contract for twenty-five years. This means that they don't just build the school but maintain it afterwards and hire the caretakers and administrators. The main argument used to support traditional models of privatization is that competition leads to more efficiency and brings lower prices and better quality services. Market signals based on profit and price information indicate how a company is doing, and when faced with the threat of extinction, forces them to improve. In addition, as the public choice theorists argue, property rights create new incentives for better performance.

The experience of more than two decades of privatization does not, however, support these claims. Contrary to the theory, competition does not always follow privatization. There may be an appearance of competition in the drive to secure initial contracts but the reality may be rather different. Global service providers who compete against one another for tenders in one country, may be collaborating in others. Just two firms – Correction Corporation of America and Sodexho – dominate the market for private prisons. They are supposed to compete for contracts but often run joint projects in different parts of the world. The European electricity market is dominated by seven main players who invested €80 billion in mergers and acquisitions in 2002–03 The result, according to one study, is that 'effective competition in the European power market is just a myth: there is no real competition on more than 90 per cent of the EU electricity market'.[55]

Natural monopolies also tend to develop in many utilities, and few people go to the trouble of changing supplier. People cannot shop around for different water suppliers and even where there is 'choice' few people exercise it in the case of essential services. The country with the highest level of change in electricity suppliers was Britain but, even here, only 12 per cent of small users changed supplier.[56] The lure of large profits from natural monopolies means that companies employ a variety of underhand tactics to win contracts. The British Office of Fair Trading has noted that companies often tender for local authority contracts 'on a predatory basis, accepting short-term losses so as to eliminate competitors with the expectation of subsequently making monopoly profits'.[57] A good example of such tactics is to be found in the case of companies like Stagecoach who sometimes flood the market with cheap bus fares until rivals are pushed out and a monopoly position is established.

The lure of big profits means that privatization exacerbates the problem of corruption. Police have estimated that 'the overwhelming majority of corruption cases in Britain are connected to the award of contracts'.[58] In France, the Suez Lyonnaise and Vivendi plus the largest construction companies, have been investigated for 'an agreed system of misappropriation of public funds'.[59] In Germany the district auditor of Hesse noted that 'there is an established system of illegal acquirement and excessive allowances for public contracts'.[60] The European Commission itself had to resign en masse in 1999 because of a corruption scandal linked to private tendering.[61]

Despite claims of its advocates, it is not the case that privatized firms automatically bring lower prices. In some areas, such as airfares and telecommunications, prices have dropped, but these have also been linked to changes in technology or a change in market positioning. In other areas such as in electricity, prices have risen both in the run up to privatization and in the aftermath.[62] In France, where it is possible to compare both private and public suppliers of water, it was found that private suppliers' charges were 13 per cent higher.[63] International evidence also suggests that privatized water monopolies in Britain are more costly for users than municipal monopolies in Sweden or Scotland. The irony of privatization is that it needs a state bureaucracy to regulate its services to ensure that it does not over-charge.

The most common consequence of privatization is major cuts in employment. In Britain, between 1979 and 1999, the number of railway employees fell by around three quarters, the electricity labour force by half, the water industry by 40 per cent.[64] The gains in productivity claimed by privatized companies arose mainly from this shedding of jobs. Beyond this, there is little evidence of a continuing dynamic productivity, as even a recent

European Commission report acknowledged, when it reported that 'no significant impact of reforms was identified with labour productivity and this seems to suggest that deregulation is associated with one off changes in the level of productivity'.[65]

The claim that privatization brings better quality services is also quite spurious. The railway service in Britain has had a notoriously poor performance since privatization. Electricity blackouts have become more frequent in the US and Europe since privatization. Privatized water companies do not take adequate precaution against drought. Private hospitals may refuse to treat patients without health insurance and private schools are free to manipulate their intake to ensure their place on school league tables. Private prisons may abuse prisoners by hiring cheaper guards and not providing adequate training for them.

Many academic studies suggest, therefore, that there is no conclusive evidence to show that privatization leads to better services. A comprehensive study by Martin and Parker, for example, which examined eleven privatized firms over five distinct periods (including nationalization, pre-privatization, post-announcement of privatization, post privatization and the recession of the early 1990s) did not sustain the hypothesis that private ownership is more efficient than nationalization.[66] A more recent study by Massimo Florio of the UK experience concluded that although the business cycle (and restructuring, while the company is under public ownership) has a discernable effect on a company's performance, privatization per se has no visible impact. He found no statistical evidence to show that productivity in the UK increased substantially as a consequence of ownership changes at privatization compared to the long term trend.[67]

Somewhat different arguments are used to justify public-private partnerships (PPPs) Typically it is suggested that private finance can 'plug a gap' in public funding and that private sector management techniques can deliver a better service. The evidence from Britain again, however, points in a different direction.

Far from plugging a financial gap, PPPs cost the public more for a variety of reasons. It is cheaper for the state to borrow because there is less risk of it defaulting on a loan. The cost of borrowing for the private sector is normally between 1–3 per cent higher and, cumulatively, over twenty-five years this can amount to a considerable amount of money.[68] Fees for lawyers, financial advisors, consultants and tendering costs add 3–5 per cent to the price of a PPP. Expected returns for shareholders impose an additional cost on top of these expenses. There is also a consistent pattern of cost overruns in PPP projects from the initial proposal through to the final business plan. In five PPP hospital schemes reported to the Select Committee of the British House of Commons, costs jumped by between 65 and 171 per cent between the different stages.[69] Extra costs also accrue because the state is locked into commitments that may no longer be appropriate to the population's needs. If, for example, there were to be a decline in a local population and the state no longer required a particular school or the full use of particular hospital services, it would still be required to pay all the outstanding debt, interest and foregone profit of the PPP consortium.[70]

There is also no conclusive evidence to show that private sector management techniques are necessarily superior to those employed in the public sector. It is simply not the case that the public sector is mired in a bureaucracy from which the private sector escapes scot-free. While about 7.5 per cent of jobs in the British public sector are classified as managers or senior officials, the corresponding figure for the private sector is 17.2 per cent. In finance and business services, that are supposed to be at the cutting edge of the new turbo capitalism, the figures rise to 27 and 21 per cent respectively.[71] The private sector is often driven by increasingly crude benchmark measures, which stress immediate financial returns over wider long-term planning. Once these benchmarks are in place, top management often jettison all other criteria and look no further. These types of practices explain how AIB – who, co-incidentally, are heavily involved in PPP projects – managed to lose $691 million when one of its currency traders, John Rusnak, defrauded it. If ever there was an example of inefficiency, this must surely be it!

PPPs in Britain have led to wide-scale dissatisfaction, as many feel that they have received poorer services for the amount of public money invested. In the London Underground, in one of the largest PPP schemes, private companies won a £15 billion contract to improve the service. Christian Wolmar, the historian of the underground, has described the result as 'an expensive mess, a reduction in accountability, an apparent black hole for taxpayers and few benefits for passengers'.[72] In the health sector, cost cutting by private companies has led to an estimated closure of 3,800 beds in eleven hospitals. The chair of the government's own Commission on Architecture, Stuart Lipton, has complained that some hospitals faced leaking sewage, unstable rooms and no air conditioning. Pressure to save money has led to the construction of corridors that are too narrow to turn trolleys and nurses' stations from which patients cannot be seen.[73]

PPPs produce a growing democratic deficit as public services come to be treated like private commodities. Whereas citizens once claimed the right to public information about their schools or hospitals, the private consortia now protect themselves with rules of commercial secrecy. The public is not even being given the full details of contracts negotiated between their state and private companies as these become covered by rules of commercial secrecy. This denial of information and knowledge can only please market fundamentalists, seeking to reduce the public sphere.

Privatization is the logic of Friedrich Hayek's vision to turn us into atomized individuals, preoccupied with our own bank balances while neglecting society at large. Arguments about pricing, efficiency and better service are incidental and can be disproved. The real issue is the complete corporate take-over of the social world. Ireland has embarked on this route somewhat later than its immediate neighbour, but despite all the soft words spoken about caring and social inclusion, the same corporate take-over is underway.

NOTES

1. J. O'Leary, 'Effects of Irish Ferries case will be positive', *Irish Times*, 16 December 2005.
2. J. Power, 'Wealth creators targeted as union tax demands turn rich lists into hit lists', *Irish Independent*, 28 October 2004.
3. M. Friedman, *Capitalism and Freedom* (Chicago: University of Chicago Press, 1982), p.vi.
4. R. Sidelsky, *John Maynard Keynes: The Economist as Saviour* (London: Penguin, 1992), p.235.
5. A. Ebenstein, *Hayek's Journey: The Mind of Frederich Hayek* (Basingstoke: Palgrave, 2003), p.96.
6. Ibid.
7. F. Hayek, *The Road to Serfdom* (London: Routledge, 1997), p.52.
8. F. Hayek, *Law, Legislation and Liberty: Vol. 1, Rules and Order* (London: Routledge and Kegan Paul, 1973), p.2.
9. F. Hayek, *The Constitution of Liberty* (London, New York: Routledge, 1993), p.105.

10. Ibid.
11. N. Bosanquet, *After The New Right* (Aldershot: Heinemann, 1984), p.39.
12. S. George, 'How to win the War of Ideas: Lessons from the Gramscian Right'. *Dissent*, Summer 1997.
13. 'The Road to Serfdom: Inside Story of a 50-year phenomenon'. On Laissez faire Books website www.lfb.com/index.
14. A. Ebenstein, *Friedrich Hayek* (New York: Palgrave, 2001), Chap.18.
15. James Pierson, 'Investing in Conservative Ideas'. *Commentary*, May 2005.
16. H. Hazlitt, 'The Early History of the FEE'. *The Freeman*, 34, 3 (March 1984).
17. Pierson, 'Investing in Conservative Ideas'.
18. M. Friedman, *There is No Such Thing as a Free Lunch* (LaSalle, IL: Open Court, 1975), Introduction.
19. G. Becker and J. Elias, 'Introducing Incentives in the Market for Live and Cadaveric Organ donations'. Working paper, University of Chicago, 2003 http://home.uchicago.edu/~jelias/organs_becker_elias.pdf.
20. See J. Valdes, *Pinochet's Economists: the Chicago School in Chile* (Cambridge and New York: Cambridge University Press, 1995).
21. P.Constable and A. Valenzuela, *A Nation of Enemies: Chile Under Pinochet* (New York: Norton, 1973), p.171.
22. Ibid.
23. G. Becker, 'Latin America owes a lot to its "Chicago Boys"'. *Business Week*, 9 June 1997.
24. T. Gylfason, 'Interview with Assar Lindbeck'. CESifo Working Paper Series No.1408.
25. See John Blundel, *Waging the War of Ideas* (London: Institute of Economic Affairs, 2001), p.42.
26. See The Powell Memo: to Eugene Sydnor, Chairman of Education Committee, US Chamber of Commerce 23 August 1971 in media transparency.org.
27. Quoted in E. Andrew, 'Education and the Funding of Research'. *Techne*, 9, 1 (Fall 2005), pp.44–6.
28. 'The Very Foundation of Conservatism'. *New York Times*, 28 November 2005.
29. L. Lapham, 'Tentacles of Rage'. *Harpers Magazine*, 309, 1852 (1 September 2004), p.2.
30. Ibid., p.4.
31. http://www.mediatransparency.org/grantsearchresults.php?searchString=Law+ and+ Economics
32. *Buying a Movement: Right Wing Foundations and American Politics* (Washington: People for the American Way, 1996), p.16.
33. 'Covert Industry Funding Fuels the Expansion of Radical Right Wing Think Tanks'. *Corporate Europe Observatory*, July 2005.
34. For an interesting account of Pinera's role in right-wing think tanks see 'The Siren of Santiago'. *MotherJones*, March/April 2005.
35. See J. Stiglitz, *Globalization and Its Discontents* (New York and London: Norton, 2002) and P. Krugman, *Peddling Prosperity: Economic Sense and Nonsense in an age of Diminished Expectation* (New York and London: Norton, 1994).
36. See C. Lapavitas, 'Mainstream Economics in the Neoliberal Era', in A. Saad-Filho and D. Johnston, *Neoliberalism: A Critical Reader* (London: Pluto Press, 2005), pp.30–41.
37. Commanding Heights: Interview with Milton Friedman on Public Broadcasting Service, 10 January 2000, www.pbs.org/wgbh/commandingheights/shared.minitext/int_miltonfriedman.html.
38. See G. Stigler, 'Director's Law of Public Income Redistribution'. *Journal of Law and Economics*, 13, 1 (1970).
39. Thomas Frank, *One Market under God* (New York: Random House, 2000), p.69.
40. J. Gelinas, *Juggernaut Politics: Understanding Predatory Globalisation* (London and New York: Zed Books, 2003), p.119–20.
41. M. Holborow, 'Language and Ideology: Interconnections between English and

NeoLiberalism', in J. Edge (ed.), *ReLocating TESOL in the Age of Empire* (London: Palgrave, 2006), pp.96–7.
42. M. Friedman, *Capitalism and Freedom* (Chicago and London: University of Chicago Press, 1982), p.13
43. T. Friedman, *The Lexus and the Olive Tree* (New York: Anchor Books, 2003), p.115.
44. G. Soros, *The Crisis of Global Capitalism* (London: Little Brown, 1998), p.45.
45. Common Cause, Campaign Contribution by Tobacco Interests, September 2005, www.tobaccofreekids.
46. L. Elliot and D. Atkinson, *The Age of Insecurity* (London: Verso, 1998), p.100.
47. D. Bollier, *Public Assets, Private Profits: Reclaiming the American Commons in an Age of Market Enclosure* (Washington: New America Foundation, 2001), p.52.
48. J.M. Keynes, *General Theory of Employment, Interest and Money* (London: Macmillan, 1973), p.156.
49. G. Hardin 'The Tragedy of the Commons'. *Science*, 162 (13 December 1968), pp.1243–8.
50. Ibid., p.1247.
51. J. Buchanan and G. Tullock, *The Calculus of Consent* (Michigan: University of Michigan Press, 1962).
52. M. Barlow and T. Clake, *Blue Gold: The Battle Against Corporate Theft of the World's Water* (London: Earthscan, 2002), p.125.
53. See S. Weber, 'The Political Economy of Open Source Software'. Berkeley Roundtable on the International Economy Paper 140 2000.
54. J. Sulston and G. Ferry, *The Common Thread* (London: Bantham Press, 2002).
55. C. Kjaer and O. Schafer, The Myth of Effective Competition in European Power Markets (European Renewable Energy Council, 2004), p.18.
56. D. Hall, 'Evaluating the Impact of Liberalisation on Public Services' (London: PSIRU, 2004), p.7.
57 Public Services Privatisation Research Unit, *The Privatisation Network* (London: PSIRU, 1996), p.12.
58. Quoted in D. Hall, 'Privatisation, Multi-national and Corruption'. *Development in Practice*, 9, 5 (November 1999), p.5.
59. Ibid., p.7.
60. Ibid.
61. Ibid., p.8.
62. See for example, D. Cahill and S. Beder, 'Regulating the Power Shift: The State, Capital and Electricity Privatisation in Australia'. *Journal of Australian Political Economy*, 55 (June 2005), pp.5–22.
63. D. Hall, 'Services of General Interest in Europe – an evidence based approach' (London: PSIRU, 2001), p.4.
64. J. Kay, Privatisation in the United Kingdom 1979–1999, http://www.ukprivatisation.com/.
65. European Commission, 'Horizontal Evaluation of the Performance of Network Industries providing Services of General Economic Interest'. EC SEC (2004) 866, p.151.
66. S. Martin and D. Parker, *The Impact of Privatisation: Ownership and Corporate Performance in the UK* (London: Routledge, 1997).
67. M. Florio, *The Great Divesture* (Massachusetts: MIT Press, 2004)
68. D. Whitfield, 'Private Finance Imitative: The Commodification and Marketisation of Education'. *Social Justice*, 1, 2 (1999) pp.2–12.
69. A. Pollock, D. Price and S. Player, *The Private Finance Imitative: A Policy Built on Sand* (London: Unison report, 2005), p.8.
70. D. Dawson, 'The Private Finance Initiative – a Public Finance Illusion'. *Health Economics*, 10, 6 (September 2001), pp.479–86.
71 Trade Union Congress, *Bowler Hats and Bureaucrats: Myths about the Public Sector Workforce* (London: TUC, 2005), pp.4–5.
72. 'Down the Tube: how PPP deal is costing London'. *Guardian*, 21 February 2005.
73. 'PFI is here to stay'. *British Medical Journal*, 324, 1178 (18 May 2002)

Chapter Three

For Sale: Recently Refurbished State

During the Irish Ferries dispute, something unusual happened at the Independent Group of newspapers. Justine McCarthy was so annoyed by the blatant injustice of sacking the staff that she wrote a column on corporate greed. She questioned why there was adulation for Ryanair when it banned unions and charged its disabled passengers for access to their planes. She also wrote about the warrior managerial culture that pervaded the Celtic Tiger in search of huge profits. Her column reflected a wider mood of disquiet but hardly anyone saw the article because it was spiked. She was subsequently dropped as a columnist and another journalist, Gerry Flynn, was also 'stood down' as industrial correspondent after he had reported that Irish Ferries had threatened to tear-gas their workers.[1] Management at the *Irish Independent* did not seem too pleased about the journalists' coverage of the dispute.

'The free press is essential to democracy' – this is a familiar refrain when someone wishes to praise the tolerant culture of Western democracy. Censorship is normally seen as something that occurs in backward, dictatorial societies where the rulers have little popular legitimacy. It is usually taken to mean state action – although Islamic protests against offensive cartoons depicting the Prophet Mohamed were also commonly treated as examples of censorship. Rarely, however, is private ownership seen as a source of censorship.

Yet the Irish Ferries case indicated a problem. Contrary to impressions, the firm was not a maverick company but one that was deeply embedded in the networks of corporate Ireland. Its board included John McGuckian, the chairperson of Ulster Television; Peter Crowley, the chief finance officer of IBI Finance, the leading corporate finance advisor operating in Ireland, and Bernard Somers, who runs one of Ireland's main 'change-management' firms. In fact Somers was on the board of both the Independent News and Media PLC (INM) and Irish Ferries. Coincidently, Al McGrath, the Human Resource Manager of Irish Ferries, was a former Human Resources manager of INM. Many corporate executives were sympathetic with the Irish Ferries management, but waited to see if they could beat the unions. They knew that restructuring at Irish Ferries differed only in degree from similar practices taking place elsewhere in Irish industry. The *Irish Independent* itself got rid of 205 jobs and then outsourced its clerical work to two contractors – SWS in Cork and AnswerCallDirect in Armagh[2] – so it was hardly surprising that the newspaper might indicate displeasure with journalists who were overly critical of Irish Ferries.

All of which raises important questions for the functioning of democracy. In a democracy, people are supposed to have a right to have their views heard. But what if there was a systematic bias towards one particular, corporate view of the world? Or despite claims about 'balance', views that were critical of corporations are crowded out? Independent Newspapers bestrides the Irish print media like a colossus, publishing the largest selling daily, the *Irish Independent*, and the Irish edition of the *Daily Star*. It directly owns two out of five Sunday newspapers, the *Sunday Independent* and the *Sunday World*, and effectively controls a third, the *Sunday Tribune*. It owns the only national evening newspaper, the *Evening Herald*, and controls approximately 20 per cent of local and regional papers. In all, Independent Newspapers effectively controls about 80 per cent of the Irish print media.[3] The company, which is mainly owned by Tony O'Reilly, thus wields enormous political influence.

There are some indications that corporations who dominate the media are by no means averse to using that influence. The British Prime Minister, Tony Blair, has met with Rupert Murdoch on a number of occasions to assure him of support and to ask for a favourable hearing from his media. Blair presumably did this because it was in his interest. Might not Independent Newspapers also try to influence politicians and the decision-making process? Two examples indicate that they do.

In late 1996, John Bruton, the then Fine Gael Taoiseach, met Tony O'Reilly at the latter's summer residence in Glandore, Cork. There a series of 'gripes' was conveyed to the Taoiseach about the failures of his government to uphold some of O'Reilly's commercial interests. Subsequently, Bruton's senior advisor, Sean Donlon, had a meeting with executives of Independent Newspapers on these same matters. He told the Moriarty Tribunal that he was left 'in no doubt about Independent Newspapers' hostility to the Government parties if outstanding matters were not resolved to their satisfaction'.[4] O'Reilly followed up the meetings with a letter to Bruton outlining his disappointment about the government's failure to act and indicating his displeasure. None of this, it transpired, was an empty gesture. On Election Day on 6 June 1997, the *Irish Independent* duly ran a front-page editorial, which urged people not to vote for Bruton's incumbent government.

A more ominous case was the treatment that Independent Newspapers meted out to investigative journalist Frank Connolly. His decision to help found the Centre for Public Inquiry set off alarm bells within elite circles as it threatened further exposures of the golden circle that linked politics and money. The Centre was modelled on the Washington-based Centre for Public Integrity which conducts investigative journalism in the public interest. Its reports on the influence of money on politics have become bestsellers. Connolly was known as a thorn in the side of the corporate elite ever since he revealed that the Fianna Fail Minister Ray Burke was involved in planning corruption in North Dublin. The story set off a chain reaction that led to the establishment of the Flood tribunal of inquiry. One of those who were due to answer questions was Tony O'Reilly because his company, Fitzwilton Investments, had made a £30,000 donation to Ray Burke. The tribunal was to investigate if there was any link between this and re-broadcasting licences that Burke had issued.[5]

As soon as the Centre for Public Inquiry (CPI) was founded, the *Sunday Independent* ran a headline on 'Gardai Probe new watchdog boss Connolly'. Some months later they ran another story quoting a Unionist peer in the House of Lords who used parliamentary privilege to attack Connolly. After the CPI launched a report on Trim Castle, the *Sunday Independent* ran another piece headlined 'Ahern fears Frank Connolly's links'.[6] Finally, in an extraordinary case, *Irish Independent* journalist Sam Smyth ran a story based on leaked Garda documents about a passport application Connolly had allegedly made before travelling to a Revolutionary Armed Forces of Columbia (FARC)-controlled area of Colombia. The documents had come directly from the Minister for Justice, Michael McDowell. Earlier McDowell had been informed that the Gardai had decided not to prosecute Connolly on charges of travelling with a false passport but the Minister still wanted to discredit the journalist and used access to official information to do so.[7] The 'scandal' that was manufactured between McDowell and the *Irish Independent* was designed to inflict the maximum damage on the CPI – and it worked. It was too much for the wealthy US philanthropist Chuck Feeney, and his company Atlantic Philanthropies, who withdrew funding for the Centre, forcing its closure. The 'free press', it appears, was used to crush one of Ireland's best-known journalists.

These examples indicate a relationship between the ownership of Independent Newspapers and some journalistic coverage where issues of direct interest to the company are concerned. However, there is also a much deeper connection between press ownership and ideology. The term ideology is used sometimes in a narrow, pejorative sense to refer to being motivated by a wider political agenda and is often used to marginalize particular beliefs. Hence someone who argues against social partnership is labelled 'ideological' whereas supporters of social partnership are assumed to be simply promoting the national good. There is, however, a wider more fruitful use of the term that defines it as a partial view of the world that bolsters and helps to sustain particular interest groups. Neo-liberalism from this perspective is an ideology because it is a belief system that promotes the interests of the corporate elite. It also pervades the mass media and, in particular, major right-wing press groups such as Independent Newspapers.

Herman and Chomsky have argued that the raw material of the news passes through five interrelated filters that interact and re-enforce each other. These are:

1) the size, concentrated ownership, owner wealth and profit orientation of the dominant mass media firms; 2) advertising as the primary income source of the mass media; 3) reliance of the media on information provided by government and business 'experts' funded and approved by these primary sources and agents of power; 4)'flak' as a means of disciplining the media and 5)'anti-communism' as a national religion and control mechanism.[8]

These filters give the media a bias towards corporate interests and are mainly self explanatory. 'Flak' refers to the type of technique whereby writers such as Frank Connolly are subject to systematic attack to discredit alternative views. Herman and Chomsky's argument, however, needs one amendment: 'anti-communism' has been replaced by neo-liberalism as the national religion of today.

Independent Newspapers is one of its more aggressive exponents. The majority of its columnists provide regular arguments to beef up the foot soldiers on ground level. Some, such as Moore McDowell and Shane Ross, specialize in expert economic arguments to justify market solutions and typically use their columns to attack public sector workers. The newspaper group as a whole played a major role in the defeat of the ASTI strikes in 2001 by whipping up a virulent campaign against them. Others, such as Ruth Dudley Edwards, Eoghan Harris, Alan Ruddock and Brendan O'Connor, concentrate their fire on marginalized groups such as Muslims. The latter figure, for example casually claimed that the ' fundamental principles (of Islam) will only be satisfied when its followers have wiped out Western civilisation'.[9] The effect of this type of ranting is to construct social groups as outsiders who are then deemed to be 'threats' or 'spongers' that society must unite against. This type of press coverage assists the neo-liberal project by diverting attention from 'spongers' in some very high places. (That designation might be better applied to members of the corporate elite, including the owner of Independent Newspapers, who has designated himself as a 'tax exile' from Ireland since the 1960s.) But this scapegoating also feeds into a law and order agenda that relies on regular panics to construct a more repressive state apparatus.

However, while Independent Newspapers plays a major role in promoting the neo-liberal creed, it would be wrong to assign it a power above its station. One of the problems with the Herman/Chomsky model is that while it correctly draws a link between ownership and corporate propaganda, it tends to view the media audience as more susceptible to 'brainwashing' than is actually the case. Modern rulers can exercise considerable control over the dissemination of information but they cannot determine how it is received. If an ideology is constantly pumped out with monotonous regularity, many come to read between the lines and to contrast their own experience with the message. As the Italian writer Gramsci put it, people develop a contradictory consciousness which combines a 'common sense' that is often shaped by their rulers and a 'good sense' which arises from experiences of struggle and solidarity.[10] The attempt by Independent Newspapers to shape coverage of the Irish Ferries dispute, for example, did not prevent tens of thousands marching in opposition.

A conventional understanding of politics can also lead to an over-focus on the media. Here, it is assumed that voters elect governments who, in turn, carry out policies for which they have a mandate. The modern voter, it is sometimes argued, has embraced consumerist values because of constant advertising and propaganda and this, in turn, shapes government policy. Hence the media becomes the prime mover in promoting a neo-liberal direction in politics. However, this is a naive view on how democracy functions in a highly unequal society. It ignores just how limited it is and arises because there is confusion between the government and the state. This is understandable because the wider state is silent, whereas the government regularly pronounces. Yet the two are not synonymous.

Surrounding every elected government is a state that claims to itself a monopoly on the use of violence and is constructed around a permanent administrative apparatus. Each elected minister is encircled by a team of unelected higher civil servants who are plugged into global and EU networks of decision-making. Decisions are made within a framework determined by wider economic forces that neither politicians nor their unelected administration control. On almost every relevant issue under discussion, the views of 'the market' or, more precisely, unelected boards of directors, will be conveyed to the senior civil servants and, through them, to the Ministers. Should the corporations be displeased, there is always an implicit threat that the 'markets will react badly'. The whole framework is set up so that only 'realistic' decisions are made. Of course there is still a variety of opinion between Left and Right, but it is a variety within a dominant unchallenged framework.

If the political decision-making is seen in this way, it becomes clear that the news media are not the key force in shaping society. They are, rather, the primary mechanism by which an elite wins legitimacy for decisions that have already been made. In the past, the elite reached out to their populations through church institutions or through other social networks where their middle-class supporters transmitted their arguments. The atomization of modern society, however, means that the mass media now plays that role. But the neo-liberal agenda still comes from a wider re-structuring of the state in response to pressure from the 'corporate' elite.

RESTRUCTURING OF THE STATE

Broadly speaking, the Irish state has gone through three major phases in its relationship to business.

From 1932 to 1959, there was a populist project aimed at building up native capital. The dominant party, Fianna Fail, forged a coalition composed of small farmers, industrial workers and native capitalists to challenge the agro-export model that the first Cumman na nGaedheal presided over. In a speech in 1928, De Valera argued that this model turned Ireland into an 'outgarden' of its former empire by supplying it agricultural produce, and would keep it in a state of permanent underdevelopment.[11] After they came to power in 1932, Fianna Fail adopted protectionist policies to build up native industry. Companies such as Jefferson Smurfit and Cement Roadstone were allowed a space to establish themselves in a captive market created by protectionism. The weakness of native capital, however, also meant that the state itself had to step in to supply the necessary infrastructure to assist development and a host of semi-state companies such as the ESB and Bord na Móna were formed.

The programme to strengthen native capital involved considerable hardship, and was sustained principally through policies geared to preserving the loyalty of the small farming bloc. The dominant political discourse often reflected the worldview of small farmers, with its emphasis on sturdy independence, Catholic social values and suspicion of landlordism and ostentatious display of wealth. The state was also officially committed to re-distributing land between small farmers. In the cities, the nationalist discourse was used to split and de-anglicize the labour movement by drawing unions into a closer relationship with Fianna Fail and the state. Demands for social reform were characterized as British left-wing imports and marginalized. Yet, ironically, the state structure itself was inherited from the former empire. The core apparatus of civil servants was tightly organized around a dominant secretariat in the Department of Finance, whose principal function was to maintain a tight rein on public spending. Corruption appeared to be fairly limited and the Catholic Church was the main external agency that enjoyed extensive informal access to state officials. Behind the scenes, the regular communication between de Valera and the Archbishop, John Charles McQuaid, often determined policies.[12]

After 1958 this changed, and a new corporatist project emerged to integrate native and foreign capital. Protectionism was dropped and the Control of Manufactures Act, which limited the role of foreign capital, was repealed. The Irish state set out to attract foreign investment and find a niche in global markets. One sign of the change was the creation of one of the first export processing zones at Shannon airport to attract US capital. The state did not, however, drop its support for native capital, as some have implied,[13] but, rather, sought to integrate its interests with those of foreign companies. The political elite had no intention of becoming a 'neo-colony' again but felt that foreign capital would add a new dynamism to the economy, from which native industry would also benefit.

The impetus for the change came from a state bureaucracy that had recently become involved in the IMF and the World Bank. But once the change got underway, the state began to restructure itself to suit the new requirements of capital. The 'modernizers' gradually pushed back the Catholic Church from a central role in decision making. The Industrial Development Authority (IDA) emerged as a semi-autonomous agency that was able to make quick decisions to suit foreign capital. Initially, these decisions concerned the award of grants and training opportunities, but the agency expanded its role to become a strong voice for foreign capital within the state structure itself. Native capital raised few objections as it, too, benefited from policies of doling out 'corporate welfare' to business. Anyway, it had its own avenues into the state apparatus. Alongside the more formal ways of making representations, Fianna Fail, principally, but also Fine Gael, offered a direct, informal route for patronage. The former party dropped its image of rustic frugality, embracing big business with such gusto that corruption and greed ate away at a political leadership which had once extolled the virtues of sacrifice. The remarkable feature of Ireland's spate of scandals is just how many major firms were involved. From Cement Roadstone, from whose head office the Ansbacher accounts were effectively run, to Allied Irish Banks, who wrote off the debts of Charles Haughey, there was an understanding that palm-greasing was a normal way to get a special hearing from the state.

The tensions generated by the integration into the global economy were reduced through social partnership. This began in rudimentary form in the 1960s, with the formation of the Commission on Industrial Organisation and a host of industrial Adaptation Boards that organized trade unions and employers into discussions on how to prepare Irish industry for the competitive age. By the late 1970s, National Understandings emerged briefly to co-opt union leaders and contain the threat of working class militancy. Then, after 1987, a more extensive form of social partnership developed and has survived to the present. It became the principal mechanism for aligning the major economic interest groups to the goal of 'national competitiveness'. The unions embraced a form of 'business unionism' that asserted their common interests with employers, and, in return for wage restraint, the state agreed to a vague social agenda which involved no extra costs on business. Alongside the parliament new structures were created for discussions on national economic priorities. This mechanism did not, however, shift the priorities of the state but became an important tool for de-mobilizing opposition. Anger that blew up over corruption scandals, for example, was defused as the unions refused to offer a focus for opposition.

The final phase of state restructuring has been the emergence of the neo-liberal state. This was facilitated by social partnership and developed rapidly during the Celtic Tiger years. The phrase 'neo-liberal state' may at first appear as an anomaly, as some neo-liberals boldly assert the state is a relic to be displaced by market forces. However, this assertion is only made by the wilder, utopian supporters of the ideology. Far from seeking to displace the state, the large corporations want to re-shape it so that it becomes a handmaiden, available to look after their every immediate need. This occurs at a number of levels.

In the first instance, the social tensions caused by neo-liberal policies necessitate a more repressive state that is sealed off from many democratic pressures. Far from declining, the state becomes more active in attacking opposition. New laws have been passed so that trade unions can no longer simply withdraw their labour but must go through a long series of obstacles before they can legally strike. Strikes over the victimization of individual shop stewards are banned while political strikes are supposed to be outlawed. Corporations have gained more extensive powers to take out court injunctions against those who interfere with their property, as the Rossport Five found to their cost. More broadly, the scope for elected representatives to make decisions is restricted as power is shifted to unelected officials at local level and the EU Commission at supra national levels. Bush's 'war on terror' has further increased the drift to a security state. Laws such as the Public Order Act, that were supposed to deal with anti-social behaviour, are now frequently used against demonstrators that the police choose to disperse.

The unleashing of turbo capitalism on a global scale also means that the corporations need closer ties with their local states to gain 'competitive advantage'. Sometimes this means pressure to ensure that Ireland lobbies for more favourable directives at EU level. Or it may simply mean the proofing of all proposals for national legislation in advance so that they do not adversely affect business. Or, crucially, it may mean creating more tax shelters or regulation-lite zones to give corporations based in Ireland an extra advantage over rivals. The corporations not only require more of this type of measures, but they also want it delivered in a smoother, frictionless way that does not rely on old style corruption. This does not mean that they favour a hands-off, transparent relationship that removes the possibility of corruption for ever. Rather they want modern and 'open' mechanisms to ensure that the machinery of the state is immediately available for help. The Haughey era has become a terrible embarrassment because its crudeness encouraged an anti-corporate sentiment throughout society. The ad hoc nature of the corrupt payments also led to fears that one corporation could gain an 'unfair' advantage over others. In the do or die world of global competition, the neo-liberals require a rule-bound way through which the state automatically responds to the needs of business.

The corporations also want a state that reduces overall taxation and turns public services into commodities from which profits can be made. This is not simply a matter of privatizing a few semi-state companies but a much deeper change that obliterates notions of 'social rights'. Ideologically, the citizenry must be convinced that there is 'no such thing as a free lunch' and that they must pay for services. Economically, the public sector must be re-modelled to reflect market pressures. Business techniques must infuse its management and the virus of trade unionism that spreads outwards from the public sector needs to be contained. Above all, large sections of the economy that grew up under the aegis of the state have to be depoliticized. The citizenry must understand that state run services – where they continue to exist – function according to the 'laws of the market' rather then being responsive to political pressure.

Let us now look at some of the mechanisms by which this neo-liberal state functions today.

LOBBYING

Lobbying has become an increasingly common way by which corporations intercede with the Irish state to get results. Lobbying refers to a practice of using an outside professional agency to advance either individual or collective interests. Occasionally, corporations present themselves as the equivalent to Non Governmental Organizations and claim that they merely lobby in the same way that the Combat Poverty Agency makes pre-budget submissions or Trocaire seeks to increase aid to developing countries. The comparison, however, is extremely misleading. Corporations are able to deploy far more resources to get their voices heard. They are not confined to a regular schedule of meetings organized well in advance but tend to have more immediate access to decision-makers. Unlike NGOs, they are also involved in promotion of policies from which they directly benefit. And they are frequently making arguments that go with, rather than against, the grain of the neo-liberal ethos.

There are now a variety of ways in which corporate lobbying takes place. One method used is the employment of specialist lobbying firms. These are a relatively new phenomenon in Ireland but appear to be growing with some speed. Typically, they appear as Public Relations firms that also offer a 'public affairs' or lobbying function. They tend to recruit individuals who have been members of the political elite or who have worked closely with government ministers or top party officials. These individuals are prized for the connections they can open for clients.

Alan Dukes, the former Fine Gael Minister for Finance, works as a public affairs consultant with Wilson Hartnell Public Relations and was involved in lobbying TDs about Babcock and Brown plans for the purchase of Eircom.[14] Drury Communications offers clients a range of public affairs services including, 'putting key clients and key decision makers together'.[15] The head of this lobbying unit is Iarla Mongey who once worked closely with Mary Harney as deputy government press secretary. Q4 is another PR firm that offers a lobbying service to corporate clients. It is headed up by two former key figures within Fianna Fail – Jackie Gallagher, a former special advisor to the Taoiseach Bertie Ahern and Michael Mackin, a former General Secretary of Fianna Fail. The lobbying activity of MRPA Kinman is headed up by Stephen O'Byrnes, a former key figure in the Progressive Democrats and a member of the RTE Authority.

US corporations look for a little more punch and have two key lobbying agencies: The American Chamber of Commerce and the US Ambassador. The American Chamber of Commerce hosts a number of business lunches and special conferences with key decision makers. It boasts that it has 'excellent access to Irish and European policy networks' and can 'keep Irish decision makers focussed on the factors that contribute to the continuing attractiveness of Ireland as a location for foreign direct investment'.[16] The Chamber vigorously lobbied against an EU directive, which would oblige employers to consult their staff and provide them with information on issues affecting them. Instead of an automatic right to such consultation, they demanded that it could only be triggered by a written request signed by 10 per cent of workers. In this way, the names of the employees might be noted by the very management which was reluctant to consult them in the first place! The Irish state duly agreed and the Employees (Provision of Information and Consultation) Act bore, according to *Industrial Relations News*, the 'indelible stamp' of the American Chamber of Commerce in Ireland.[17]

The Chamber works very closely with the US Ambassador who, it appears, intervenes extensively to lobby for US business interests. A dramatic example of the clout that this particular lobbyist yields was evident in the chewing gum affair.

In a rare moment in 2003, the former Environment Minister Martin Cullen and his successor Dick Roche appeared to be on the verge of imposing an extra cost on business after he was handed a consultancy report on litter. The report proposed a special €4–5 million levy on chewing gum and fast food firms and banks that used ATM machines to help bear some of the cost of cleaning up litter. The levy on chewing gum was to be raised by a 5 cent consumer tax on every packet. The justification was quite straightforward. Anyone who takes a cursory walk through the streets of any major city will find dark spots on most pavements that are the remnants of discarded chewing gum. These require special equipment to clean them off. The levy would be the chewing gum companies' contribution to defray costs. Wrigley's, however, approached US Ambassador James Kenny, who duly set up a meeting between the company, government representatives and himself. The result was the withdrawal of the proposed levy.

When a sovereign government appears unable to impose a minor chewing gum tax, there should be concerns about the fate of its democracy. But when it is casually explained that this type of intervention is perfectly normal, one really wonders. The US embassy in Dublin explained that 'The ambassador makes these interventions in a whole range of sectors in pursuit of US interests and on behalf of US firms. This was just a case where the ambassador saw US interests at play and decided to get involved.'[18] 'US interests', it seems, are synonymous with large corporations such as Wrigleys and McDonalds.

Irish industry tends to rely on organizations such as the Construction Industry Federation (CIF) and Irish Business and Employers Confederation (IBEC) to lobby state agencies. These have a major advantage over the unions as their members command the resources that determine whether or not investment takes places. Not only can they engage in extensive research and forward planning but they also have access to information that is normally shrouded in 'commercial secrecy'. In a rare interview about their lobbying activities, one IBEC executive gave a glimpse of the information asymmetry which employer organizations enjoy,

> I am surprised how often they (ministerial civil servants) ring me up looking for data ... Maybe it's just a matter of us having access to several thousand members, and they (the members) trust us, so we survey them. I think we are a good source of data.[19]

Control of information about business decisions means that IBEC lobbyists can constantly exaggerate the negative implication of any government regulation. 'We can tell them pretty much anything – how would they know?', is how the anonymous IBEC executive rather crudely put it.[20]

IBEC's ability to scupper plans for regulation testify that there is an important grain of truth in this. At one point Ireland's rising level of carbon dioxide emissions seemed to lead to an emerging consensus in policy-making circles about the need for a carbon tax. But a negative lobbying campaign by IBEC led to its withdrawal. IBEC has also lobbied for a removal of 'unnecessary' planning delays on major infrastructural development – and has been rewarded with the Planning and Development (Strategic Infrastructure) Bill (2006). More broadly, IBEC has consistently lobbied against 'costly' and 'cumbersome' regulation and its efforts have borne fruit with the Department of the Taoiseach's paper on 'Regulating Better' which sought to reduce 'red tape'.[21]

On major issues of economic policy, IBEC and the CIF have consistently been able to come up with initiatives that win acceptance from state officials. One of the most crucial decisions made about state services has been the formation of Public Private Partnerships. This proposal, however, originated in a joint IBEC/CIF document in April 1999, which was drawn up by a committee composed of representatives of National Toll Roads, AIB, Arup Engineers and a number of legal and finance houses. Although these groups are precisely those who stood to gain commercially from these projects, their plans were accepted right down to very specific details.[22]

Most of this lobbying activity takes place behind closed doors and in an arena where 'connections' and 'networking' play a vital role. It is a depoliticized arena that is less subject to democratic scrutiny – and this is precisely why it benefits the corporations.

OUTSOURCING OF GOVERNMENT

Another key feature of the neo-liberal state has been the hollowing out of the parliamentary system and a transfer of greater powers to unelected semi-autonomous public bodies. 'Governance' is a term that has come into vogue to describe an apparent de-centralization of state authority to a multitude of quasi-governmental institutions. It is sometimes assumed that the complexity of modern life requires these new forms of 'governance' but, in reality, the ethos of de-regulation plays a much greater role. Alongside the apparent delegation of authority, there is, in fact, a higher degree of centralization that reduces the role of parliament. If a host of advisory agencies are formed, it means that Ministers and top state officials can, effectively, make more unilateral decisions based on 'independent' advice. The complexity argument also tends to ignore who exactly gets to dominate many of these new public bodies.

A study by the left-leaning TASC think tank revealed that there were somewhere in excess of 450 public bodies at the end of 2005. In the first category belong executive bodies such as the Health Services Executive, which controls a budget of €11.5 billion per year, and whose activities mean that the Department of Health has been reduced to a smaller policy-making unit. The

National Roads Authority and the Environmental Protection Agency play a similar executive function. In another category belong advisory bodies which often have a significant input into policy making. These include bodies such as the Food Safety Authority or the Enterprise Strategy Group charged with mapping the future direction of Irish industrial policy. Finally, there are ad hoc 'taskforces' that are charged with producing recommendations on a number of specific issues. Ireland now has a ratio of one public body for every 5,000 people, which is slightly over the ratio of one elected representative at national or local level for every 4,000 people.[23]

Up to half of these public bodies have come into existence in the last ten years but, despite a constant refrain about 'openness and transparency', they are sometimes very slow to share information on their decision-making process. An email from an official in the Health Services Executive (HSE), in a reply to a request by the author for information on its policy of locating private hospitals on the grounds of public hospitals, rather poignantly illustrates the contradiction:

> Apologies for the delay in responding to your request. This is an EU Procurement Process which is governed by strict principles, including openness, transparency, fairness, etc. In that context I can only issue documents and information to participants in the process. All documents and information must be issued to all participants simultaneously in order to comply with the principles outlined above. Thank you for your interest in this matter.[24]

More generally, some of these public bodies are not subject to the Freedom of Information Act and/or the intervention of the Ombudsman. Coillte, the state forestry company, has however led the way in this culture of secrecy by deliberately claiming reasons of 'commercial secrecy' to hide their activities from the public.[25]

Not all public bodies have an equal impact on decision making and some are far more important than others. It is noticeable that corporate influence appears to grow the more the public bodies discuss issues that are closer to its concerns. A number of examples illustrate this.

The National Roads Authority (NRA) has come into conflict with a number of groups who object to its policy of motorway construction. The NRA seems to take a fairly relaxed approach to heritage and has become a strong advocate of the use of Public Private Partnerships to build toll roads. Opponents charge that its proposal to build an M3 motorway through the Tara landscape will damage many archaeological sites in the area.[26] However, boards of directors of the NRA have often included a strong representation from the construction industry, but they never have archaeologists or critics of PPPs on them. Those who have served on its boards have included Liam Connellan, a key figure in the Construction Industry Federation, Bernard McNamara, a director of McNamara builders, Peter Langford, a director of Arup Consulting Engineers, who later resigned so that he could act as project director for his firm's bid for consultancy work. The current chief executive of the NRA is Fred Barry, a former managing director with Jacobs's Engineering Ireland, a company which won a contract to provide engineering services on the N6 road in Galway.

Any proposed policy changes to do with the Irish Financial Services Centre is channelled directly though the Department of the Taoiseach and a special IFSC Clearing House group has been formed to advise on changes. The composition of this Clearing House Group is totally dominated by the representatives of large corporations. It is composed of groupings such as AIB Capital Markets, Bank of Ireland, Merrill Lynch, Capital Markets, State Street International, the legal firms which service these types of companies and top state officials. There are no representatives of the trade unions, the NGOs or poverty groupings to propose ways in which a levy could be placed on some of these huge financial transactions to bring greater benefit to Irish society.

One of the key advisory groups on migration policy is the Expert Group on Future Skills Needs (EGFSN). It is chaired by a director of Computer Placement Resources PLC, one of the largest recruitment and outsourcing agencies in the state and its board includes the Training and Communications Manager of Waterford Crystal, the Human Resources Director of Cement Roadstone; the Government and Human Affairs manager of Hewlett Packard, the Managing Director of Arkaon as well as one IBEC representative, two trade unionists and a number of public officials. Few people have heard of the EGFSN but it works with FAS in detailed manpower planning. Rather bizarrely, in a society that promotes market forces, it employs what can only be described as Soviet-style planning methods to ascertain how many workers with specific skills will be required in the coming years. The level of detail can be astounding. By 2008, for example, it is suggested that Ireland will need an extra 600 mushroom pickers, thirty propagation workers for plant nurseries and fifty food technology agronomists.[27] The group advocates policies that treat migrants as simple economic units that are at the disposal of business. It argues, for example, that ministers 'should retain discretionary powers to either refuse or cancel permanent residency'.[28] Many of its recommendations have found their way into legislation.

The Enterprise Strategy Group has played a key role in developing Ireland's industrial strategy. Its document on 'Ahead of the Curve' sets the framework that guides much of government policy in this area. It calls for a continuation of the 'attractive tax regime', a new strategy to commercialise research in higher education; extra funds to encourage business networks and, bizarrely, special cabinet meetings twice a year on entrepreneurship to which four senior business people will be invited. However, these pro-business recommendations are hardly surprising when you consider its composition. It is made up of the managing directors of Wyeth, Combilift Ltd, Delta Partners, Masonite Ireland, Eurostyle Ltd, Aderra Limited, the CEO of the Kerry Group and Zalco Investment; the Chief Risk Officer of the AIB, a Vice President of Dell, five pro-business academics and one former trade union official.

Other more sectional bodies also reveal a strong corporate influence. The Taskforce on the Mushroom Industry is composed entirely of representatives of the mushroom producers, state officials, a consultant and an IFA figure. There are huge concerns in trade union circles about low wages that are paid to migrant workers and heath and safety standards within the industry, but there is no trade unionist on the taskforce. The Dublin Docklands Development Authority is responsible for one of the most lucrative pieces of property in the Celtic Tiger that also happens to border poor inner city areas. The Board is composed of a representative of Anglo-Irish bank, McKinsey & Co Inc, Alexsam Corporate Finance, Byrne Curtin Kelly, OHM Group, Arup Consulting Engineers, Interactive Project Mangers and a top civil servant. There are no representatives of local working class communities.

These examples reveal an extraordinary level of corporate influence. But there is one other crucial way in which government policy making is being outsourced.

In the seven years before 2005, the Irish government spent €174 million on consultants' reports.[29] Some of the money went on publicity campaigns as the state embraced a style of glossy packaging that had long been cherished by corporations. Some was spent on 'business managements systems' that were often related to information technology projects. But a considerable amount was also spent on buying expert advice from supposedly independent sources. This combination of activities meant that, for example, the Department of Communications and the Marine has averaged about one consultancy or PR contract per week since 1998. However, while the level of sheer waste in public spending itself was extraordinary, there was also another, more fundamental, process at work.

Consultancy reports are often commissioned when governments do not want to take direct responsibility for decision making. A former assistant director of the Central Bank explained that 'consultants can provide covering fire, can serve as flak catchers and diffuse responsibility'.[30] This can make the hiring of consultants extremely attractive to the political elite. In addition to functioning as 'flak catchers', consultants can also help to depoliticize decision-making. Recommendations on vitally important issues for society are reduced to technical options that are produced by supposedly independent experts. However, although consultants may be independent of the state, they are certainly not independent of the large corporations.

The Irish state tends to hire consultants who are linked to major accountancy firms or, in the case of environment issues, engineering firms. Accountancy today is dominated by a global oligarchy composed of four firms – Deloitte, KPMG, Price Waterhouse Coopers and Ernst and Young. In Britain every one of the 100 largest corporations, bar one, use these firms to verify their accounts, while in the US all the major firms who account for 99 per cent of listed sales use the Big Four. This level of concentration means that they charge absurdly high fees but, more importantly, they develop a close symbiotic link to the bigger corporations. As a profession, accountants have become one of the most aggressive promoters of neo-liberalism – often under the guise of seemingly technical or organizational prescriptions. Neo-liberalism assumes that every thing can have a price and accountants have been recruited to assist in the process of commodification by claiming to be able to quantify all forms of resource allocation. Far from being independent, therefore, managerial consultants and those linked to accountancy firms invariably propose corporate solutions.

THE BUSINESS-POLITICAL COMPLEX

A third major element of the neo-liberal state has been the closer integration of the political and business elite. In the past, the state relied on a bureaucracy that was trained in civic duty as its primary motivation. It saw itself as having a different ethos to the private sector – one that was built on trust that arose with a professional ethic. Money was not seen as a primary motivation for entering the state service and a hands-off relationship was considered appropriate with the private sector. The different internal dynamics of business and the state was most obvious in the way each was made accountable.

> Accountability in the market domain comes through Exit and the threat of Exit. That is how producers are made accountable to customers, and how consumers ensure they are not exploited by market power or vested interests.
>
> In the public domain, however, accountability through Exit is, by definition, not available. The relationships of the public domain are necessarily long term. The loyalties, which are fundamental to it, could not take root, and would not survive, a regime of Exit. It follows that, in the public domain, accountability can only come though Voice – in other words, argument, discussion, debate and democratic engagement.[31]

Marquand's description is somewhat one sided and idealizes a professional ethic which stressed civic duty. Nevertheless, it neatly captures how state officials saw themselves in the past.

The neo-liberals, however, refuse to accept a distinction between the organizational philosophy that applies in corporations and in the public sector. Instead, they insist that both have customers and both must be managed through business plans and incentives to motivate top managers. Instead of professional trust that cultivates an ethos of civic responsibility, they insist on audits and benchmarking to monitor compliance to business style targets. In brief, they advocate a more direct intermeshing of the political and economic elites.

The Irish state has boldly embraced this ethos. Top civil servants rarely make explicit declarations about how the state is internally organized, but a number have in recent times. Brendan Tuohy, the Secretary General of the Department of Communications, Marine and Natural Resources, has called for a 'greater movement between business, academia and public service'.[32] Dermot McCarthy, the Secretary General to the government and the Department of the Taoiseach, has called for a two-way movement between the public and private sectors and has pointed out that provisions to allow such recruitment are already in place.[33] Increasingly, performance management techniques have been linked to pay and bonus payments to mimic the private sector in 'incentivising' effort. In 2005, two hundred of the top civil servants received average bonus payments of €11,500 each. The chief executive of the NRA was recruited on a salary of €300,000 plus a bonus, while the chief executive of the HSE received a €32,000 bonus on top of his salary package of €400,000 in 2005. When questions were raised about this, he was reported to be amazed about the 'fuss'.[34] It is still relatively small beer compared to the private sector but the aim is clearly to shift the organizational philosophy.

The new business-political complex, however, also works at much deeper levels. One element of the Irish state, which has effectively been colonized by the corporations, is the three development agencies – the Industrial Development Authority, Enterprise Ireland and Forfas. This is reflected in both their organizational structures and in their wider ethos. Enterprise Ireland, which is charged with developing Irish industry, is chaired by Patrick Molloy who is also chair of Cement Roadstone, and a director of Waterford Wedgewood. Seven of the other eleven members are either company directors or senior managers. The IDA is charged with attracting foreign investment and its board is composed of company directors, senior civil and public servants, a top accountant and a partner in Deloitte and Touche. Forfas, which has an overall advisory role on industrial development, is chaired by the managing director of Aderra and its board has a similar composition being composed of a former key figure in Diageo, the chief executive of a major recruitment agency, the managing director of William O'Brien Plant Hire and the Sia group, the CEO of GE Money, and a number of senior public officials. These three agencies are housed close together and function as the most explicit voice of business within the state machinery itself. If IBEC and the American Chamber of Commerce lobby the state from the outside, these three state agencies echo their points from the inside.

The growing fusion between the economic and political elites is evident in the career paths of many former top public servants. This pattern is not historically unusual in Ireland but it appears to have grown apace in recent years. A pattern of elite circulation has developed whereby former top public officials and executives of state firms move over onto the boards of banks and large Irish-owned corporations. Sometimes they function as non-executive directors but the effect is to create an interlocking web of elite networking. So Gary McGann, the former Chief Executive Officer of Aer Lingus, is now the CEO of Smurfit Kappa. David Kennedy, another former Aer Lingus CEO, is now a director of Cement Roadstone. The former attorney general of the government, Dermot Gleeson is now chairman of Allied Irish Banks. Another former attorney general, Peter Sutherland, is now the chair of BP Amoco. Michael Buckley, the former secretary general of the Department of Social Welfare, was another who became CEO of Allied Irish Banks, while Paul Haran, who was former secretary general of the Department of Enterprise Trade and Employment, joined the board of the Bank of Ireland and Glanbia. Kieran McGowan, the former head of the IDA holds directorships in Cement Roadstone, United Drug and Irish Life. The most dramatic case, however, must surely be Seamus Pairceir, the former chair of the Revenue

Commissioners who reduced Dunnes Stores tax bill by €23 million and now works as a tax advisor for ... Dunnes.[35] The career paths of former individual public servants are of significance only as an indicator of the changing culture of the state bureaucracy. When combined with the growth of other forms of corporate influence it suggests that business is likely to get a much more receptive hearing from the state than ever before. And demands of business are not particularly modest, as we shall see when it comes to taxation and regulation.

NOTES

1. C. Murphy, E. Browne, J. Byrne and V. Browne, 'Attack on Corporate Greed Censored'. *Village*, 1 December 2005.
2. 'Independent Outsourcing'. *Village*, 1 December 2005.
3. Tasc, Discussion paper on media as political mediators, TASC website. http://www.tascnet.ie/showPage.php?ID=69
4. C. Keena, 'Bruton tells how Coalition was Pressurised by O Reilly'. *Irish Times*, 24 March 2004.
5. P. Cullen, *With a Little Help from my Friends: Planning Corruption in Ireland* (Dublin: Gill and Macmillan, 2002), pp.185–6.
6. C. Murphy, 'Independent Newspaper and Centre for Public Inquiry'. *Village*, 15 December 2005.
7. Irish Council of Civil Liberties Press Release, 'Ministerial Actions must be Investigated for Constitutional and Human Rights Violation', 14 December 2005.
8. Quoted in J. Klaehn, 'A Critical Review of Herman and Chomsky's "Propaganda Model"'. *European Journal of Communications*, 17, 2 (2002), p.158.
9. B. O'Connor, 'Why Terrorism Still Won...'. *Sunday Independent*, 13 August 2006.
10. A. Gramsci, 'Notes for an Introduction and an Approach to the Study of Philosophy and the History of Culture: Some Preliminary Reference Points', in A. Gramsci, *Selection from Prison Note Books* (London: Lawrence and Wishart, 1971), pp.323–43.
11. Dáil Debates, Vol.25, Col.478, 12 July 1928.
12. For fuller discussion see Kieran Allen, *Fianna Fail and Irish labour: 1926 to the Present* (London: Pluto Press, 1997).
13. P. Bew and H. Patterson, *Sean Lemass* (Dublin: Gill and Macmillan, 1982).
14. 'Dukes to lobby on behalf of B&B'. *Sunday Business Post*, 19 March 2003.
15. Drury Communications website www.drurycommunications.com/face_government/face1.htm.
16. American Chamber of Commerce Ireland. http://www.amcham.ie.
17. C. Dooley, 'US Influence on Employee Bill denied'. *Irish Times*, 1 August 2005.
18. A. Beesley, 'Roche gives up Chewing Gum'. *Irish Times*, 16 March 2003.
19. P. Bernhagen, 'Business Political Power, Information Asymmetry and Structural Constraints on Public Policy: Two cases from environmental politics and banking regulation in Germany and Great Britain'. Paper prepared for Annual National Conference of the Midwest Political Science Association, 3–6 April 2003, Chicago, p.9.
20. Ibid., p.10.
21. 'A Chink of Light'. *IBEC News*, May 2005.
22. IBEC and CIF, Public Private Partnerships (PPPs) Briefing paper, April 1999.
23. P. Clancy and G. Murphy, *Outsourcing Government: Public Bodies and Accountability* (Dublin: TASC/New Island 2000), p.17.

24. Correspondence from HSE official to author 28 July 2006.
25. Office of Information Commissioner, *Annual Report 2005* (Dublin: Office of Information Commissioner, 2006), p.28.
26. E. Bhreathnach, C. Newman and J. Fenwick, 'The Impact of the Proposed M3 Motorway on Tara and Its Cultural Landscape'. Working Paper, Department of Archaeology, University College, Galway, 20 March 2004.
27. EGFSN, *Skill Needs in the Irish Economy: The Role of Migration* (Dublin: Forfas, 2005), p.91.
28. Ibid., p.141.
29. M. Brennock, 'Government Routinely Seeks External Advice'. *Irish Times*, 8 October 2005.
30. M. Casey, 'Public Service must cut back on Consultants'. *Irish Times*, 22 August 2005.
31. D. Marquand, *Decline of the Public: the Hollowing Out of Citizenship* (Cambridge: Polity, 2004), pp.92–3.
32. B. Tuohy, 'SMI: Ten Years On: Presentation to Policy Institute'. Trinity College, 22 February 2005.
33. J. McManus, 'Transferees may unlock Puzzle of Decentralisation'. *Irish Times*, 10 April 2006.
34. 'Heading for Calmer Water'. *Irish Medical Times*, 18–25 August 2006.
35. 'Former Revenue Chief gave Advice to Dunne'. *Irish Times*, 15 June 2005.

Chapter Four

The Atlantic Tax Haven

Imagine a giant aircraft carrier parked off the Irish coast with airplanes roaring in every day, carrying hundreds of young troops. They get out for a few hours and stretch their legs as they wander around the specially designed leisure points and shops. Then they take off in big troop carriers to occupy a country with a well-organized insurgency. The country is, of course, Iraq and the troops come from bases like Fort Bragg in the US. There is, however, no giant aircraft carrier off its coast but, instead, Ireland has gone one step further. It has granted the US military full freedom to use its second most important airport at Shannon.

The US authorities are grateful. In the words of Richard Haas, the former special envoy to Northern Ireland and a top strategist at the US State Department, 'Shannon is extremely useful', because of its capacity and location. 'Are there alternatives or substitutes? Yes. Would they be as good? No. Shannon is one of the most capable facilities in this part of the world.'[1]

Shannon has become one of the major hubs for the US occupation of Iraq. In 2005, over 330,000 US troops passed through the airport – which was the equivalent of 904 soldiers per day.[2] Most came on military charter flights but some also came on special civilian carriers such as World Airways. Shannon has also been used to transport military cargo such as mortars, radar seekers, helicopter parts and, of course, personal arms and ammunition. On one occasion, twenty-eight Patriot missiles passed through Shannon as part of a covert operation involving the US and Israel.[3] Most disturbingly, the airport has also been used to transport prisoners on special 'rendition' exercises to countries like Egypt. This refers to the practice of US authorities to outsource interrogations to countries that use torture.

How could a neutral country with its own experience of occupation be involved in this? Irish neutrality grew out of opposition to colonialism and, though applied inconsistently, this meant abstention from military adventures. Until the late 1980s, Ireland refused to have any part in even foreign military exercises. The Fine Gael Minister, Patrick Cooney, summarized government policy in 1983, 'The over flights or military landings must not be an integral part of training manoeuvres by foreign military aircraft; likewise, clearance is not granted where a troop-carrying aircraft is en route to military exercises.'[4]

This makes it all the more extraordinary that Shannon has effectively replaced airports such as Frankfurt as the European hub for US military operations. Even more astoundingly, Irish taxpayers are picking up the bill. Over the last five years, they have paid out €10 million in charges for air-traffic control and communications services for aircraft passing through Irish-controlled airspace.[5]

Economically, Ireland has by far the highest level of US investment per manufacturing worker in Europe – the capital deployed being a full seven times the European average. The Celtic Tiger was primarily driven by a huge influx of US investment that sought a base inside the EU to get around the entry barriers that were erected for the single market. America has also become Ireland's second export market – but significantly, most of this trade comes from the internal transactions carried out in US multi-national companies.

However, it does not follow that because there is such a high level of US investment, the Irish state had 'no choice' but to allow the US army into Shannon. Contrary to impressions, a country is not necessarily punished economically for political disagreements. The French case illustrates this neatly as it was initially the main opponent of the US war on Iraq. Such was the political hatred between the two countries' elites that on one occasion the US House of Representatives changed the name of the 'French Fries' in their canteen to 'Freedom Fries'. Yet in that very same year, US investment flows to France rose by more than 10 per cent. A recent report summed up the pattern,

For transatlantic relations, 2003 was a year of political bust and economic boom. Even as transatlantic bickering engendered by America's war with Iraq plunged political relations to their lowest point in six decades, the economic ties that bind the United States and Europe together only grew stronger in 2003.[6]

The reason should be obvious. US corporations are primarily concerned with the bottom line, with their rate of profit. If profit rates are high, they will live with most forms of political disapproval. If they are low, even the most obsequious political behaviour will not attract them. The rate of return on US-owned direct investment in Ireland was three times higher than the rate of overall US direct investment abroad from 1999 to 2003.[7] This means that the Irish government had ample scope to oppose US foreign policy – and US investment would still continue to flow.

It suits politicians, however, to disguise political choices as technical necessities. It is almost as if they had borrowed a fatalistic form of Marxism to 'read off' political developments from the economic base. Yet, in reality, the opening of Shannon to US troops has far more to do with the strategic geo-political priorities of the Irish elite. They wish to align themselves with the dominant Anglo-American imperial power block, and as part of that bloc, they try to play a minor role as a bridge-builder between the US and Europe. Although a relatively small state, Ireland strives to align the foreign policy priorities of the US and EU. The US ambassador to Ireland, James Kenny, made this point with some flattering hyperbole,

> No European government is more capable of advancing US-EU partnership than Ireland. With its economic and cultural links to America and common views, Ireland is well placed to serve as a transatlantic bridge and to strengthen the 'irreplaceable relationship'.[8]

By claiming they had 'no choice' the Irish elite merely try to absolve themselves of guilt for collaborating in a bloody war. Yet the reality was that Shannon was opened to US troops as a gesture of political loyalty to the US empire. Like all empires, the US regularly demands tangible tokens of willing submission. The modern token is the military base or a 'lilly pad' where US troops can move in to and out of quickly. Chalmers Johnson summarizes the pattern,

> Once upon a time, you could trace the spread of imperialism by counting colonies. America's vision of the colony is the military base. By following changing politics of global basing, one can learn much about our ever-larger imperial stance and the militarism that grows with it.[9]

What is interesting, however, is the manner in which Ireland embraces the empire but still presents an image that it has a caring, 'independent' foreign policy. Irish foreign ministers still make much of Ireland's past and its sympathies, for example, with the cause of the Palestinians. Ireland projects itself as a supporter of the developing world, sometimes promoting debt relief or increases in aid. Top politicians continually praise the United Nations and claim that a 'peace process' is the way to resolve conflicts. Yet, despite this rhetoric, they are active supporters of the US war on Iraq.

This conundrum illustrates how the Irish elite have become remarkably adept at double speak. They have learnt not to talk straight or spell out their policy but to coat their actions in a special gloss that takes off the harshness. They are thus able to both serve an empire, and still present an image of 'neutrality' to the wider global public. When the contradictions grow, the discourse of economic nationalism is used to cover over the cracks. The message is that the first duty of the state is to win jobs and investment for the Irish and glaring inconsistencies may be the price that has to be paid. Cuteness, it appears, is the special talent that compensates for the historic economic and military weakness of the Irish elite.

Shannon is an important metaphor for Ireland's wider role in the global economy. Ireland provides not only a 'lily pad' for the US empire but it is also a bridgehead for US capital within Europe. Physically, it is the location for more than 600 US companies and the total stock of US Foreign Direct Investment stood at $73 billion in 2004. Although a tiny country with only 1 per cent of the EU population, it has attracted a quarter of US investment in new or 'greenfield' sites between 1993 and 2000.

As a result, Ireland tops the 'transnationality index' of the world.[10] This index measures the importance of Foreign Direct Investment and employment in foreign firms for the wider national economy. Put more simply, Ireland is more dependent on foreign investment than any country in the world and this arises from its particular dependence on US investment.

These economic ties have led to a greater alignment between the Irish and US elites in their understanding of the world. The pivotal point of that understanding is that corporations must be given the maximum of freedom. One pro-business writer sums up the nature of this growing synchronization between Ireland and the US,

> The intensive trade and investment relationship between Ireland and the USA, and the daily contact between executives from large US companies and Irish government officials, often gives Irish officials an inside track in understanding the challenges to US-EU relationship. Given this 'special' economic relationship, US officials and business executives (as well as Irish enterprise agencies) have been eager to see Ireland play a more active role on policy issues of importance to US-Irish economic relations, such as e commerce governance and taxation, biotechnology and financial services.[11]

Ireland has, thus, become one of the foremost exponents of US corporate interests inside the EU. It used its presidency of the EU in 2004 to try to push through a software directive that would have given Microsoft even more scope to take out patents and hinder the free flow of programming ideas. The company was an official sponsor of the Irish EU presidency and had its logo on the official EU presidency website. Responsibility for the software directive continues to fall on the Irish Internal Market Commissioner, Charlie McCreevy, who, some argue, is too close to the large US corporation.[12] The Irish government also typically abstains on votes on genetically modified food because it is caught between its own public opinion at home and a US administration that has pressurized it to become a player in the biotechnology industry. Inside the EU, representatives of the Irish state promote greater use of market mechanisms. There is now a consistent pattern whereby Ireland seeks to block labour reforms that benefit workers and when these measures go through, it seeks to delay their implementation.

So Ireland showed extreme reluctance about the EU parental leave directive that entitles parents to three months leave to care for children up to the age of 8. Then, when it was agreed, it tried to impose an upper limit of 5 years for children and delay its wider implementation. It failed to meet the deadlines for implementing the Part Time and Fixed Term Work directives that prohibits discrimination against part time and contract staff and continued to discriminate against these workers on occupational pension rights. It has opposed EU directives to protect agency workers and alongside two other countries, Britain and Hungary, insisted that agency workers get little protection. This was entirely consistent with its policies at home, as it failed to implement its own legislation that compels recruitment agencies to register the number of employees they have on their books.[13]

Publicly, however, as in the case of Shannon, Irish politicians use the softer language of 'social solidarity' to put a gloss on these harsh economic measures. This style of double speak developed with the long experience of social partnership. Behind the rhetoric of social solidarity, Ireland comes second to the US for having the most unequal society in the developing world.[14] The political elite has learnt that the best way to get on with the real job of making the country suitable for business is to use a little soft soap. The result is that corporate interests now dominate Irish economic and social policy. This can be illustrated by looking at two key areas of concern to corporations – tax and regulation.

THE ATLANTIC TAX HAVEN

Every year an important ceremony takes place when the Minister for Finance poses with his family to present the budget. There follows a long speech in the Dáil as the Minister reads out a script prepared by his civil service. Later, the press dutifully picks up on the details about changes to the 'old reliables' and income tax bands. For the next day or so, these are the main topics of conversations throughout the country. There is, however, one extraordinary omission from the script: no detail is given about the changes on how corporations will be taxed and, instead, this is left to the seemingly 'technical' adjustments in the Finance Bill that follows. A whole industry has been created for interpreting each precise nuance in the wording of this Bill. Before the Bill is produced various 'lobby groups' make private representations to the Minister, often over seemingly small changes which can save the corporations millions in tax. These measures have helped to create an Atlantic tax haven that rivals Bermuda or the Cayman Islands. The public has been effectively excluded from knowing the full details through the simple device of making only a cursory mention to 'other taxation' in the main Budget day script.[15]

Explaining Ireland's role as the foremost tax shelter of the world is difficult because you need to enter a world dominated by large accountancy firms who charge for 'privileged' information. KPMG, for example, collected €124 million in fees between 1997 to 2001 for devising tax shelters that cost the US government at least €1.12 billion in lost revenue.[16] Firms like KPMG explore the fine detail of financial legislation of various states and then advise corporations on the best methods to achieve 'tax efficiency'. In the words of a US Republican Senator, Norm Coleman, they have 'developed, implemented and mass marketed ... tax shelters to rip off the (US) Treasury of billions of dollars in taxes'.[17] It is no wonder that many US public representatives have become concerned because resources that could be used to alleviate poverty are being stashed away in foreign tax shelters. It is estimated that if corporations paid the same effective tax rate now that they paid in the 1950s, corporate tax settlements to the US Treasury would be $380 billion a year higher than they actually are.[18]

Ireland, it appears, figures highly on the list of tax shelters. Between 1999 and 2002, profits from US companies in Ireland doubled from $13.4 billion to $26.8 billion. This did not occur because of a huge surge in real investment – but rather because more US companies declared their profits in Ireland to benefit from its low tax regime. In 1997, a new double taxation agreement was signed between the US and Ireland which widened opportunities for exemption from US taxes. The Irish government succeeded in effectively exempting items such as royalties, profits earned from international transport and interest from

The Corporate Takeover of Ireland

TABLE 4.1
THE RISE OF TAX HAVENS, 1999 AND 2002 COMPARED
(PROFITS ARE IN MILLIONS OF US DOLLARS)

Rank	Country	1999 Before Tax Profits	Effective Tax Rate	Rank	Country	2002 Before Tax Profits	Effective Tax Rate
1	Britain	29,368	30%	1	Ireland	26,835	8%
2	Canada	21,244	22%	2	Bermuda	25,212	2 %
3	Netherlands	19,390	10%	3	Netherlands	20,802	9%
4	Ireland	13,355	8%	4	Britain	19,717	31%
5	Switzerland	11,690	6%	5	Canada	19,626	26%
6	Germany	11,636	27%	6	Luxemburg	18,405	1%
7	Japan	9,010	43%	7	Switzerland	14,105	4%
8	Bermuda	8,529	3%	8	Japan	11,526	39%
9	Mexico	7,049	31%	9	Mexico	7,699	37%
10	CaymanIsland	5,638	3%	10	Singapore	7,533	11%
14	Singapore	4,370	12%	13	Germany	5,371	27%
16	Luxembourg	4,032	2%	21	Cayman Island	2,809	5%

Source: M. O Sullivan, 'Data Shows Dramatic Shift of Profits to Tax Havens'. *Tax Notes*, 104, 12 (2004), pp.1190–6.

tax. Similarly, it was agreed to reduce the normal US withholding tax on dividends from 30 per cent to 15 per cent in some cases and 5 per cent in others.[19]

US tax expert, Martin Sullivan, has argued that a 'seismic shift' occurred in the late 1990s in international taxation when subsidiaries of US corporations declared 58 per cent of their profits earned abroad to be in tax havens such as Ireland or Bermuda.[20] Ireland differs from Bermuda in that real business activity takes place there – as against being a location for front companies. However, precisely because of this, it is a more respectable destination that allows corporations to slip below the radar screen of public opprobrium. As a result, Ireland now tops the list of global tax havens for US companies.

The key to Ireland's role as a giant tax shelter is a headline figure for corporation profits tax of 12.5 per cent. According to *Forbes*, the leading business magazine, this is one of the lowest rates in the world.[21] The Industrial Development Authority uses a slightly different measure and boasts that Ireland's headline figure is second in Europe, after Cyprus.[22] To put matters in perspective, the US has a corporation profits tax rate of 35 per cent.

Ireland's extreme generosity to the corporations has triggered a new race to the bottom and, in recent years, Portugal, Netherlands, Germany, Austria and Poland have all cut their taxes on profits substantially. According to KPMG, OECD countries have cut corporate tax rates by nearly 7 per cent between 1996 and 2003.[23] This, in turn, has delighted right wing politicians in America who see this as a lever to reduce corporate taxes in their own country. Thus, US Treasury Secretary, John Snow has said of the Irish government, 'I applaud them and believe they ought to be emulated'.[24] The accelerated race to the bottom, however, also means that the Industrial Development Authority must use this headline figure as a way of advertising more hidden tax incentives.

One of the big advantages that Ireland offers the corporations is that taxation on profit is by self-assessment. Corporations can also suggest how their income is to be broken down into categories such as trading, deposits or foreign income. A very relaxed attitude is taken to the filing of annual audits. The *Wall Street Journal* summed up the contrast with the US, when it noted that 'a late filing would require an explanation and possibly large penalties. In Ireland, the regulators don't even ask. The penalty for late filing: €3.60 a day.'[25] The Revenue Commissioners have up to four years to request an independent audit of companies, but these are extremely rare. The total number of random audits has fluctuated from a mere 192 in 1999 to 740 in 2001 to a new low 274 in 2003.[26] The number of returns that are screened has dropped consistently from 23,119 in 2000

TABLE 4.2
TAX WRITTEN OFF

	Overall Total Written Off		Bankruptcy/Receivership Liquidation		Ceased Trading/ No assets	
	No of Cases	€m	No of cases	€m	No of Cases	€m
1997	*	357		193		27
1998	*	274		118		67
1999	4,501	88	475	28	2,347	33
2000	3,975	82	397	20	1,432	33
2001	36,654	140	382	27	578	17
2002	157,255	178	360	31	2,236	43
2003	42,741	119	337	29	2,277	32

Source: Comptroller and Auditor General Annual Reports various years. Figures for number of cases written off in 1997 and 1998 are not available.

to 10,913 in 2003 and 4,811 in 2004.[27] When one considers that there are more than 150,000 registered companies in Ireland, this is only a scratch on the surface.

Not surprisingly, companies are responsible for the bulk of tax write-offs. The Comptroller and Auditor General has noted that 60 per cent of the total tax write-offs between 1997 and 2001 came from two categories: 'liquidation/receivership/bankruptcy' and 'ceased trading'.[28] In other words, predominantly from the corporate sector. Table 4.2 illustrates the pattern.

The sheer scale of tax avoidance through the simple device of liquidation or bankruptcy has alarmed the Comptroller and Auditor General. After an in-depth study of the corporate sector, he decried the practice of 'phoenix companies', which fall and then rise again to escape their tax liabilities. He noted that there were 'substantial abuses of the tax system by individuals through abuse of the principle of limited liability or the 'corporate veil'.[29] However, his most damning indictment was of the Revenue Commissioners who used a narrow 'case based' approach to examine corporate tax records. They had often failed to check returns for corporation tax against information from their own databases on VAT returns or their property file. They did not cross check information on directorships with the Companies Registration Office. He concluded that 'the monitoring of Corporation Tax compliance appeared to have a low priority ... in comparison with the high yielding VAT and PAYE'.[30]

The general ethos of the Revenue Commissioners is thus extremely business-friendly. The same large accountancy firms who advertise their tax avoidance skills can also make representations to the Revenue Commissioners about seemingly technical questions. When 'tax professionals' request a meeting with Revenue officials to discuss their client's affairs, they are usually facilitated.[31] In one famous case, the serving Taoiseach Charles J. Haughey even set up a meeting between the chairman of the Revenue Commissioners and the supermarket magnate Ben Dunne, to discuss whether the company could continue its status as a trust – and thus save millions in tax. And this is not simply a case of the dark old days. Firms that specialize in helping tax avoidance are still represented on state bodies that are supposed to oversee the corporations. So KPMG advertise to their clients that they are represented on the Taoiseach's advisory committee on the International Financial Services Centre – even though one of their business activities is helping companies to avoid the small taxes that are charged there.

Once the figure for profits is submitted to the Revenue Commissioners, there are numerous ways in which corporations can claim allowances to reduce their tax liability. A corporation has the same rights as a person – but when it comes to taxation, it can claim far more privileges than the flesh and blood PAYE taxpayer. Let us list out the main forms of corporate welfare.

- *Corporations can write off spending on machinery and industrial buildings*
  The Revenue Commissioners assume that a machine lasts only eight years and so each year a company can write off one eighth of its value. If companies buy software programmes, they can also write these off. This provision also acts as a hidden tax subsidy to the banks because if they present themselves as the formal owners of factory or office machinery and lease it out, they can gain extra capital allowances to set against their vast profits. In one absurd case, a consortium of Irish businessmen were able to claim capital allowances for the purchase of a luxury yacht formerly owned by Aristotle Onassis – and then gain extra allowances for the costs of its re-furbishment. Companies can also claim tax allowance for depreciation of industrial buildings and, provided they can sell them after the ten year tax life is over, they do not face any 'clawbacks' even though the property price appreciated dramatically.

- *Corporations can write off their losses for tax purposes – in some cases indefinitely*
  If a company loses €10 million one year, it can remove this figure for taxation the next year. If it loses €10 million in one year, €5 million in the second year and €3 million in the third year, the cumulative loss of €18 million can be written off against future profits. If losses occur in one company in a group, they can be used to create a tax shelter for another profitable group member. All of which begs a question: how can entrepreneurs be truly described as 'risk takers' when even their losses can be used for tax purposes?

- *Royalties, licence fees and income earned from patents are tax-free*
  Licence fees charged by IBM or Microsoft for using certain software is written off for tax purposes. Patents which are often taken out for twenty years by the pharmaceutical companies on their drugs are entirely tax free – if the work can be claimed to have been done in Ireland. No wonder that 40 per cent of all PC package software and 60 per cent of all business applications software sold in Europe is produced in Ireland.

- *Ireland allows huge tax breaks on dividend payments*
  Officially, there is a withholding tax of 20 per cent of dividends but there are so many exemptions that it is laughable. Large corporations, who set up holding companies to buy and sell shares or receive dividends, avoid tax on their speculative activities. A new provision in 2004 allows companies with headquarters in Ireland to sell off shares on global stock exchanges – and pay no capital gains tax on their profits. They can even borrow money to engage in such activity and write off the interest for tax purposes. There are also exemptions for 'certain collective investment funds' – many of which are situated in the Irish Financial Services Centre.

- *Shipping companies no longer have to pay tax on actual profits, but on a notional profit based on ship tonnage*
  Irish Ferries which laid off Irish workers to replace them with cheaper foreign contract staff cut its tax bill by nearly €3 million, paying a mere €300,000 tax on profits of €23 million.[32]

- *There is no specific law on transfer pricing*
  Transfer pricing means that multi-nationals manipulate their pricing structure in order to artificially declare higher profits in countries where there is a low tax regime. So they might artificially reduce the price of certain components coming into Ireland to make it appear that higher profits are made there. Alternatively, they might charge parent companies in the US artificially high prices to make it look higher profits were made in Ireland. A report by the US Senate in 2001 claimed that multinationals used transfer pricing to evade up

to $45 billion in taxes. In one dramatic case a firm sold tooth-brushes between subsidiaries for $5,655 each![33] Transfer pricing is so common in Ireland that there is a major question mark over some Irish economic statistics. Yet there is no unit within the Revenue Commissioners to deal with the issue. Nor are there any specific laws against transfer pricing, unlike other countries.

The overall effect of these policies is to create a giant magnet to pull in capital. The Internet search engine firm Google provides a good example of how it works. In the first quarter of 2005, it raised its profits to €342 million from €155 million the previous year. Yet it still managed to cut its effective tax rate from 59 per cent to 19 per cent. Its chief financial officer, George Reyes, explained that this was due to 'a greater proportion of our earnings in 2005 being recognised by our Irish subsidiary. These earnings are taxed at a substantially lower rate than the combined effect of our US federal and state income taxes.'[34]

However, the major beneficiary of these schemes is Microsoft, which uses Ireland to help shave $500 million off its annual tax bill. Microsoft operates in Ireland through a small subsidiary company, Round Island One Ltd, which is supposed to control $16 billion of its global assets. The legal address of this firm is in the headquarters of the Dublin law firm Matheson, Ormsby Prentice that advertises its expertise in helping corporations use Ireland as a tax shelter. Round Island One license rights to Microsoft's software that is sold in Europe, the Middle East and Africa and this allows the corporation to route its sales through Ireland. It then claims considerable exemption on taxes by taking advantage of Ireland's low tax regime on patents.[35]

Wealthy individuals who control the corporations also enjoy tax breaks in their own right. If they claim to live outside Ireland for more than 183 days of the year, they are designated as 'non-resident' and do not pay Irish taxes. Under a special 'Cinderella rule', a day is not counted if the person leaves the state before midnight. Unlike social welfare recipients, however, there is no monitoring of their movements to see if they comply with this provision. Private planes can come and go from Irish airports without the tax exiles having to register their entry or exit. Bertie Ahern introduced the 'tax exile' rule while he was Minister for Finance in a rather underhand way. It appeared as an amendment at 5.00 p.m. on a Friday afternoon and Ahern claimed that it was designed to help semi-state workers who worked abroad for short durations. In fact it has been put to great use by the Irish rich. The most famous beneficiary is the multi-millionaire Denis O'Brien, who saved up to €55 million in tax by moving to Portugal before he sold Esat in 2000 for €2.3 billion. Mr O'Brien however, did not seem particularly grateful for this, stating that

> There is too much shite going on inside Ireland at the moment. I think people are too negative towards politicians, Government, and entrepreneurs. We are fast turning into a communist state. We are fast moving towards communist doctrine. People in this country should be thankful for what they achieved in the last ten years. Instead I come back to Ireland and people are screaming like spoiled children.[36]

Another major tax break for the wealthy comes through special arrangements for pension provision. Up till recently, owners of firms could take large sums of money out of their businesses and set up a special pension fund for themselves – and pay no tax! The pension fund could then be used to borrow money and buy and sell property, all completely tax-free. There was no limit on how much owners of business could put into these Approved Retirement Funds but it is now limited to €254,000 a year. Before the figure was capped, 79 of the richest people in Ireland built up tax free pension funds with an average value of €8 million each under this scheme.[37]. So, for example, the racehorse owner, John Mulhearn, was the beneficiary of a €3.5 million payment into his pension fund just before he sold Clayton Love Distributors. The pension was equal to 50 per cent of the net assets of the company at the time.[38] Another way for the wealthy to reduce tax liability was to get paid through stock options. Companies often reward their directors through an option to buy shares at a specified price. Once cashed in, they are taxed as Capital Gains rather than as a PAYE tax. The advantage is that the Capital Gains Tax is set at the absurdly low level of 20 per cent while a PAYE worker earning more than €30,000 must pay a tax rate of 42 per cent.

On top of all these there are a myriad of other tax scams. If wealthy individuals face a 'credible threat' and hire bodyguards, put bullet-proof plating on their company cars, or take out home security systems, they do not have to pay benefit-in-kind liability.[39] There are even tax reliefs for the importation of private pleasure boats and aircraft. Income earned from stallion fees has been tax free and will only finally be phased out in 2008 – even though the fees for the successful impregnation of a mare by a stallion could be just less than €10,000. One of the wealthiest men in Ireland, John Magnier, the owner of the Culmore Stud, benefited enormously from this particular scheme.

A host of property based tax incentives have been used to create shelters for speculators. Owners of hotels, sports injury clinics, student accommodation, nursing homes, multi-story car parks and private hospitals have all benefited from special tax exemptions. One effect was to produce an extraordinary rush to build hotels as these could be converted to apartment blocks after seven years. Between 2000 and 2004, an extra 987 hotels were built with a tax subsidy of €196 million.[40] Money that could have been used elsewhere has been used to subsidize property speculation, a scheme that is only now being gradually phased out. There are also tax reliefs for donations of heritage items but just seven people took advantage of it in 2003, each benefiting by an average of €400,000.[41] There are reliefs for small-business people under the Town Renewal Scheme, the Rural Renewal Scheme and the Urban Renewal Scheme. By the end of July 2006, when these are due to be phased out, the costs of the tax subsidy to the Exchequer will have amounted to €1,933 million.[42]

Ireland's status as the most important tax haven in the world is celebrated by the political elite as a cute stroke benefiting all of society. Even critics, such as the Labour Party's Joan Burton, tend to focus on the more 'parasitic' property-based schemes and do not question the fundamentals. So there is a consensus that stretches from the Progressive Democrats to the Labour Party on maintaining a reduced Corporation Profits Tax and other tax subsidies to attract global corporations. However, Ireland's status as a tax haven damages Irish society in three crucial ways.

First, it helps to create extreme inequality and so vests even more power in the hands of a wealthy elite. Figures released in 2004 showed that 242 people who had earnings of between €100,000 and €1million paid no tax. A further 149 paid an effective tax rate of 20 per cent or less.[43] By being able to accrue so much tax-free income, the top 400 people in Irish society are able to invest more money in subsidizing right-wing politicians who introduce further policies that benefit them. They no longer necessarily give direct donations but they control the media and can offer all sorts of patronage to ensure their continued domination over Irish society. The interests of the poor are quite simply marginalized and growing inequality becomes a permanent feature of Irish life.

Second, tax cuts to the wealthy have contributed to Ireland having a very low overall tax base. Total taxes represent only 29 per cent of Gross Domestic Product compared to an EU average of 40 per cent.[44] This, in turn, means that there is less money available for public services or, to put it differently, the population subsidize the corporations by putting up with poorer services. This burden naturally weighs more heavily on the poor who rely more on public services. Ireland's public health system has traditionally been so under-funded that more than half the population have voluntarily taken out private health insurance. There are virtually no state-run crèche facilities; schools are under-resourced, lacking the most basic scientific equipment; treatment facilities for conditions like cystic fibrosis are abysmal.

TABLE 4.3
MAJOR COMPONENTS OF TOTAL TAXATION IN IRELAND AND EU AVERAGES, 2002
(FIGURES IN PERCENTAGES)

	Ireland	EU-15	EU-25
Direct Taxes	41	34	33
Indirect Taxes of which:	43	34	35
- (VAT	25	17	17)
- (Excise and consumption taxes	12	6	6)
Social Insurance of which:	16	32	32
Employers Social Insurance	10	18	18

Compiled from *EU Commission Structures of the taxation systems in the European Union*.

Third, the cost of running the normal functions of society is increasingly shifted on to indirect taxes and 'stealth taxes'. Taxes in the EU are classified into three categories – direct taxes, which include both PAYE tax and Corporation Profits tax; indirect taxes such as VAT and excise duties; and social insurance contributions paid by both employers and employees. Indirect taxes make up 43 per cent of the overall tax burden in Ireland compared to 34 per cent in the EU, as Table 4.3 illustrates.

One of the main reasons for the reliance on indirect tax is that VAT rates are high in Ireland and accounts for a quarter of the total tax take. This is the second highest level in the EU after Estonia. VAT also falls on the population at large rather than the corporations because, as PricewaterhouseCoopers put it rather bluntly, when advising its corporate customers, 'In practice, VAT is not a cost for most business since VAT may be passed onto consumers'.[45] This tax regime produces a highly inequitable situation where both the poor and the rich pay the same VAT rates on consumer goods. So a working-class family will pay the same 21 per cent VAT rate on their telephone service as a millionaire. But even though the poor may use the phone less, they will still feel the tax rate more as it represents a higher proportion of their income. One economist has estimated that indirect taxes cost lower income families 21 per cent of their income but just 10 per cent of the income of the top earners.[46]

Lower income earners suffer even more directly from a wide range of 'stealth taxes' or 'user fees' on public services. These have grown as the overall tax take has proven to be insufficient to fund basic public services. Admission charges to accident and emergency units have risen from zero to €55 a visit. The amount that has to be paid for medicines each month has risen from €25 to €85. The charge for overnight in-patient stay has risen to €55 a night. Bin charges fluctuate but can reach between €400 and €500 a year. There is also the increasing phenomenon of apartment and housing estate charges when estates or complexes are not taken into local authority care.

Another side of this deeply inequitable taxation system is a hidden subsidy for corporations in the form of reduced social insurance contributions. As Table 4.3 shows, social insurance makes up only 16 per cent of tax revenue in Ireland compared to an EU average of 32 per cent. Within this reduced coverage, employers pay far less than their counterparts in the rest of Europe. There is no legal obligation on corporations, for example, to contribute to a pension scheme for their staff. This means that in the private sector, pension coverage is abysmal, with only 38 per cent of employees covered for pensions. Overall Ireland has one of the lowest levels of spending on pensions, at only 3.7 per cent of GDP as against, at the other extreme, 14.7 per cent in Italy.[47] One result is that Irish workers have longer working lives, with the average exit age at 64.4 as against an average of 61.0 across the EU.[48] Whereas workers on average incomes in other countries can expect their post tax pension to be worth just under 70 per cent of their earnings after tax, Irish workers can expect a replacement rate of less than 40 per cent.[49] Once again, it would appear there are significant costs borne by the population at large for the tax breaks that corporations enjoy.

The Irish state has created a respectable tax haven for the corporations on the edge of Europe. It has done so in the cute manner – talking about combating social exclusion while systemically creating a neo-liberal Valhalla for the corporations. Contrary to consensus within the wider political elite, this has not benefited Irish society at large. Rather, it has exacerbated inequality to an extraordinary degree and has led to grossly under-funded public services. And by allowing employers to evade their elementary social responsibilities, it has condemned many of the elderly to extreme poverty at the end of their days.

REGULATION LITE

Sedat Yigit had his wits about him as he recorded the hours he worked. 'There were weeks I worked up to 90 hours. We worked in every type of weather condition; there were no stops for rain. For the first one and half months, I worked every single day. There was no day off, not even Sundays.'[50] Many of his fellow workers at GAMA were paid a mere €2.20 an hour even though this is well below the legal minimum wage and the Registered Employment Agreement for the construction industry that set wages at €12.95 an hour. They were housed in barrack-like conditions and when they protested they were subject to threats of physical violence. Only after a seven-week unofficial strike and a sustained campaign by the Socialist Party TD, Joe Higgins, did the workers finally receive some gains. They received a lump sum equal to €8,000 per year of service in a 'pragmatic settlement'[51] that saw most return to Turkey as their work permits had been revoked.

The GAMA case revealed a dreadful form of 'bonded labour' in the Celtic Tiger. But it also raised other questions about Ireland's claim to be regulated by an extensive body of labour legislation that is supposed to protect workers from abuse. GAMA is a major corporation that specializes in state construction projects and has won contracts from the ESB, National Roads Authority, South Dublin Council, Ballymun Regeneration Limited and Clare County Council. Yet no one seemed to ask any questions about how it was able to tender far more cheaply than its rivals – in the case of Clare their tender was €14 million cheaper than the original estimate![52] Alternatively, if questions were asked they were met with a reassurance that the company had been given the all-clear by the appropriate regulatory authority. As early as 2003, for example, Mary Harney, the then Minister for Enterprise, Trade and Employment, was informed by the Bricklayers Union about GAMA's system of under-payment. Ms Harney had originally travelled to Turkey to encourage GAMA to come to Ireland after a wave of union militancy swept the building sites. But she claimed that a report from a senior official in her department found that the BATU (Building and Allied Trades' Union) allegation was 'without substance'.[53]

The Irish elite talks profusely about 'proper standards' and 'transparency', yet the very structure of many of their regulatory systems allows a darker side to flourish. The GAMA case was a more dramatic example of how 'regulatory standards' are often used for appearance while, in real life, a different ethos can prevail. This occurs particularly in the construction industry, where sub-contracting is rife. No socio-economic system could operate without coded rules that guide the activities of its officials. The Irish system of light regulation, however, allows for enough loopholes to give corporations the satisfaction of claiming to adhere to standards – while enjoying get-out clauses when necessary. This point may be illustrated by looking at both labour regulation and corporate regulation.

TABLE 4.4
INSPECTION AND PROSECUTIONS CARRIED OUT BY LABOUR INSPECTORS

Year	Inspections/Visits	Prosecutions Initiated
2001	6,474	23
2002	8,323	25
2003	7,168	20
2004	5,160	14
2005	5,719	25

Source: Annual Reports, Department of Enterprise Trade and Employment.

Labour Standards

At the time of the GAMA dispute Ireland had twenty-one labour inspectors to cover a workforce of 1.6 million; this was then increased by ten, which was announced as the scandal broke. To put matters in perspective, there were fifty dog wardens to look after the welfare of the 150,000 strong canine population. There were also forty-one inspectors whose sole function was to enforce the smoking ban in pubs. The situation was even worse than these tiny figures would suggest because not all the positions had been filled. In July 2005, for example, there were only 16.5 personnel working as labour inspectors due to a high turnover of staff – leaving each inspector responsible for 116,381 members of the workforce.[54] It was absurd to assume that such a small handful of inspectors could possibly ensure that labour laws were implemented. In fact, as Table 4.4 illustrates, the number of inspections has shown a consistent tendency to decline, while the number of prosecutions of employers is derisory. When prosecutions do occur, they generally result in fines that range from €500 to €2,000.

The tiny number of prosecutions does not suggest there is a strong inspectorate that is willing to take on employers. One of the reasons is that the powers of the inspectors are relatively limited. Under the Organization of Working Times Act, they can visit workplaces and request copies of the records which employers keep. But if they find anything is wrong they themselves cannot take a prosecution case but must refer it to another agency such as the Rights Commissioners. In general, the ethos is to convince an employer to make amends, but if they refuse to pay up for work carried out by employees, it will take a long time to extract the money from them.

A leaked document to the *Irish Times* on the inspectorate revealed considerable demoralization among the staff of the labour inspectorate. Due to a high turnover, the average length of experience was only 15 months, even though the inspectors themselves only felt fully confident to carry out their duties after a 12–18 month period. Training for the post is extremely 'haphazard' and, bizarrely, knowledge of labour legislation was not one of the necessary requirements for recruitment. Elementary resources such as computer systems are inadequate, and there is no regional presence except in Cork.[55] The number of labour inspectors is due to increase to ninety-one by the end of 2007, but even if that figure is reached, it is still grossly inadequate.

The state has also shown little enthusiasm to properly regulate the building industry. Instead, employers have been able to hire sub-contractors to circumvent their responsibility to ensure wage agreements are adhered to and contributions are made to employee pension schemes. A Department of Enterprise and Trade report found that 130,000 construction workers were not covered by the industry pension scheme. The main reason was the widespread use of sub-contracting. A firm such as Collen Construction that took out a court injunction that led to the jailing of three Ballybrack bricklayers is a good example. For the twelve months ending March 2005, it was registered as having seventy-one operatives and foremen on their sites, along with fifty office workers. Yet, at most times, Collen Construction operates between ten and fifteen large sites with several hundred working on them.[56]

Legally there is insufficient regulation of recruitment agencies – they merely have to be set up by people of good character, to pay an initial licence fee and then to submit returns on placements. But even this is not adhered to properly. The Department of Enterprise Trade and Employment (DETE) claim that the practice of collecting data on the numbers of workers who are registered with temporary agencies was discontinued after 1995 and only fragmentary figures exist.[57] This is an extraordinary claim, as recruitment agencies are legally obliged to make these returns and it is the function of the Department to enforce the law. One study, however, using data from the European Foundation's Third European Survey on Working

Conditions by Conroy and Pierce in 2002 suggested that Ireland had the highest percentage of workers employed on a temporary agency contract (5.2 per cent) in the EU, whereas the average across the then fifteen states was 2.2 per cent.[58]

The most damming indictment of the lack of protection offered to migrant workers, in particular, came from a study commissioned by the Labour Relations Commission. After analyzing the experiences of migrant workers taking their cases to the Rights Commissioner, they found that

> The main issue was underpayment of wages, including payment below the minimum wage; followed by non-payment of overtime (including non-payment of Sunday and public holiday premiums) excess hours and non-payment of holiday pay. Other issues were those of unfair dismissal, unlawful deductions, bullying and non-issuing of pay slips. What was particularly remarkable about the issues raised is that, in almost all cases, the claimant listed more than one and, in many cases, listed all of the above complaints.[59]

The report noted that 80 per cent of migrant workers' claims were successful in 2002, with this figure rising to 85 per cent in 2003.[60]

All of this helps to explain how no one claimed to know about the GAMA scandal beforehand. The absence of proper regulatory structures mean that the state agencies that hired GAMA could claim that as 'far as they know' the company was compliant with labour legislation and registered agreements. To deal with these troublesome issues, construction firms often turn to private firms such as Contractors Administration Services. This boasts that it has a 100 per cent success record in ensuring 'no labour disruption' or 'escalation of labour costs above national norms'.[61] It also claims to ensure that all sub-contractors comply with labour laws. State agencies such as the National Road Authority or ESB use this firm and took its claims about companies such as GAMA at face value. In addition, the state agencies could point out that a 'reputable firm' such as PricewaterhouseCoopers audited GAMA. Overall, then, the business ethos that permeates the Irish state means that companies can obtain clean bills of health with relative ease.

A similar pattern of light regulation applies to workplace

health and safety. There is no specific state agency to monitor occupational illness – as distinct from safety – in Ireland. Yet many workers suffer from longer-term conditions such as RSI or cancer as a result of their working environment. Figures of injuries at work are collected by the Health and Safety Authority based on 'reportable accidents', which are defined as causing a worker to lose three days of work. A senior Services Industrial Professional Technical Union's Health and Safety officer, however, believes that only one third of 'reportable' accidents are actually reported.[62] The number of health and safety inspectors who monitor employers is also quite low. As safety inspectors are encouraged to chalk up as many visits as possible, they often pre-notify employers so they can see everything they want. Employers, of course, use this pre-notification to ensure everything is at it should appear to be.

Corporate Standards

Regulation on business activity is also extremely light – but this time it is of benefit to the wealthy. The Irish government's approach is that regulation should be 'principle based' rather than 'rule based' so that business does not face 'unnecessary' red tape. 'Red Tape' is a derogatory term that is often used by business spokespersons who want to escape wider social scrutiny of their activities. The Minister for Enterprise, Trade and Employment summed up the general approach: 'I am conscious that when you go the foreign direct investment route in the US, what companies say is that they like the Government's agility to get things done in Ireland and that they are not over-regulated like in mainland Europe.'[63]

Officially, business in Ireland is regulated through agencies such as the Office of Director of Corporate Enforcement (ODCE) and the Irish Financial Services Regulatory Authority (IFSRA). Both these institutions have been formed recently in the wake of concerns about business ethics, but the philosophy of light regulation is deeply embodied in their ethos.

Laws governing companies are not particularly onerous but, despite this, a minority of companies do not comply. Sometimes, for example, directors will allow companies to go insolvent without calling in the liquidator, or fail to submit a return to the

Companies Office. This occurs in the construction industry, for example, when builders wish to escape future obligations. Yet despite this well-known practice, the ODCE has only obtained eight convictions of directors in 2002; twelve in 2003 and twenty-two in 2004.[64] Convictions can range from restrictions on acting as director for five years to outright disqualification, but fines are derisory in the extreme. In 2003, for example, directors of two companies, who were sanctioned for failing to submit an annual return to the companies Registration office, were fined the grand total of €250 and €100 respectively.[65]

The area that enjoys the lightest of regulation is probably the financial sector. Finance represents over 4 per cent of GDP – which is exceeded in the EU only by Luxemburg, a well-known hub for financial operations.[66] Historically, the Irish state has long supported the emergence of a 'strong' banking sector and its Central Bank has put bank 'solvency' far higher on its list of priorities than consumer rights. One result is that the average profit of Irish banks per customer is three times higher than the European average.[67] In the ten-year period from 1993 to 2003, for example, profits at the Bank of Ireland jumped from less than €29,583 per employee to €75,074.[68] The dark side of this 'success' story has been a scandalous history of over-charging and collusion in tax evasion.

Between 1996 and 2004, the AIB (Allied Irish Banks) over-charged customers in foreign currency transactions to the tune of €34 million by the simple device of claiming that it was applying a marginal rate of 0.5 per cent on each transaction while in fact it was charging 1 per cent. Senior management claimed they know nothing about this 'mistake', but when one former senior manager, Seamus Sheerin, pointed the finger at them, they settled the case out of court.[69] According to one of its own former executives, Ray Douglas, the same bank set up a special scheme for senior executives known as the Faldor scheme, to avoid tax. Yet no regulatory authority seemed to know anything about these matters until one whistleblower contacted the Irish Financial Services Regulatory Authority in 2004. To make doubly sure, he or she also informed RTE (Radio Telefis Eireann).

The National Irish Bank (NIB) was also involved in tax avoidance scams and overcharging customers. In 1992, it established a hit squad, the Financial Advice and Services Division, which toured the state seeking out branch customers who had 'hot money' and encouraging them to evade tax by putting their money into a new offshore product apparently based on the Isle of Man. The senior management were responsible for setting a culture of high targets for branch managers; the external auditors, KPMG did not make an issue of it; and no regulatory authority did anything until 1998.[70] Once again, the key intervention came from a whistleblower who contacted RTE and revealed the whole scandal. The NIB, it seemed, had important political connections as its chief executive, Jim Lacey, was chairman of Forum 2000, a Fianna Fail body that raised money from business. One of its other senior managers was Beverly Cooper Flynn, who later became a Fianna Fail TD. The NIB had also written off debts of a Fianna Fail TD, John Ellis, when his bankruptcy might have meant the collapse of the Haughey government.

Given the spate of scandals, one might have expected more stringent regulations, and the formation of the IFSRA and the introduction of a Companies (Audit and Accounting) Act 2003 and the Central Bank and Financial Services Act 2004 did indeed seem to augur changes. The latter act allowed for fines of up to €5 million on financial corporations who break the law. But when the first case of a breach of regulatory requirements emerged into public view, IFRSA revealed that it had merely reached a settlement with the firm. The Board of IFSRA is dominated by figures that are close to the corporate world. It is chaired by Brian Patterson, a former executive of Waterford Crystal, who gained a reputation as 'Mr Re-Structuring'.[71] It also includes John Dunne, former director general of the employers' federation IBEC; Alan Ashe, a former managing director of Standard Life Assurance; and Friedhelm Danz, a company chairman. There are no representatives of the trade unions or lobbyists for the poor who might take a more critical view of the financial sector. There is also a special 'consultative industry panel' who are charged with 'commenting on the impact on competitiveness of the Financial Regulator's imposition of restrictions/conditions'.[72] It is made up of representatives of the major banks, brokers, and insurance and asset management companies. The chairperson of IFSRA continues to reject any 'rules-based approach', claiming it is a system where 'you would have yards and yards of questionnaires and boxes to be ticked'.[73]

This style of light regulation is most evident in the Irish Stock Exchange and the Irish Financial Services Centre. The Irish Stock Exchange is administered by a private board that produces no proper annual report. It was unusual in the financial world for being in charge of its own regulation. The IFSRA has only recently announced that it was taking on a policing role. The whole area of finance is shrouded in a cloak of secrecy and one of the few ways the public gets access to information is when the wealthy fall out among themselves. A recent case where the giant fruit corporation Fyffes took DCC chief executive, Jim Flavin, to court over 'insider trading' raised important questions. Flavin was on the board of Fyffes and sold shares for €106 million after, it was argued, he obtained highly confidential information which indicated a decline in profits in the near future. During the trial it was revealed that DCC set up a Dutch company, Lotus Green, for the purpose of avoiding tax on the sale of its Fyffes shares. To maintain the impression that Lotus Green was controlled from Holland, minutes of a meeting were altered to delete the role played by an Irish director and to insert Dutch directors. Mr Flavin stated baldly that 'sometimes minutes might be adjusted to reflect and make sure that something is in accord with the underlying fundamentals in relation to a tax situation'.[74] But it might also be suggested that if a company could brazenly save itself €17 million in tax through the simple device of changing minutes, this indicates a confidence that state agencies did not inquire into business affairs too deeply.

The regulation-light Irish Financial Services Centre has become a major centre for international financial speculators. Its activities are divided into three main categories – asset management, banking and insurance. Officially, the centre is regulated though the IFSRA, but the scope and depth of that regulation are often quite minimal. Even the International Monetary Fund felt compelled to issue a jaundiced report on the regulation of the insurance industry, noting that whereas Ireland observes the 'basic or necessary criteria ... it may need to consider more stringent requirements'.[75] There was no formal programme to monitor the internal control systems of insurers and a statutory report was only required annually which was 'below best practice'.[76]

Not surprisingly, this has drawn the IFSC into a major scandal when AIG, one of the largest global insurance companies, tried to inflate its profits by pretending to re-insure its risk with the Dublin-based company, Cologne Re, a subsidiary of Warren Buffett's General Re.[77] The chairperson of this latter company, John Houldsworth, who pleaded guilty to drawing up the fraudulent paper work, served as chair of the highly influential Dublin International Insurance Management Association. This case led to the IFSC being labelled 'the financial Wild West', with Michael Gass, a legal expert with the Boston based Palmer and Dodge firm, stating that, 'My general understanding is that Dublin is viewed, along with the Cayman Islands and Bermuda, as a haven for reinsurance companies to set up offices and get away with doing things they would not be able to do elsewhere'.[78]

The Industrial Development Authority explicitly markets the IFSC for its ability to skim along the bottom of the international regulatory screen. It boasts that there is 'no transfer pricing legislation' and 'no thin capitalisation rules'.[79] It states that 'Ireland uses an Anglo/Saxon business model' and has 'proactive Private/Public Industry Forums'.[80] It points out that once companies are regulated in Ireland, they can then passport their services throughout the EU. It adds that while Ireland is in full compliance with the EU and OECD regulation, 'back offices activities do not require to be regulated'.[81] It states that corporations can employ a 'global resourcing strategy with offshore locations used for cost-sensitive activities'.[82]

The spate of scandals in the Irish finance industry led to a more stringent Companies (Audit and Accounting) Act in 2003. This made it legally necessary for company directors of any limited company with a turnover of over €15.3 million to submit compliance statements each year. According to the new law, they would have to state that they have in place internal control systems to ensure they obeyed the law of the land, including its tax laws. Company auditors were then supposed to sign off on whether these statements were fair and reasonable. It was all, however, just too much for Ireland's financial sector.

Even before the Act came into effect an intense lobby campaign began in elite circles to get it scrapped. IBEC claimed it would act as a 'disincentive';[83] Senator Fergal Quinn was 'horrified';[84] a senior partner in PricewaterhouseCoopers thought it was 'too radical';[85] an anonymous executive of a US corporation thought 'at the stroke of a pen it makes Ireland uncompetitive'.[86] Sean

Fitzpatrick, the chief executive of Anglo Irish Bank summed up the elite consensus, 'we need to legislate to the necessary minimum, supplemented by codes of corporate governance and good business practice'.[87] With voices like this, it did not take long for the government to suspend its own legislation. The matter was referred to the Company Law Review Group who, in a majority vote, duly recommended a more 'business friendly' approach, and drafted an amendment which limited the scope of the compliance statements. The chairperson of the Company Law Review Group was a director of the Bank of Ireland Mortgage Group, and the membership included a partner of KPMG and McCann Fitzgerald, a director of the Irish Stock Exchange, and a senior executive of the Irish Bankers Federation, an IBEC nominee, assorted legal representatives and one sole trade union nominee.

The reversal of a law that merely required company directors to state that they abided by all relevant laws tells a lot about Ireland's approach to regulation. Trade unions have campaigned for years against the Industrial Relations Act that limits their right to strike, but have been unsuccessful – yet business could get the mildest of measures reversed even before they were implemented.

Overall, then, the Irish state is trying not only to win a lead in cutting taxes but also in reducing regulations on business. But this level of freedom for the corporations carries a tremendous cost for society. Over the next five chapters we shall look at how many different areas of Irish society are affected. Ireland is by no means unique in this regard and cannot be treated in isolation. So we shall examine it in the context of a corporate takeover of our world.

NOTES

1. M. Brennock 'Airline Suspends Shannon stop for US Troops'. *Irish Times*, 5 February 2003.
2. RTE News, 5 January 2006.
3. P. Leahy, 'State Blocked US Planes carrying Landmines'. *Sunday Business Post*, 20 April 2003.
4. 'Sea Change on Shannon Flights'. *Irish Times*, 9 April 2003.
5. '"Taxpayer paid €10m over Flights Bill", says TD'. *Irish Times*, 14 May 2005.
6. 'US Investment over twice as much in Ireland as in China'. *Irish Times*, 18 May 2004.
7. Congressional Budget Office, Briefing: Why does US Investment Abroad earn a Higher rate of return than Foreign Investment in the US (Washington: CBO, 2005), p.6.
8. 'Ireland can help Bridge Transatlantic Bridge'. *Irish Times*, 6 February 2004.
9. C. Johnson, 'America's Empire of Bases' in TomDispatch.Com, 15 January 2004. http://www.tomdispatch.com/index.mhtml?pid=1181.
10. *World Investment Report 2004* (Geneva: UNCTAD, 2005), Figure 1.7.

11. A. McDowell, 'How Ireland Can Help to Complete the Trans Atlantic Marketplace', in Institute of European Affairs, *An Indispensable Partnership: EU-US Relations from an Irish Perspective* (Dublin: IEA, 2004), p.57.
12. F. Mueller, *No Lobbyists as Such: The War over Software Patents in the European Union* (Starnberg, Germany: SWM Software Market, no date).
13. K. Allen, 'Double Speak: Command and Control Models in a Neo-Liberal Economy', in B. Fanning (ed.), *Immigration and Social Change in the Republic of Ireland* (Manchester: Manchester University Press, 2007) pp.96–103.
14. See *UN Human Development Report 2004* (New York: UNDP, 2004), pp.150–1.
15. See for example Financial Statement of Minister for Finance, Brian Cowen, 1 December 2004 (Dublin: Department of Finance, 2004).
16. D. Johnston, 'Sceptical Hearing for Audit Firm'. *New York Times*, 19 November 2003.
17. L. Drutman, 'Citizen Works Shines a Light on Corporate Tax Avoidance'. Press Release, 14 April 2005 (Washington: Citizen Works, 2005).
18. R. McIntyre, *Tax Cheats and Their Enablers* (New York: Citizens for Tax Justice, 2005), p.14.
19. See Revenue Commissioners Press Release, 'Signature of New Tax Convention between Ireland and the US', 28 July 1997.
20. M. O Sullivan, 'Data Shows Dramatic Shift of Profits to Tax Havens'. *Tax Notes*, 104, 12 (2004), pp.1190–6.
21. 'Tax Misery and Reform Index'. *Forbes*, 23 May 2005.
22. See IDA website on http://www.idaireland.com/home/index.aspx? Id=659.
23. KPMG, Corporate Tax Rate Survey 2003, p.2.
24. 'European Nations Vie to Win Investments via Tax Cuts'. *Wall Street Journal*, 28–30 January 2005.
25. G. Simpson, 'Irish Subsidiary lets Microsoft slash taxes in US and Europe'. *Wall Street Journal*, 7 November 2005.
26. Comptroller and Auditor General Annual Report 2003, Table 9. (Dublin Stationery Office, 2003).
27. Correspondence from Revenue Commissioners to Author.
28. Comptroller and Auditor General Report 2001, p.20. (Dublin Stationery Office, 2001).
29. Ibid., p.32.
30. Ibid., p.26.
31. Correspondence between author and Revenue Commissioners.
32. Irish Continental Group, Financial Report, Preliminary Statement 12 Months to 31 December 2003.
33. 'A Taxing Battle'. *The Economist*, 31 January 2004, p.72.
34. K. Barrington, 'Even US may Question low Tax Regime'. *Sunday Business Post*, 1 May 2005.
35. Simpson, 'Irish Subsidiary lets Microsoft Slash Taxes'. *Wall Street Journal*, 7 November 2005.
36. 'O'Brien turns his back on Negative Ireland'. *Irish Times*, 24 October 2003.
37. L. Reid, 'More than 100 have pension funds worth €5m plus', *Irish Times*, 24 November 2006.
38. 'Revealed: The Greatest Tax Break of all – and it's Legal'. *Sunday Tribune*, 6 February 2005.
39. 'Tax Break for Endangered Business People'. *Sunday Business Post*, 20 March 2005.
40. Indecon, *Review of Property based Tax Incentive Scheme: Report for Department of Finance* (Dublin: Government Publications, 2006), pp.ii and 20.
41. 'The Tax Loophole Rip-off'. *Village*, 20–26 November 2004.
42. Goodbody Consultants, *Review of Area-Based Tax Incentive Renewal Scheme: Final Report* (Dublin: Government Publications, 2005), p.ii.
43. RTE News, '11 Millionaires Paid No Tax', 22 October 2004.
44. Eurostat, *Structures of the Taxation Systems in the European Union* (Luxembourg: Office of Official Publications of the European Communities, 2004).
45. PriceWaterhouseCoopers, *Doing Business and Investing in Ireland* (Dublin: PWC, 2005), Chap.7.
46. Combat Poverty Agency, 'Promoting Equity in Ireland's Tax System'. Policy Statement, April 2006.

47. Eurostat, *Europe in Figures: Eurostat Yearbook 2005* (Luxembourg: European Commission, 2005), p.138.
48. European Commission, *Employment in Europe 2005* (Luxembourg: Office of Official Publications of the European Communities, 2005), p.59.
49. OECD, *Pensions at a Glance: Public Policies across OECD Countries* (Paris: OECD, 2005), p.2.
50. 'GAMA Staff Threaten Hunger Strike'. *Irish Times*, 20 May 2005.
51. 'Workers in GAMA Vote to Accept Labour Court Ruling'. *Irish Times*, 28 May 2005.
52. 'Clare County Council accused over GAMA Contract'. *Irish Times*, 10 May 2005.
53. 'GAMA Wages Scandal Splits Employers and Trade Unions'. *Sunday Business Post*, 17 April 2005.
54. Reply to written parliamentary question of Pat Rabbitte, Labour Party Press Office, 3 July 2005.
55. 'Labour Inspectors Condemn Lack of Resources'. *Irish Times*, 8 April 2005.
56. S. Miller, 'Workers and Taxpayers hit by Builder Sub-contracting-union'. *Village*, 9 March 2006.
57. Correspondence from Employment Agency Section of DETE to author, 7 December 2005
58. P. Conroy and M. Pierce, *Temporary Agency Work: National Reports Ireland* (Dublin: European Foundation for Improvement of Living and Working Conditions, 2002), p.16.
59. Labour Relations Commission, *Migrant Workers and Access to the Statutory Dispute Resolution Agencies* (Dublin: LRC, 2005), p.15.
60. Ibid., p.15.
61. Contractors Administration Services Website, August 2005. http://www.cas.ie/system.htm.
62. Interview with author.
63. 'ISE Review likely after Fyffes case'. *Irish Times*, 21 June 2005.
64. Correspondence from ODCE to author.
65. ODCE Annual Report 2004, p.58.
66. 'Banking on a Promising Future'. *Public Affairs Ireland*, No.13 (July 2004).
67. 'Irish Banks make three times more per Customer'. *Irish Examiner*, 15 October 2004.
68. 'Profits per Employee soar at BoI and AIB'. *Sunday Business Post*, 24 April 2005.
69. 'Scandal to get more Air-time at AIB Talks'. *Irish Examiner*, 27 April 2005.
70. Report on Investigation into the Affairs of National Irish Bank Ltd and National Irish Bank Financial Services by High Court Inspectors Justice Blayney and Tom Grace, http://www.odce.ie/new/article.asp?NID=326&NCID=42.
71. 'Mr Re-Structuring: Brian Patterson, IFSC Regulatory Authority Chairman'. *Sunday Business Post*, 28 April 2002.
72. http://www.ifsra.ie/frame_main.asp?pg=/consultative_panels/cpl_intr.asp&nv=/consultative_panels/cpl_nav.asp
73. 'Regulator Underlines Concerns about Debt'. *Irish Times*, 27 July 2006.
74. 'Lotus Green Board Minutes Altered, court told'. *Irish Times*, 16 March 2005.
75. IMF, *Report on the Observance of Standards and Codes (ROSC) Ireland: Insurance Supervision* (Washington: IMF, 2001), p.1.
76. Ibid., pp.8–9.
77. 'Spitzer Rides into Town'. *Sunday Times*, 24 April 2005.
78. Ibid.
79. IDA, 'The IFSC'. Package of material sent to author.
80. Ibid.
81. Ibid.
82. Ibid.
83. IBEC Press Release, 'Government White Paper on better Regulation', 20 January 2004.
84. 'Quinn expresses "horror" at Auditing Bill'. *Irish Times*, 17 April 2003.
85. 'Auditing Proposals "too radical"'. *Irish Times*, 16 June 2003.
86. 'Section 45 will kill Irish Competitiveness'. *Irish Times*, 25 February 2005.
87. 'Bill will stifle Business – banker'. *Irish Times*, 21 May 2003.

Chapter Five

Catching Them Young

One of the great inventions of modern society is childhood. Children, of course, have existed since time immemorial, but childhood as a protected zone between infancy and adulthood is comparatively new.

In medieval society a child joined adult society as soon as he or she could live without constant care from their mother or nanny. They did not wear a special dress or have special rooms but worked alongside adults, and even married at extraordinary young ages. One of the women in a Chaucer poem written in the fourteenth century casually comments that 'since the age of twelve, thanks to God whose life is eternal, I have taken a husband five times at the church porch'.[1] Although it may appear shocking to modern sensibilities, parental indifference to children was widespread. Common manifestations included knocking infants to sleep through 'forceful shaking', boarding out infants to wet nurses or leaving them alone for long periods.[2] Medieval parents were not morally inferior to their modern counterparts, but high infant mortality meant that they did not allow themselves to become too attached to their children.

Modern childhood began to emerge from the seventeenth century onwards through schooling and the creation of the nuclear family. Early medieval schools were often known as 'cathedral schools' and their purpose was to train both the young and the old for the clergy. Later their function changed and they focussed on the moral development of children. Initially, it was the sons of the middle class who attended, but gradually the practice spread throughout society. Later still, the organization of lessons and classes, according to the child's age, suggested a new concept of childhood: that it was a sheltered period of preparation for adult life.

Simultaneously the nuclear family separated itself off from the wider society by retreating from extended networks to build 'the wall of private life' between itself and society. 'Privacy' became one of the most cherished values of the new middle class, symbolized by gardens walls or hedges. Within the family the mother-child bond became primary, and this meant that it was no longer solely seen as an institution for regulating property relations, but became an emotional haven from the outside world. Henceforth childhood was deemed to belong to an age of innocence, and painters such as Joshua Reynolds depicted it with glowing, soft and vulnerable imagery. Children were to be protected by their parents and subject to a sort of quarantine before being able to join adult society.

This image of childhood innocence is, of course, a quintessentially Western romantic concept. Although it originally brought many benefits – not least the escape from child labour – it has become a dangerous myth because it assumes that children are outside of society, driven by instinct and living in their own imagination. The myth leads to the idealization of the middle-class child and to a rejection of other 'rougher' children as outcasts who hang out on the streets. It harks back to an age of the stay-at-home mum and a return to family values. In the hands of a cynical tabloid media, the mythology creates moral panics about child molestation and internet 'grooming' by paedophiles, as if these were principal dangers facing the modern child. No sensible person would suggest that paedophiles are not a menace but the US cultural critic, Henry Giroux, suggests there may be greater dangers for most children:

> Consider the following contradictions. Pornography on the Internet is held up as an imminent danger to childhood innocence but nothing is said about the corporations and their middle-class shareholders who relentlessly commodify children's bodies, desires, identities, in the interest of turning in a profit. Mainstream media critics who focus on the disappearance of childhood endlessly argue that the greatest threat to childhood innocence is rap music rather than media

conglomerates such as Time-Warner (which produces many rap artists), General Electric, Westinghouse or Disney.[3]

The commodification of children is replacing the age of innocence as the forces of global capitalism transform young lives. In Ireland this begins at a very early age, as childcare now inhabits a twilight zone between the traditional Catholic family and the 'individual responsibility' in a free market.

In the past, Ireland had the lowest number of women in the workforce but the Celtic Tiger changed all that as it sought new sources of labour to fuel its dynamic economy. Women below the age of 30 joined the labour force in spectacular numbers as rising house prices destroyed the idea of a stay-at-home mother for the majority. Yet the Irish state insisted on a novel combination of the traditional and the modern, asserting a fictitious belief that childcare was the sole responsibility of the individual family. The message to parents was that they had to rely on their own resources to take care of their children. When children reached the magic age of four, the state assumed responsibility for their social rights and granted them free access to formal education in a primary school. Before that age, however, they were not social beings but the property of their families.

In 2000, an Equal Opportunities Childcare Programme was launched and modest sums were made available to community or non-profit organizations to provide about 25,000 childcare places.[4] However, this was focussed on the socially excluded and was a scheme designed to draw more women into the labour force by attaching crèche facilities to training programmes. Beyond that, there was denial that good childcare is beneficial for a child's development – both for their cognitive, language and academic skills and for their wider social skills. This was despite the fact that 40 per cent of families with pre-school children rely on someone other than the parents to look after their children.[5] The exact figures are somewhat of a mystery, as many rely on relatives or friends who do not have to register with the state if they look after less than three children. For the rest, childcare has been turned into a private commodity that is supplied by small businesses.

The result is one of the dearest childcare costs in Europe. A survey conducted by the *Sunday Business Post* in January 2005 found that costs for a six-month-old baby ranged from €6,120 a year in Donegal to €11,024 a year in Dublin.[6] Two qualifications need to be made about this figure. First, the six month old would face difficulty getting into a crèche in the Dublin area because regulations specify that one carer is needed for every three children under the age of 1 year.[7] Places have to be booked up to six months in advance, sometimes before the baby is born. Second, childcare costs tend to rise much faster than inflation – in fact by about three times the rate of general inflation. Ireland's childcare costs now rival mortgage payments as one of the main drains on personal expenditure. A recent Forum on the Workplace of the Future report noted that not only are Ireland's childcare costs the highest in Europe but they also consumed a bigger proportion of parents' income. Irish parents pay on average 20 per cent of their annual income on childcare, which is far higher than the EU average of 12 per cent.[8]

The privatized childcare system also fares worse for quality. There is no professional corps of inspectors who have specific training in childcare.[9] Some services are housed in unsuitable premises – in some cases community halls, where materials have

TABLE 5.1
RANKING OF EU 15 ACCORDING TO HOW SUPPORTIVE THEIR CHILDCARE SYSTEM
IS TO A DUAL EARNER MODEL

Country	Score
Denmark	88.55
Sweden	78.86
Finland	56.69
France	51.30
Belgium	48.10
Luxemburg	43.09
Germany	39.76
Austria	6.50
Italy	35.66
Netherlands	34.63
United Kingdom	33.63
Portugal	23.13
Greece	19.47
Spain	18.37
Ireland	5.64

Source: The rationale of Motherhood Choices: Influence of Employment Conditions and Public Policies (MOCHO Project). Report of the Forum on the Workplace of the Future.

to be put away after each session.[10] There is a scarcity of qualified staff who have undertaken courses in Early Childhood Care and Education and a lack of subsidized refresher courses to help staff up-skill and rekindle enthusiasm. There are no developmental and educational goals set by the state as a curriculum. There are voluntary guidelines to encourage developers to make provision for childcare facilities in housing estates that have more than seventy units. But like many guidelines for business there is little evidence that they are adhered to.[11]

Contrast this with the Nordic model where childcare is seen not only as a public service but where a pedagogue is employed with training and salary levels similar to teachers. In this model, there is also a strong emphasis on health care, socialization, well being and active learning.[12] Table 5.1 ranks the childcare facilities across Europe according to costs, staff-child ratios, opening hours and private or publicly funded facilities. It indicates that Ireland comes at the bottom of the list by a long shot.

The privatization of childcare is only one aspect of the neo-liberal model that suggests that there are only individuals who make rational 'choices' about their lives – including choices about parenthood. Society as a whole, it is assumed, and business in particular, is not responsible and should bear only minimal costs. By contrast, a growing number of EU countries offer parents paid, job-protected maternity or paternity leave for at least one year to care for their children. Even the OECD argues for a paid, flexible and job-protected maternity and paternity leave as essential components to support working parents with very young children. Their motivation is not a particular concern about children's rights but part of a strategy to increase labour supply.

However, the Irish model of neo-liberalism does not even go that far and, instead, shuns any possible cost to employers. The scale of the problem has caused an outcry but the official response has been minimal. Instead of taking some responsibility for childcare, it has offered a special supplement to parents of just €19 a week. New tax reliefs have been granted to child minders to register and set up a business, but few have done so. Paid maternity leave, from March 2007, will still amount to only twenty-six weeks and is drawn from a wider social insurance fund rather than from employers. There is an additional entitlement to sixteen weeks unpaid leave but low paid workers can hardly afford to avail of this. There is no legal right to career breaks and there is no parental leave. Despite twenty years of social partnership where participants claimed they were developing a 'social agenda', Ireland continues to lead the race to the bottom on childcare.

CORPORATE INVASION OF SCHOOLS

Up till recently, schools were seen as a commercial free zone. Aside from contracts for school uniforms, there was thought to be little scope for profit. But the neo-liberal assault is removing all barriers and schools are becoming commercial hunting grounds.

It began back in June 1998, when the government decided to use education as a pilot project to test market opportunities for Public Private Partnerships. Five schools were 'bundled' together into a deal which offered a private sector company a fee to design, build and operate them for twenty-five years. It was claimed that the new arrangement would offer better value, and allow school principals to concentrate on core educational functions rather than worry about maintenance. The five schools chosen for the new pilot project were in Ballincollig, Clones, Dunmanway, Shannon and Tubbercurry. A wedge had been opened to allow corporations to start reshaping the school system.

The contract to run the schools was given to the British multinational, Jarvis. This happened to be the same company who was responsible for the Potters Bar rail accident in Britain, where seven people died because of inadequate track maintenance. Jarvis initially tried to shift the blame by producing photographs that claimed the line had been tampered with, but finally had to admit culpability.[13] Its record in maintaining schools was not much better. In the Huddersfield area, where it was responsible for twenty schools, the deputy leader of Kirkless council described that record as 'woefully bad'.[14] Aside from Jarvis, the other main firm involved in the first PPP deal was Farrell, Grant and Sparks, which the Department of Education and Science hired to advise it on procurement procedures for the five schools and for the Cork School of Music. The same firm also crossed the table and advised Bovis Lendlease on a PPP contract for the National Maritime College in Cork.

Most of the claimed improvements that the PPPs were

supposed to bring never materialized. There was no 'value for money' bonus because, as the Comptroller and Auditor General noted, the final deal cost between 8 and 13 per cent more than if the schools had been built by more traditional procurement methods.[15] The true costs may be even higher as they can only be estimated over the twenty-five year cycle. The schools were built to bigger specifications than the state originally intended and higher costs were accordingly awarded. Far from the private sector taking many risks, its fee was secured even when the expected student enrollment did not occur. In the Ballincollig case, the school numbers fell from the expected 1,000 to 570 pupils, but the state continued payments for school maintenance as if there were 1,000 pupils in attendance. Nor were school principals left free to concentrate on purely educational matters but sometimes found themselves inveigled into bizarre arrangements with the 'facility management' team. Students and teachers, for example, were not allowed to install software into computers as the machines belonged to Jarvis and they had to contact the company first and pay an installation fee.[16] Problems also arose because caretakers and janitors were no longer answerable to the school principal, but to a centrally-operated helpdesk.

Schools which are built under the PPP arrangement are transformed from public facilities into private commercial concerns and this has damaging implications for the wider relationship between the school and the community. The schools were only given one additional hour per day for the use of the building for extra-curricular purposes. Beyond that the schools had to be rented out at commercial rates to local sporting bodies or community associations, and the rental income shared between the company and school management. The main purpose of many of these arrangements seemed to be to guarantee Jarvis a healthy return of 13 per cent on its capital. They had good reason to be pleased because, as David McWilliams put it, 'For an investor ... PPPs offer a risk free bet. In fact it operates like an underwriting service. The investment via PPP offers the investor a return well over the rate of interest.'[17]

Despite many criticisms of its pilot project, the Department of Education and Science is determined to turn the PPP system into a normal method of procurement and twenty-three more secondary schools and four primary schools are to be commissioned under this scheme. No doubt, it will expand even further and eventually schooling will no longer be simply about education, but will increasingly become a commercial operation.

The corporate invasion of schools does not stop at the building facilities – it is now directly targeting children as consumers. Schools have been historically under-funded in Ireland because of the failure to tax wealth. But corporations are now using the desperation of schools for better equipment to create new business opportunities, and so benefit twice over. Ample space has been created by cuts in grants for PE equipment and the failure of the state to provide basic computer equipment to schools.

Tesco has pioneered the way with its 'Computer in the School' scheme which has been running for nine years. For every €10 spent in their supermarkets, a parent will get a voucher which can be exchanged by schools for prizes. But it takes a lot of 'pester power' to collect the vouchers. To get a 'free' standard computer for a classroom, which might normally retail for about €700, a school needs to generate €215,000 worth of shopping. To get a 'free' packet of floppy discs retailing at €12.50, schools must generate €4,000 of shopping. To make matters worse, parents have just ten weeks between March and May to collect the vouchers.

Just before the Tesco scheme kicks in, schools can take part in the SuperValu 'Kids in Action' scheme which operates on the same principle, but offers vouchers for sports equipment. Or they might have used McDonald's Catch and Kick programme which partners the king of junk food with the Gaelic Athletic Association (GAA). This claims to provide school teams with 'eight coaching inputs' – such as footballs, pumps and tracksuit, all with the McDonald's logo. Children are assured that 'Catch and Kick is "crazy" "cool" and "kickin" and will soon be in over 300 primary schools all over Ireland'.[18]

Schools are an ideal market for corporations in a number of ways. They represent a mass audience that no other institution can command on a daily basis. Moreover, children are key to influencing all sorts of parent purchases including, strangely, cars. Schools also conveniently group children according to market segments that can be identified according to age, gender, class and ethnic background. Corporations can send customized messages to precise target groups by selecting boys or girls in particular classes, and focusing on schools in particular areas if they want to target social class and ethnic background. They also offer the intangible ethos of authority which can flow from the teacher to a particular product. Young children tend to take a teacher's word as truth, and when teachers endorse something, however implicitly, they become powerful sales people. When this power of authority is allied with the competitive ethos that prevails in schools, the child is defenceless. Tesco, for example, supplies schools with wall charts to gauge each child's efforts to collect vouchers and encourages inter-class competition, with prizes for those who collect most vouchers. It puts children under huge pressure to conform.

Corporations, however, have to tread carefully and cannot simply use standard methods to sell their wares. Traditionally, advertising works through entertainment and fantasy whereas school promotes enlightenment and learning. They, therefore, have to present themselves either as 'socially responsible' philanthropists or suppliers of educational material to gain entry. Tesco, SuperValu and McDonald's are good examples of how 'philanthropy' is used to gain maximum exposure for their logos. Other companies used sponsored educational materials (SEMs) which purport either to provide teaching materials or assist activities associated with learning objectives. Unilever runs a competition to write a 'wacky 40 second radio ad' to help transition year media studies students – and, co-incidentally, promote its Pot Noodle brand. Le Crunch runs an art competition to encourage healthy eating – and particularly Le Crunch apples.

One extraordinary example of an SEM operation is the AIB 'Build a Bank Challenge' which purports to help transition year and fifth year Business Studies students get to grips with running a real live bank. Schools who take part in this scheme agree to set aside a classroom that is converted into an AIB Bank. Teenagers are recruited for the AIB group and their duties include sourcing new customers to open AIB accounts through the school bank. They also encourage classmates to use new ways of banking such as phone and internet banking – and so win life-long customers for the AIB because people tend to stick with the first banks they sign up to. AIB's strategy has been created by Real Events, one of Ireland's first advertising agencies that help corporations target schools. In the US, these agencies have become a big business in themselves.

Schools are generally regarded as a safe environment where

children should be protected from manipulation. Formally, the state appears to support this stance and a Department of Education circular, which has been distributed widely since 1991, requests that 'schools consider carefully the implications of allowing any situation to develop which would result in parents being put under undue pressure to purchase a particular product'.[19] Yet this set of 'general principles' has little direct practical consequence because the Department also deems it 'inappropriate to prohibit marketing or sponsoring initiatives' and does not monitor school codes in relation to commercial promotions.[20] The former Minister of Education, Noel Dempsey, personally endorsed one sponsorship scheme even while he held office. This was the Irish Independent/CIE 'Building for the Future' scheme which purported to support 'community activity'. To enter the competition schools had to ensure that each student collected thirty tokens from the *Irish Independent* or the *Sunday Independent*. A relatively large primary school had to collect over €20,000's worth of tokens from Independent Newspapers while a smaller one needed about €10,000's worth. The same newspaper opposes any increase in the type of wealth taxes that might help fund schools.

CATCHING THEM YOUNG

The corporate invasion of the schools is only one aspect of a wider commercialization of youth that has destroyed the myth of the 'age of innocence'. Children have become a mass market in late capitalism and are targeted by the most sophisticated and powerful organizations on the planet. Mattel and Hasbro share the toy market between them, with eight of the top ten toys sold in the US in 2002 coming from them. Video games are dominated by Nintendo, Sony and Microsoft. In soft drinks it is Coke and Pepsi; in sweets it is Cadbury's, M&M and Hershey; in fast food it is McDonald's and Burger King.

The marketing gurus have segmented childhood into distinct niches such as 'toddlers' (0–3), 'preschoolers' (2–5), 'kids' (6–8), 'tweens' (from 9–12) and 'teens' (13–15) with different products targeted at each. As children suffer from 'age aspiration' and try to emulate older groups, the 'tween' market has begun receiving the most recent attention, with advertisers targeting them with products previously geared to teenagers. In Britain, this age group is estimated to have a personal disposable income from pocket money, odd jobs and gifts of around €2.7 billion dollars while their US counterparts have €20 billion. Yet these raw figures hide the potential which they offer the big corporations because, as marketing guru James McNeal argues, they represent three different markets – the direct money they spend; the spending they influence and, the most significant off all, the future market created by brand loyalty.[21] McNeal is credited with being the first to discover the kids market when he published his book *Children as Consumers* in 1986. He bluntly told business that they had only two sources of new customers: 'Either they switched from competitors or they are developed from childhood ... Growing customers from childhood is a less common source of customers, but one based on good business logic'.[22]

The result has been a sustained assault on the brains and emotions of children. The average American child now views approximately 40,000 commercials annually and makes 3,000 requests for products and services.[23] They have become the ideal customers as they spend many hours watching television, often in the privacy of their own bedroom. In the US, a third of children live in homes where parents leave the TV on most of the day – whether anyone is watching or not.[24] Most ominously, the first BabyFirstTV has been launched for children under 2 years of age, claiming to be 'educational', even though the American Academy of Paediatrics recommends no television for children under 2.[25] There has been a slight decrease in television viewing by children in many countries, but this is often because they have switched to the internet and interactive games. Together, television, the internet and interactive games are ideal media for gaining unhindered access to children.

At its most basic level, advertising uses the power of repetition to instil recognition into young minds. There is nothing intrinsically interesting about Kellogg cereals but the constant appearance of the name in all manner of scenarios encourages brand recognition. 'Ad creep' is now so extensive that children cannot participate in public life without being targeted at sports events, rock concerts, public transport or at school. By the age of 3 years, before they can read, many American children are making specific requests for brand name products.[26] By the age of 10 years the average British child has memorized between

300–400 brand names – about twenty times the number of wild birds they could name.[27]

The advertising market is becoming so saturated that companies have to seek alternative ways to sell. One older practice which has grown enormously is the practice of sponsoring films. The sponsors have gone way beyond product placement and are now involved in developing plots and writing dialogue to ensure their products are meaningfully interwoven into the film.[28] And they are developing ever closer 'synergies' to associate their products with films that children enjoy. Coca Cola paid €150 million for exclusive marketing rights to Harry Potter so that it could feature its imagery in advertising for its drinks. Nickelodeon has partnered with both McDonald's and Burger King and its characters can be found on many products with low nutritional value. Disney had a ten-year exclusive pact with McDonald's which lapsed recently, but the relationship continues on a project by project basis. Vivendi Universal, which owns Universal Film studios, did a deal with Toyota which gave it first refusal to place its products in films such as *Men in Black* or *Spiderman*. Music videos and reality television have become another form of insidious marketing with a video from Britney Spears, for example, deliberately featuring a Mazda car. One James Bond film, *Die Another Day*, was so full of branded products that even *Time* magazine labelled it 'Buy another Day'.[29]

A recent advertising tactic has been 'buzz' or viral marketing which operates on the principle that teenagers are influenced by peer pressure. The aim is to create a buzz about a particular product by targeting select audiences who spread the word. Procter and Gamble, for example, have recruited 250,000 teens who are identified as market research leaders to create a buzz about its long line of products.[30] The industry is also using 'advergaming', computer games built around a particular product; 'guerrilla marketing', using public space as a venue for advertising; and mobile phone ads. The aim is to create brand loyalties from as early as possible. As Kids 'R' Us President, Mike Searles put it, 'If you own this child at an early age ... you can own this child for years to come'.[31]

Corporations have also borrowed from a 'new age' outlook to establish mystical links between their 'brands' and their customers. Thousands of company executives attend conferences to hear about 'living the brand' or 'respecting their brand roots'. It is a form of emotional manipulation that associates particular products with powerful feelings of self. As one marketer put it, the aim is to 'develop brand loyalty by creating authentic emotional connections that bypass the brain and go straight to the heart, tapping into powerful feelings about self-image, fantasies, aspirations and dreams.'[32] Increasingly, companies such as Starbucks go beyond the emotional fantasies and try to link the brand 'molecules' to sensory feelings such as touch, taste and smell.[33] However, branding for children increases the possibility of manipulation immeasurably.

Underlying the many new techniques to create brand loyalty is a pseudo-scientific psychology that ties discoveries in child development to the needs of consumer capitalism. An army of psychologists and anthropologists are now hired to dissect the brains of young children. A recent book by the psychologist Dan Acuff, *What Kids Buy and Why*, shows techniques that corporations use to sell their products to children as young as 2 years old. Acuff advises companies such as Disney, Hasbro and Kraft, and uses child developmental research to suggest that advertisements include animals or animal characters. They should also, he argues, feature characters that are round or curvy and proceed at a slow pace that most adults would find tedious. His recommendations are based on studies which indicate that up to 80 per cent of young children dream of animals, and associate curvy shapes with 'good guys'.[34]

Ethnographic researchers are also employed to scrutinize children's private lives in their bedrooms and bathrooms so they can get at deep intangible feelings and fantasies that can be used in marketing. Emma Gilding, a senior partner at Ogilvy and Mather's Discovery Group in New York, says this is going beyond standard practice. 'It's not research; we live with them. It's not anthropology; we're in the frame.'[35] Anthropologists like Paco Underhill, the author of *Why We Buy*, concentrate on videotaping children and adults as they navigate shops in order to discover the laws of impulse buying. Levi Strauss has pioneered the concept of 'kid engineers', who are focus groups that help companies discern what is 'cool', and this has later been taken up by many companies. Nickelodeon, for example, hold about 250 focus groups annually, as well as telephone interviews, in-home research, in-store observations and research at pre-school.

There is little doubt that the purpose of this complex apparatus is manipulation of young minds and sometimes this will be candidly admitted. According to Nancy Shalek, then president of Shalek Agency,

> Advertising is at its best in making people feel that without their product, you're a loser. Kids are very sensitive to that. If you tell them to buy something they are resistant. But if you tell them they are a dork if they don't, you've got their attention. You open up emotional vulnerabilities, and it's easy to do with kids because they are most vulnerable.[36]

Concern about the effects the advertising industry is having on children is growing. In 1999, sixty prominent psychologists sent a letter to the President of the American Psychological Association (APA) seeking some sanction on colleagues who engaged in these practices. The result was the establishment of an important APA Task Force on Advertising and Children. Its principal conclusion was that children below the age of 8 do not have the cognitive ability to comprehend advertisements. In order to attain a mature comprehension of advertising, children must, firstly, be able to distinguish at a perceptual level an advertisement from a television programme. They must then be able to attribute persuasive intent to advertising and apply a degree of scepticism. The sum of the evidence indicated that most children below the age of 3–4 'do not consistently discriminate between a television programme and commercial content'.[37] By about 4–5, they do distinguish, but only at a perceptual level, recognizing differences in terms of short or long running time, or that ads are 'funnier than programmes'. The ability to recognize persuasive intent does not develop before 8 years of age, and 'even at that age, such capacity tends to emerge only in rudimentary form, with youngsters recognising that commercials intend to sell, but not necessarily that they are biased messages which warrant some degree of scepticism'.[38]

ADVERTISING AND THE IRISH CHILD

The modern Irish child watches 2.3 hours of television per day[39] and it might, therefore, seem reasonable for the state to step in and offer some protection from the manipulation we have just described. Since 1991, for example, the Swedish government has banned all kinds of advertising directly before or after children's programmes. Axel Edling, Sweden's Consumer Ombudsman, has explained the rationale quite simply. According to the international code of standards which govern the industry all over the world, advertising should be easily identified as such. The target group should be able to distinguish an advertisement from other media contexts, and through this principle a fair balance of power can be struck between the consumer and the advertiser. But children are unable to do this and, therefore, there cannot be fair game.[40]

Bob Quinn, who was nominated to the RTE Authority in 1995, tried to get RTE to enforce such a ban. On one occasion he even got the RTE authority to view their output of children's television and then proposed that they cease treating children as 'targetable consumers'.[41] By 1999, he felt he had to resign from an institution that wanted to exploit children and, along with his friend, Brian McGabhainn, went on to found STAC (Stop Television Advertising to Children) to alert the public to the issue. Bob Quinn describes himself as a 'maverick', but he was raising a vital issue that was of concern to many parents. Yet his argument has not been successfully rebutted.

One attempt to do so came from Professor Farrel Corcoran, the former chair of the RTE Authority. In an otherwise excellent book, he used the language of media studies to claim that advertisement did not function like a 'hypodermic syringe' and that critics should not underestimate the ability of children to evaluate and cognitively process commercials.[42] However, this ignores evidence collected by bodies like the American Psychological Association. His other argument was that even if RTE imposed a ban, the advertisers would go elsewhere and vital revenue would be lost. But this is hardly relevant. If a ban directly benefits the health and well being of children, it should be imposed – regardless of where the funds go. It may well be argued that this might require a change in government policy, but this would have significant impact on two counts. Despite globalization, 44 per cent of 4–17 years olds in Ireland watch Irish channels and so a ban would offer considerable sanctuary.[43] Moreover, as the smoking ban in pubs has demonstrated, it would have an important 'demonstration effect' abroad and encourage others to follow suit.

Even if a blanket ban on advertising to children was ruled out, there are good grounds for considering specific prohibitions of two products – junk food and alcohol. However, the debate around these two cases demonstrates just how deeply the corporate take-over of Irish society has gone.

a) Junk Food and Obesity

The number of obese children in Ireland has tripled in the past ten years, and today one in five Irish children carries excess body fat. It is part of a global epidemic caused by a variety of recent developments such as the 'burgerization' of food, the decline in physical exercise; and the use of fat-enhancing materials such as high fructose corn syrup and palm oil to add bulk and 'freshness' to food.

Despite its best efforts to deflect responsibility, the global food industry must take a lot of the blame. Its advertising budget is €40 billion a year – more than the GDP of 70 per cent of the world nations. For every dollar spent by the World Health Organization on diseases caused by Western diets, $500 is spent by the food industry promoting these diets.[44] Today it is assumed that children must be catered for separately to please their distinctive palate, but the foods they receive mainly consist of highly processed, long-life foods loaded with fat, sugar and salt. The food industry targets children principally through the medium of television, but the Hasting Report, which is the most comprehensive study on the literature in this area, showed that:

- Most television food advertising to children promotes the 'Big Five' – pre-sugared cereals, soft drinks, confectionary, savoury snacks and fast food.
- Food advertising to children contained little by way of nutritional information, but used animation or mixed formats to convey humour.
- There is casual link between exposure to food promotion and children's food knowledge and preferences.
- If television viewing is used as a proxy for exposure to advertising, there is a clear link to obesity.[45]

Through the IBEC sponsored group, Food and Drink Industry Ireland, which brings together the main food companies, the industry is fighting back. It has mainly employed the rhetoric of social partnership to argue that all 'stakeholders' need to cooperate in developing voluntary codes. This rhetoric works on two levels. By adopting a voluntary code which they write themselves, the food industry hopes to avoid regulation. And by claiming that everyone is a 'social partner', they imply that there is no conflict of interest with health specialists and parents. Some public health communities have, unfortunately, embraced this approach because they believe that, unlike alcohol, food is an essential, and so the industry must be brought on side. The report of the National Task Force on Obesity reflected some of this outlook when it failed to call for the ban on food advertising to children. Others have, however, become a little cynical about the partnership approach. Dr Donal O Shea, a prominent consultant who runs a weight reduction clinic, has pointed out that during the taskforce deliberations, Mars/Snickers agreed to get rid of their supersize bars. Afterwards, however, they replaced the giant bar with a 'Duo' of both Mars and Snickers – which carries over 500 calories, or a third of daily requirements.[46]

The food industry also attempts to use 'evidence based research' to question the link between advertising and obesity. Evidence here is defined as quantitative research which shows a direct causal link between two variables that could not be influenced by extraneous factors. The focus on a single cause, however, allows for an endless debate which can create the required level of uncertainty. If a link is established, for example, between time spent watching television and obesity, it can still be argued that other factors are at work, such as lack of physical exercise, or staying in a sedentary position for a long time, and so this invalidates the hypothesis of causality. However, this is a mechanical understanding of research that breaks down the totality of life experience to a set of isolated factors that have little connection to each other. By casting some doubt over one direct causal link, the industry tries to get off the hook. However, it does not follow that just because obesity is also influenced by lack of physical exercise, that advertising is not also a cause.

Finally, the food industry also relies on the standard 'rational choice' argument of neo-liberalism. Obesity is an individual problem and attributed to 'parental responsibility' because they fail to inculcate good eating habits into their children. As the mantra goes, there can be no 'nanny state' for this would be 'discriminatory' against the food industry and impinge on 'competitiveness'. The irony is that the advertising industry knows that neither children nor their absent parents are rational calculating machines because it uses 'humour' and 'fun' to engage children in a relationship that flies under the radar of parental authority.

Many of these arguments were played out during the Broadcasting Commission's deliberations on a code to deal with children's advertising for Irish television. The Broadcasting Commission of Ireland itself has an unusual composition. Its chair, Conor Maguire, had, according to one newspaper, 'good political connections with Fianna Fail'.[47] Its other members include a director of an advertising agency; a senior partner in the accountancy firm, Accenture; a barrister who was a former Fianna Fail press officer; a business man involved in community radio and a director of a private school. There are no representatives of parents or trade unions or children' rights advocates on the Commission.

On the surface, the BCI consultation process was extensive, starting in April 2003 and going through a series of drafts and submissions until the final code was drafted more than a year later. However, it provided an important example of how an apparent process of consultation can be structurally biased towards corporations in a number of subtle ways. An outright ban on advertising to children was ruled out from the very start and did not appear as an option in the first round of consultations. All representations to the BCI were afforded equal weighting and no priority was assigned to public health agencies such as the Irish Heart Foundation or even The Food Safety Promotion board over, say, the advertising agencies.[48] Individual submissions were counted as one, irrespective of the numbers represented therein, and this meant that smaller organizations representing industry were put on a par with bigger mass organizations.[49] Even within these parameters the voice of the majority did not count. The BCI noted, for example, that 'a significant majority (of the submissions) sought prohibitions on the advertisement of food and drink which contained high levels of sugar, additives, artificial sweeteners, salt and fat'.[50]

But little importance was assigned to the view of this majority. The issue was framed as a balanced debate between two sides, with the commission in the middle. Ranged on the side of 'the freedom to advertise' were the food industry, the advertisers and the television networks – in other words, vested interests that made profits. Ranged on the side of 'prohibition' were parents, public health agencies and the Green Party. From an early stage, the Commission accepted the industry side's arguments on opposing prohibition. In a catch-22 style argument, it claimed that a ban on 'junk' food would raise questions about the definition of junk food, and asked who would arbitrate between 'bad' and 'good' food. However, an alternative proposal to ban all food advertisement to children was ruled out because it would punish the 'good' and the 'bad' equally.[51] The Commission also accepted the industry argument that the relationship between advertising and obesity is very 'complex' and so they wanted a 'less restrictive position'.[52]

Once prohibition on advertising junk food was out of the question, the issue became one of general principles with few specific obligations. Between the first draft of the actual code and the final one, the food industry fought tooth and nail to remove any serious restrictions on their activity. The Food and Drink Industry Ireland objected to an early draft to ban the use of 'children's heroes' in advertisements – and out the restriction went.[53] A proposal to prohibit advertisements for products that made them look 'magical' was dropped because, as the Association of Advertisers in Ireland and the Institute of Advertising Practitioners in Ireland argued, 'fantasy, including animation, is appropriate for younger as well as older children'.[54] A proposal to include 'fizzy drinks' and confectionary in the category 'can damage teeth' was described as 'discriminatory' by the food industry.[55] A proposal from the National Taskforce on Obesity that advertisements carry messages about the size and portions of the fast food met with an objection from McDonalds. They questioned how 'fast food' would be defined and then asserted that, anyway, 'nutrition experts concur that there is no such thing as good or bad food, there are only good or bad diets'.[56]

The Children's Advertising Code that emerged was full of high-minded statements but very short on specific prohibitions. Warnings on 'balanced diets' and 'can damage your teeth' were only to be read out for under sixes to save advertising time. The advertising industry continued to kick up and talk of restrictions, but revenue increased the following year. Behind the fake consultation and bluster, one thing was clear: profit came before children.

b) Alcoholism

'Ireland is, of course, Guinness's original and spiritual home market', claimed Tim Kelly, marketing director of the company.[57] The country itself has become a brand image for the Diageo corporation and its 'mystique' is used to sell drink across the globe. The visitor who enters an Irish souvenir shop will be encouraged to buy Guinness cups, leprechauns, towels and T shirts. The 'Irish pub' has also become a marketing concept for selling the Guinness product abroad. The Irish population has been sold the brand image so successfully that, until quite recently, Guinness was seen as good for your health. At one time, children used to be encouraged to drink 'egg flips' composed of Guinness and beaten egg to help their growth. The origins of this peculiar custom went back to an original company advertisement which, under the heading 'Its Health Giving Property', asserted that 'Guinness builds strong muscles. It feeds exhausted nerves. It enriches the blood. Doctors affirm that Guinness is a valuable restorative after influenza and other weakening illness. Guinness is a valuable natural aid to insomnia.'[58] These claims do not belong entirely to an innocent past. A recent statement by Jonathan Guinness still asserted that Guinness is good for you because it 'assists the cheering effect'.[59]

Unfortunately, there is growing evidence that Guinness and other alcoholic drinks manufacturers have quite a negative effect on Irish society. Ireland ranks second after Luxemburg for alcohol consumption in the EU,[60] and during the Celtic Tiger years drinking shot up dramatically. Between 1993 and 2003, alcohol consumption increased by 40 per cent, a trend that runs counter to the rest of Europe and is unique in the world.[61] Binge-drinking is so popular that out of every 100 occasions that the Irish male drinks, fifty-eight turn into a binge-drinking session. Unfortunately, this culture is also having a devastating effect on adolescents. Irish boys and girls who are aged 16 are among the highest alcohol abusers in Europe in terms of binge-drinking and drunkenness.[62] Contrary to impressions, alcohol drinking amongst the young has more harmful physiological effects. The American

Medical Association Report on the adverse effects of alcohol on the brains of adolescents notes that drinkers scored worse than non-drinkers on vocabulary, information recall, memory and depression.[63] More generally, alcohol consumption in Ireland causes five times the health damage as that from illicit drugs.[64]

The scale of the problem means that the Irish state can no longer hide behind a disease concept of alcoholism, which either pities or blames the victim. Alcoholism has some social causes and cannot be seen simply as an individual problem defined by either genetic disposition or by 'choice'. A new public health perspective has grown among professionals and this has helped to switch the focus back from alcoholism to alcohol itself. This perspective calls for government intervention to control the sale and promotion of alcohol, and runs directly counter to the neo-liberal model of 'individual responsibility' and 'freedom to compete'.[65] The public health viewpoint has been influential in the two reports of the Strategic Task Force on Alcohol which called for limits on where alcohol advertisements could be placed, and for a ban on drinks industry sponsorship of adolescent leisure time activities.[66]

For a short period it looked like the political elite would respond. While he was Health Minister, Micheál Martin attacked the fact that companies like Guinness were sponsoring major GAA tournaments, and predicted that there would be a full ban on this activity within five years.[67] An Oireachtas Joint Committee on Health and Children, whose majority membership was drawn from Fianna Fail, Fine Gael and the Progressive Democrats, recommended,

> a complete ban on all alcohol advertising within a three-year period and a complete ban on acknowledgement or credit, including the use of logos or labels, for sponsorship of sports events, clubs or teams that cater for members under 25 years of age, by any area of the alcoholic drinks industry.[68]

The Department of Health did not favour a complete ban but stated that it intended to introduce legislation to outlaw advertisements which suggest that alcohol can enhance your life or make it more attractive. It would also require alcohol advertisements to carry a health warning. Sponsorship of events involving under18-year-olds were also to be banned.[69] These proposals were a retreat on the proposals of the Joint Committee, but nevertheless they represented a shift away from the ethos of voluntary regulation to legal measures. They also caused a stir in the international drinks industry, especially after the Taoiseach told a European Brewery Convention in Dublin that,

> The Minister for Health will shortly be bringing forward legislation to protect young people from over-exposure to alcohol marketing including advertising, sponsorship and sales promotions. This will include restricting advertising of alcohol products on public transport, in youth centres and at sporting events where young people under 18 are participating. It would also prohibit broadcasting of alcohol advertising on TV and radio before 10am, and in cinemas where movies are being shown for children and young people under 18 years of age.[70]

The heads of an Alcohol Product Bill were drawn up and the bill was due for presentation in the Dail in October 2005. But in what can only be described as a textbook case of corporate influence on political decision making, this legislative agenda was scuppered and a system of voluntary regulation was restored.

The drinks industry's campaign began with the issuing of a minority report which differed from the Strategic Task Force's report on Alcohol. It disputed 'the contention that a reduction in overall consumption of alcohol will lead to a reduction in alcohol related harm'.[71] More broadly, the industry asserted that alcohol advertising was simply about brand switching rather than increasing overall consumption. Instead of bans on advertising, it pressed for more educational programmes to promote a better understanding on the use of alcohol. In line with this, the industry moved quickly to set up the Mature Enjoyment of Alcohol in Society, and this was presented as a form of corporate social responsibility to promote a more educated use of drink. However, Dr Joe Barry, a senior lecturer in Public Health at Trinity College Dublin, had a different view: 'What MEAS is about is to avoid effective political interventions and push the easy side of responsible drinking. It has a bottom line that is different to those of us concerned about public health.'[72]

To strengthen the case for a voluntary code of advertising, the drinks industry worked with the advertising industry to set up Central Copy Clearance Ireland to pre-vet advertisements on alcohol. This was designed to deal with the argument that advertisements might have outlived their currency by the time that objections to them had been heard. However Central Copy Clearance Ireland could not deal with the fact that their code allowed manufacturers to imply that drink increased sexual opportunities or sociabilty. Thus, a Bavaria advertisement which exhorted people to drink Bavaria and 'Make New Friends' or 'Look Really Cool' passed the Central Copy Clearance system. So did an ad for the alcopop WKD featuring slogans 'Official sponsors of Christmas kissing'. These types of slogans have become the stock and trade of the drinks industry to capture a young market. While voluntary codes can easily state that drink must not be associated with sex, this can mean little because advertisements work at a subliminal level. The total failure of voluntary codes was demonstrated by an important study of teenage attitudes which showed that the way they read the ads was that 'drinking will help them to make friends and to become popular ... and enhance their ability to socially interact with the opposite sex'.[73]

The sharpest move that the drinks industry made was to hire MRPA Kinman Communications as its lobbying agency. MRPA Kinman boasts that 'it has unrivalled experience' of lobbying, as two of the firms partners 'worked at the coalface with one of the leading political parties'. The two had, in fact, been closely associated with the Progressive Democrats in the past – which coincidently was the party to which the Minister for Health, Mary Harney, belonged. Ray Gordon, the managing director of MRPA Kinman, was press officer with the Progressive Democrats from 1987 to 1992, while Stephen O Byrnes worked as a Policy Director with the party before becoming the party's government press secretary. The chairman of MRPA Kinman is Brian Geoghegan, a former Director of Economic Affairs at IBEC and the husband of Health Minister, Mary Harney. With this team on board, the drinks industry certainly had access to the corridors of power.

Their campaign worked because, by the start of October 2005, it became clear that the government had capitulated and had withdrawn the Alcohol Products Bill. In its place a special code of practice was accepted – just as the drinks industry had requested. Junior Health Minister Sean Power, who happens to be a publican, claimed that the industry was told about the draft law and was asked their opinions. As they agreed to implement an improved voluntary code drawn up under the aegis of the Department of Health, it was decided to 'delay' the introduction of the Bill. Rather curiously, he added, 'The Department approached representatives from the relevant industries – not the other way around'.[74]

The cynicism of this statement was revealed, however, when the journalist, Fintan O'Toole, showed that the new voluntary code for advertising alcohol in cinemas was written by none other than Carlton Screen Advertising. The Department of Health was so subservient to the industry that they even used the same grammatical errors as the original version supplied by the company![75] Instead of even a voluntary ban on drink advertising before 10.00 p.m. on television, the Department agreed to a system of audience profiling which had been proposed by the advertising industry. Under this system, advertisement for alcoholic drinks could continue to be shown on television so long as less than 33 per cent of the audience were under 18. The initial suggestion was that there could be no advertisements if children under 18 made up 25 per cent of the audience – but even this was too much for the drinks industry and they got an even milder voluntary code. No bans were imposed on the sponsorship of sport and the GAA, after some initial reflection, renewed its contract with Guinness for another year.

The drinks industry had won – game, set and match.

NOTES

1. P. Aries, *Centuries of Childhood* (London: Pimlico, 1996), p.318.
2. E. Shorter, *The Making of the Modern Family* (London: Collins, 1976).
3. H. Giroux, *Stealing Innocence: Corporate Culture's War on Children* (New York: Palgave, 2000), p.17.
4. National Women's Council of Ireland, *An Accessible Childcare Model* (Dublin: NWCI, 2006), p.32.
5. Central Statistics Office, *Quarterly National Household Survey Module on Childcare, Quarter 1 2005* (Dublin: CSO, 2006), p.1.
6. L. McBride, 'Crèche Course in Care Costs'. *Sunday Business Post*, 23 January 2005.
7. 'Childcare Costs', *Consumer Choice*, October 2005.
8. *Working to Our Advantage: A National Workplace Strategy: Report on Forum of Workplace of the Future* (Dublin: National Centre for Partnership Performance, 2005), p.62.
9. C. Corrigan, *OECD Thematic Review of Early Childhood Education and Care: Background Report, Ireland* (Paris: OECD, 2005), p.41.

10. NESF, *Early Childhood Care and Education, Report 31* (Dublin: NESF, 2005), p.39.
11. SIPTU, *Childcare in Ireland: A Trade Union View* (Dublin: SIPTU, 2005), p.8.
12. NWCI, *An Accessible Childcare Model*, p.16.
13. 'Jarvis Admits Liability for Potters Bar Crash'. *Guardian*, 28 April 2004.
14. 'Profile: Jarvis'. *Guardian*, 28 April 2003.
15. Comptroller and Auditor General Report on Value for Money Examination, *The Grouped Schools Pilot Partnership Project* (Dublin: Government Publications, 2004), p.11.
16. Committee of Public Accounts Minutes, *Dáil Debates*, Vol.80, 21 April 2005.
17. D. McWilliams, 'Our Educational Assets deserve a Proper Deal'. *Sunday Business Post*, 2 October 2005.
18. Information leaflet accompanying McDonald's Catch and Kick Scheme.
19. Department of Education and Science, Circular 38/91.
20. H. Curley, 'We're Educators, not Providers of Cannon Fodder for Multi-nationals'. *Village Magazine*, 2 September 2005.
21. J. McNeal, *Kids as Consumers: A Handbook of Marketing to Children* (New York: Lexington Books, 1992), p.232.
22. Quoted in A. Quart, *Branded: The Buying and Selling of Teenagers* (London: Arrow, 2003), p.66.
23. J. Schor, *Born to Buy* (New York: Scribner, 2004), p.20.
24. Kaiser Family Foundation Report, *The Media Family: Electronic Media in the lives of infants, Toddler Pre-schooler and their parents* (Washington: Kaiser Foundation, 2006), p.32.
25. Statement of Campaign for a Commercial-Free Childhood on Baby First TV http://comercial freechildhood.org/pressreleases/babyfirsttv.htm.
26. J. McNeal and C. Yeh, 'Born to Shop'. *American Demographics*, June (1993), pp.34–9.
27. E. Mayo, *The Shopping Generation* (London: National Consumer Council, 2005), p.2.
28. A. Kanner, 'The Corporatised Child'. *California Psychologist*, 39, (January/February 2006), pp.1–2.
29. J. Wasko, *How Hollywood Works* (London: Sage, 2003), p.154.
30. Kanner, 'The Corporatised Child'.
31. Quoted in M.F. Jacobson and L.A. Mazur, *Marketing Madness* (Boulder,CO: Westview Press, 1995), p.21.
32. M. Weisnewski, 'Bypass The Brain and Go Straight to the Heart: Connecting with emotion builds a brand is vital'. In Brandpapers http://www.brandchannel.com/papers_review.asp?sp_id=1232.
33. B. Nissim, 'Brand Loyalty: The Psychology of Preference'. In Brandpapers http://www.brandchannel.com/ppaers_reviews.asp?sp_id=680.
34. D. Acuff, *What Kids Buy and Why* (New York: The Free Press, 1997).
35. Schor, *Born to Buy*, p.101.
36. G. Ruskin , 'Why They Whine: How Corporations Prey on Children'. *Mother*, 97 (1999), p.42.
37. *Report of APA Task Force on Advertising and Children* (Washington: APA, 2004), p.6.
38. Ibid., p.9.
39. BCI, *Children's Advertising Code : Research into children's view patterns in Ireland* (Dublin: BCI, 2006), p.6.
40. A. Edling, Speech on TV Advertising to Children, London, 23 November 1999. Script in possession of author.
41. B. Quinn, *Maverick* (Dingle: Brandon, 2001), p.35.
42. F. Corcoran, *RTE and the Globalisation of Irish Television* (Bristol: Intellect Books, 2004), p.169.
43. BCI, *Children's Advertising Code*, p.36.
44. T. Lang and M. Headsman, *Food Wars* (London: Earthscan, 2004), p.206.
45. G. Hastings, M. Stead, L. McDermott, A. Forsyth, A. MacKintosh, M. Rayner, C. Godfrey, M. Caraher and K. Angus, *Review of Research on the effects of Food Promotion to Children* (Glasgow: University of Strathclyde, Centre for Social Marketing, 2003).

46. N. Hunter, 'Government, Industry slammed on obesity'. Irishhealth.com http://www.irishhealth.com/index.html?level=4&id=0300.
47. S. Carswell, 'Turning out in the North West'. *Sunday Business Post*, 5 July 2003.
48. BCI, 'Children's Advertising Code: Phase Three Consultation Document – Review of Adult Submissions Received' (June 2004), p.3.
49. Ibid., p.3.
50. BCI, 'Children's Advertising Code: Phase Two Consultation Document: Review of Adult Submissions Received' (March 2004), p.56.
51. BCI, 'Statement of Outcomes Phase Two Development of the Children's Advertising Code' (2004), p.11.
52. Ibid., p.13.
53. BCI, 'Children's Advertising Code; Consultation Document Phase 3: Review of Adult Submissions' (2004), p.26.
54. Ibid., p.9.
55. Ibid., p.29.
56. Ibid., p.31.
57. T. Kelly, 'Guinness Ireland: Broadening the Brand Franchise without Destroying the Mystique', in F. Gilmore, *Brand Warriors: Corporate Leaders Share their Winning Strategies* (London: Harper Collins, 1999), p.105.
58. Quoted in J. Timms, 'Philanthropy, Integrity and Guinness: A Study of the Corporate Social Conscience' (MA Thesis, Department of Sociology, UCD, 1998), p.47.
59. J. Guinness, *Requiem for a Family Business* (London: Macmillan, 1997), p.6.
60. Strategic Task Force on Alcohol, *Second Report* (Dublin: Government Publications, 2004), p.6.
61. Dr Conor Farren, National Drugs Strategy Presentation, 1 March 2006 in Presentation to Joint Committee on Arts, Sport, Tourism, Community and Gaeltacht Affairs in Dáil Committee Proceedings No 46, 1 March 2006.
62. B. Hibell, B. Andersson, S. Ahlstrom, O. Balakiereva, T. Bjarnason, A. Kokkevi and M. Morgan, *The 1999 European School Survey Project on Alcohol and Other Drugs Report: Alcohol and other drug use among students in 30 European countries* (Stockholm: The Swedish Council for Information on Alcohol and other Drugs, 2000).
63. American Medical Association, 'Effects of Alcohol on Brain of Adolescents', reprinted in Oireachtas Joint Committee on Health and Children, *Report on Alcohol Misuse by Young People* (Dublin: Houses of Oireachtas, 2004).
64. Farren National Drugs Strategy Presentation, 1 March 2006 in Presentation to Joint Committee on Arts, Sport, Tourism, Community and Gaeltacht Affairs in Dáil Committee Proceedings No 46, 1 March 2006.
65. See S. Butler, 'How Local is Local? Assessing the Prospects for local Alcohol Policy in Ireland'. Paper to Addiction Research Centre Conference, Trinity College Dublin, 26 September 2002.
66. Strategic Task Force Report on Alcohol, *Interim Report* (Dublin: Government Publications, 2002), p.20.
67. D. Fahy, 'Martin wants to end link between Alcohol and Sports'. *Irish Times*, 16 February 2001.
68. Joint Committee on Health and Children, *Report on Alcohol Misuse by Young People* (Dublin: Houses of Oireachtas, 2004), p.35.
69. L. Reid, 'Proposal to ban Alcohol Adverts ruled out'. *Irish Times*, 16 June 2004.
70. 'Irish to Restrict Alcohol Advertising'. *Food and Drink Europe*, 21 May 2003 http://www.foodanddrinkeurope.com/news/ng.asp?id=17538-irish-to-restrict
71. Drinks Industry of Ireland Minority Report on Government Task Force on Alcohol in Strategic Task Force Report on Alcohol, *Interim Report*, p.23.
72. M. Houston, 'Alcohol Lobby Group Criticised'. *Irish Times*, 6 December 2004.
73. C. Dring and A. Hope, *The Impact of Alcohol Advertising on Teenagers in Ireland* (Dublin: Health Promotion Unit, Department of Health and Children, 2001), p.7.
74. Dáil Debates, Vol.607, 6 October 2005.
75. F. O Toole, 'Caving into the Drinks Industry'. *Irish Times*, 20 December 2005.

Chapter Six

The Enclosure of Knowledge

For hundreds of years, universities provided a space where a small minority of people had some freedom to explore ideas. Despite current imagery about 'fanatical', 'intolerant' Muslims, universities trace their origins back to the Islamic world. One of the earliest precursors was the House of Wisdom founded in Baghdad in 830 by the caliph Ma'mun. This contained an observatory, a laboratory and a translation service that took ideas from other cultures. From the tenth century onwards, this institution spread to Europe with the formation of cathedral schools that were financed by local bishops. Through a process that still remains obscure, some of these schools became autonomous and their school masters organized themselves into guilds – or *universitas* – in order to regularize instruction and establish adequate standards for students.[1]

Some also took advantage of schisms in church-state relations to create a space for critical inquiry. That space was, of course, tiny, and no real questioning of church authority was possible, but teachers drew on new influences to develop intellectual inquiry. One such mode of intellectual inquiry was the teaching method of the Christian scholar Abelard, who said that 'through doubt we are led to inquiry, through inquiry we reach the truth'.[2] Another was the rationalist approach of the great Islamic scholar Ibn Rush'd or Averroes, as he became known, who proclaimed that 'intelligence is nothing but the perception of things with their causes'.[3] Still another influence was that of the Jewish philosopher Maimonides, who used the fact that there was no hierarchy of rabbis to defend the idea of intellectual speculation.

From this conflux of different cultures, the idea of critical inquiry emerged.

The notion of academic freedom should by no means be romanticized. In a deeply hierarchical society, the claim to academic freedom was often bogus. The modern university uses the rhetoric of being 'value free' and 'objective', but the reality has often belied the rhetoric. Celebrated scandals have included the philosopher Martin Heidegger, who joined the Nazi Party and informed on his colleagues, or the psychologist Cyril Burt, who doctored his results to strengthen his case against comprehensive education. However, the problem goes much deeper than a few bad apples. The academic hierarchy mirrors the wider society in class, race and gender and its dominant ideas reflect this social background. Individuals within universities may have had the freedom to debate but the university as a whole accepts the authority of the state, and places a premium on abstract forms of knowledge that do not imply any practical criticism. All manner of individualistic eccentricity is encouraged under the rubric of 'originality', while the early enlightenment idea that knowledge is at the service of humanity is often lost.

Nonetheless, by the twentieth century the university had come to be seen as a public good that brought wider benefits to society. The American writer John Dewey saw the institution as essential to the formation of a thoughtful citizenry who could participate in a democratic society because it provided a training ground whereby students could develop their critical faculties through discussion and debate.[4] The university also provided society as a whole with the means to advance scientific knowledge. Individual scientists might choose their own subject for inquiry, but there was also a 'Republic of Science'[5] in which all participated. From this common pool of knowledge everyone could draw in order to advance the frontier of knowledge. Writing in the midst of the Cold War, the US sociologist Robert Merton outlined the four key norms by which scientific knowledge progressed in Western society. These were 'disinterestedness' – the scientist did not gain personally from any of their discoveries; 'universalism' – there was no French or German science, but a science for all humankind; 'organized scepticism' and 'communism', meaning knowledge did not have any owners but was shared in common.[6]

It may have taken a thousand years for these cultural practices to develop, but corporate capitalism is destroying them with an indecent haste.

KNOWLEDGE ECONOMY AND THE CORPORATE UNIVERSITY

Rather ironically, the attack on the university is fought in the name of 'the knowledge society'. During the 1990s, the term 'knowledge society' became a mainstream concept for global agencies such as the World Bank and OECD. In 1998, for example, the World Bank produced its *World Development Report: Knowledge for Development*, which argued that if poorer countries overcame the 'knowledge gap' and used Information and Communication Technology (ICT) they could leap-frog forward to development.[7] World Bank President James Wolfensohn even claimed that 'poor people know as well as anybody else that what keeps them poor is lack of competitiveness and lack of knowledge'.[8] Not, it appears, lack of capital, because knowledge itself had become a form of capital.

The intellectual roots of this rather mystical belief went back to the early 1970s when the veteran US ideologue, Daniel Bell, proclaimed the arrival of a 'post industrial society'.[9] The cigar-smoking capitalist and the grimy factory may have symbolized the old industrial society but, according to Bell, in the post-industrial society the new 'axial principle' was possession of knowledge. This in turn gave rise to a new social ethic whereby scientific experts took over from the business elite, and the universities replaced the firm as the central social institutions. Bell's book had a distinct techno-utopian quality, but with the growth of ICT his original ideas were reconfigured to variously characterize society as either 'post-fordist' or 'post-modern' or finally as a 'knowledge society'. The common feature consists of three central claims. First, mass manufacturing is in decline and with it has disappeared the 'old' working class. Second, class conflict has been replaced by individualism and a desire by all social groups for 'flexibility' and 'choice'. Third, wealth no longer relies on lumpy objects but on intangible processes embodying high levels of knowledge.

These theories gained credibility in elite circles with the resurgence of the US economy in the 1990s. Prior to this decade, there were fears that the US would be overtaken by Japan, but, it was argued, the embrace of 'innovation' and the 'knowledge economy' played a key role in its revival.[10] In particular, the commercialization of knowledge through close university-industry links allowed the US to take a lead in new sectors such as bioengineering, nanotechnology and biopharming. A key moment in the new relationship came with the Bayh-Dole Act of 1980 that was proposed as a defensive measure to help the US beat Japan in the global markets. The act allowed universities to take out patents on their research and then sell them to commercial concerns. One of its supporters summed up the philosophy:

> The public domain was a treacherous quicksand in which discoveries sink beyond the reach of the private sector. If the results of federal sponsored research were to be rescued from oblivion and successfully developed into commercial products they would have to be patented and offered up to private companies.[11]

Under Bill Clinton, funding for scientific research increased further. There was a transition from the 'defence agenda', which justified public funding for research on the grounds of the cold war, to a 'competitiveness agenda' whereby the government supported research as a mechanism to help private companies compete.[12] These developments had a major effect on the discourse of the global elite. Just as the Japanese model was in vogue in the 1980s and the world came to learn about 'benchmarking' and 'total quality management', so in the 1990s the language of the 'knowledge economy' and 'commercialization of research' spread like wildfire. In this new ideology, a link was forged between education, individual responsibility and the growth of a new 'light' economy. In the words of Charles Leadbetter, one of the British popularizers of the Third Way model and a political advisor to EU Commissioner Peter Mandelson, 'Education is the first priority; a policy for mass entrepreneurship is the second'.[13]

The concept of the knowledge society soon percolated through to the Irish elite though the medium of official EU-speak. The Irish Council of Science Technology and Innovation had picked up on the language of the knowledge economy earlier than most and stressed that Ireland needed to develop its scientific infrastructure. However, as Brian Trench, a member of the council, noted, he 'was alone, or nearly alone, in arguing the importance of the social and cultural aspects of science as against the overwhelming emphasis on economic and cultural aspects'.[14]

Despite the talk of the knowledge society there was, plainly, little interest in developing a scientific culture that encouraged a rational, empirical-based understanding of the wider world. Instead the council engaged in a 'Technology Foresight' designed exercise to predict future trends in applied technology that would be of benefit for business. It recommended that Ireland focus on biotechnology and ICT research as its key niches in the global market. It also suggested a major increase in research funding and the formation of a new foundation, the Science Foundation Ireland (SFI), to administer this funding.[15]

The SFI was set up in 2000 and was modelled on two US research agencies – the National Science Foundation and the National Institute of Health. These commanded considerable support from US business and, on one occasion, CEOs, former CEOs and presidents of sixteen major US companies even opposed calls for cutbacks in their spending programmes and took out a full page advertisement in the *Washington Post* to call for continued funding.[16] The board of the SFI reflected its close connections to the US science-industry complex, and two of its members, William Harris and Erich Bloch, had previously served in the National Science Foundation. Harris was appointed Director General of the SFI and quickly established close ties with the pharmaceutical industry. Bloch subsequently played a huge role in the restructuring of UCD when his consultancy group, the Washing Advisory Group, was commissioned to provide a report for an undisclosed sum. Another board member, Dr Martina Newell McGloughlin, was the co-director of the National Institute of Health training programme in Biomolecular Technology. The board also included figures closely associated with the business sector in Ireland. The original vice-chairperson was Frank McCabe, a former vice-president of Intel, but he was replaced by Helen Keelan, Intel's Strategic Division manager. The board also included Jim Mountjoy, the chairperson of the Prospectus Consultancy group, and John Travers, a business consultant and former CEO of Forfas. The SFI's panel on ICT was directly chaired by Eoin O' Driscoll of Lucent Ireland.[17] Significantly, there was no representative from any social movement concerned about the use to which scientific knowledge was put or any public intellectuals who advocated a wider scientific culture.

The close connections with the US reflected the way that the Irish political elite had aligned themselves with the US empire and also, of course, the domination of the US multi-nationals within the Irish economy. A further step along the road to commercializing research was taken at a US-Ireland Business summit in Washington in September 2002, which agreed to set up a US-Ireland research partnership task force. This three-day summit was attended by key political figures on both sides of the Irish border who were close to business, such as Mary Harney and Reg Empey, Robert Essner, the CEO of Wyeth corporation, Frank Carlucci, Chairman of the Carlyle Group and Michael Capellas, President of Hewlett Packard. Its focus was on US-Ireland cooperation in biotechnology, information communication technology and financial services. The clear implication was that the universities would be drafted in to help service these sectors. In 2006, Micheál Martin, Minister for Enterprise, Trade and Employment, finally announced that the new US-Ireland research partnership was now 'open for business'.[18]

Even before the formal research partnership was established, this particular conception of the 'knowledge society' began to reshape the universities in quite dramatic ways. Any notion that the university needed to retain a certain autonomy from business was discarded and so too was the tradition that scientists should adhere to a norm of 'disinterested' research. Instead the model, which appeared to work in the US, was imported into Ireland. This proposed that scientists should be given an incentive to make a profit from their research by getting a share in the licence fees from patents. One influential US study had suggested that biotechnology firms cluster around universities with 'star scientists' and a team of PhD investigators.[19] So the Irish universities also followed suit by tearing up the common pay scales for academics and paying special bonuses to recruit such 'stars'. In one unseemly spat, University College Dublin modelled themselves on football team managers and 'poached' one of Trinity College Dublin's 'star' scientists in food and nutrition.

Gone was the idea that the university had a duty to society as a whole rather than merely its commercial elements. It is now official state policy that after education and research, educational institutions have a third role: the promotion of enterprise. The new ethos has been expressed succinctly as follows:

> The exploitation of knowledge and commercialisation of research must become embedded in the culture and infrastructure of the higher education system. This requires continued emphasis on new campus company start-ups, a pro-innovation culture of intellectual property protection and exploitation, programmes in entrepreneurship, consulting services, information services, new forms of graduate development programmes and greater links between higher education institutions and private enterprise.[20]

This particular report was drawn up by the Enterprise Strategy Group which, as we have seen, was composed of business people and was hardly unbiased. At the heart of the new demands being placed on the university was a contradiction between the traditional business demand for a low tax, low public sector-economy and its desire for subsidized research services.

Ireland's political elite has recognized that foreign investment in manufacturing has begun to shift to countries in Eastern Europe and beyond to China and India. The 'race to the bottom' that they helped trigger by undercutting their rivals in Europe has started to accelerate, and they fear that they may lose out unless they move up the 'value chain' and embrace the idea of a 'knowledge economy'. However, past policies place considerable obstacles in the way. The low tax policy has left behind a weak infrastructure in which to gain competitive advantage in high-skill 'knowledge based' industries. Until recently, Irish state spending on research and development was tiny and so the number of scientific publications per million of the population is 647 compared to 1,598 in Sweden, 1,332 in Denmark and 1,309 in Finland. The number of patent applications of the population is 62 per million compared to 248 in Sweden, 151 in Denmark and 258 in Finland.[21] Yet, despite this historic under-investment in research, the large corporations want the Irish state to give them a new subsidy.

To do so, the needs of the wider society for a strong scientific culture have to be made subordinate to the immediate needs of corporations for profit. At present, investment in research and development by business is very low and falls below international standards. Business expenditure on Research and Development in Ireland is only 73 per cent of the EU average and 57 per cent of the OECD average.[22] Only nineteen foreign affiliates spend more than €5 million a year on research and these companies account for two thirds of all research and development performed by such companies.[23] Even more extraordinary, the pharmaceutical sector in Ireland, which stands to benefit the most from the corruption of the academy, spends ten per cent less on Research and Development than the OECD average.[24]

This dichotomy between the weak scientific base and the corporate desire for research 'deliverables' can only be resolved through much cruder forms of 'commercialization'. Corporations in Ireland want to redirect science away from basic research on general topics to more applied research topics that suit their immediate needs. However, these needs can be fickle or far from the cutting edge of scientific discovery – leading to quite a different situation to that pertaining in the US, from where the model is imported. In the US, 94 per cent of company spending on research goes to research centres within the industry because there is a tradition of massive privately-owned research centres. This means, as some writers put it, that 'what university research often does today is to stimulate and enhance the power of R&D in industry, in contrast to providing a substitute for it'.[25] In Ireland, however, there will be less independence and more substitution for industry.

US corporations will continue to spend the bulk of their money in their research facilities in the US and their desire for research facilities in Ireland is, in fact, mainly driven by tax reasons. In order to continue to enjoy Ireland's super-low rate of tax on patent income, US corporations must show that at least some research work was done there. The *Wall Street Journal* explains the logic.

> The research facilities are necessary to satisfy Inland Revenue Service rules on moving intellectual property abroad. To do so – and thus have profits from it be taxed abroad – a company must be able to argue plausibly that its offshore unit is at least partly responsible for the innovations.

A common device is to take successful, patented American ideas and then develop new generations of them – with the help of the offshore research division. The ownership of the new version (and profits on licensing it) can then legally be shared between the US parent company and the offshore unit.[26]

If their 'offshore' divisions in Ireland are hooked into universities, US corporations can both reduce costs and satisfy the requirement needed to enjoy low taxes. But what will be required from Irish universities are localized adaptations or newer versions of technology rather than more basic research.

The American Chamber of Commerce and the Irish Business and Employers Confederation (IBEC) have been to the fore in pressing for this type of relationship. In November 2004, both these bodies held a conference in the Royal Hospital Kilmainham for 'thought leaders' from universities and business. The conference was sponsored by AIB under the title 'Collaboration to Commercialisation'. The focus was almost entirely on the immediate 'deliverable' fruits of research that the university might bring to business. Thus, a key executive from the IDA emphasized that the aim was to 'translate research into new products, processes and services' and to 'promote innovation and entrepreneurship among researchers'.[27] Ciaran Ennis, president of the American Chamber of Commerce and an executive with IBM, warned that 'while the pursuit of knowledge is worthy in itself, it does not pay the bills or develop competitive advantage if not properly harnessed'. He wanted a process which 'converts the fruit of research and development activity back into hard cash'.[28] The idea that the ethos of university research might not just be about paying the bills of industry, but about making a contribution to the wider common good, did not figure in this equation. Similarly a joint IBEC/Irish Universities Association Conference held in Dublin City University in November 2005 was even more explicit in setting out the demands of business. The business leaders wanted forms of 'research training ... to make the student "industry savvy" by more industry-based doctoral research'. They also wanted 'easier access to academic infrastructure, resources and databases'.[29]

The new demands that corporations are placing on the

university do not stop at the science departments. They also want to re-structure the whole university so that resources are shifted from 'loss-making' humanities and arts subjects into science and business-related subjects. They want to reshape the university so that it pays homage to business culture and comes to resemble any another corporation. Welcome to the world of the corporate university.

THE CORPORATE UNIVERSITY

Privately owned for-profit universities exist all over the world and large US education 'service providers' have already entered the Irish education market. Kaplan, which is a wholly owned subsidiary of the *Washington Post* newspaper, has bought the Dublin Business School and has used it to buy another smaller college. The Georgia Tech Research Institute has established itself in Athlone and is building up a portfolio of research programmes with business that will be valued at approximately €20 million. These private universities make little pretence that their priority is anything other than money making. They develop customized programmes to suit the immediate needs of industry and subordinate general educational aims to these needs. While the main client of the Georgia Tech Research Institute used to be the US Department of Defence, with the end of the Cold War it has shifted its focus to doing applied research for industry. One writer described the ethos as follows,

> GTRI is wholly dedicated to meeting the needs of its clients and providing them with immediately usable results. Basic research and academic reputation are irrelevant. Research is not conducted by a tenure track faculty, but by a permanent staff of researchers, most of whom hold masters degrees.[30]

A similar approach to education is evident in the privately owned Hibernia College which runs a teacher training course. This whittles down the wider, more subtle experience of teacher training to an online distance programme in order to cut costs. Although students are charged just under €7,000 a year, there are no libraries, no space for students to interact, no campus – but lots of IT programmes. Education is reduced to the sale of a diploma with the private company guaranteeing minimal standards of 'quality control'. Hibernia College has also customized its courses to suit particular buyers, setting up a special e-learning contract with Pfizer to give its medics and executives a Masters of Science degree in Pharmaceutical Medicine. These types of private colleges function as 'digital diploma mills'[31] where there is little pretence that the student will be encouraged to develop their critical faculties.

The publicly funded universities were supposed to have a different ethos. They belonged to a 'commons' where there was a relatively free space from the pressures of the market. However, in the last few years, there has been a determined effort to destroy this ethos and to force publicly funded universities to embrace the wider ethos of corporations. This shift works in many subtle and diverse ways.

It often starts with the small but symbolic change of branding of the university name. Most Irish universities have introduced new logos and have used the occasion to hold a conversation about 'corporate identity'. The University Council in Trinity College, for example, has agreed that 'branding the Trinity image was important (but) … this must be done in a subtle way'.[32] UCD went one step further and organized a New Age style ceremony to 'unveil the brand'. Staff were typically cynical about such a move and asked why the money could not be used to improve resources. This question, however, rather missed the point. The money was spent to convince them that they were to 'buy in' to the new corporate culture.

The role of university presidents also changed from being a 'first among equals' among intellectuals to being a straightforward CEO. Their primary role today is to intermingle with other corporate executives and 'do deals'. University College Cork former president Gerry Wrixon was an entrepreneur in his own right, overseeing the sale of his company, Farran Technology, which made at least €5 million.[33] DCU's president, Ferdinand Von Prondzynski, was named a 'Businessman of the Week' by the *Irish Examiner* because his ambition was to increase DCU's commercial income from 10 per cent of total income to 50 per cent by 2007.[34] Typically, university presidents surround themselves with former academics from a business, science or medical background. The latter is particularly interesting because, as Jennifer Washburn points out in her study of the American university, medicine comes second to the business faculty for the closeness of its ties with industry.[35] Three of the six vice-presidents in UCD come from a medical background as did its president, Hugh Brady.

The state strategy to create corporate universities is being spearheaded by development agencies such as the IDA, Enterprise Ireland and Forbairt who, as we have seen, function as lobby groups for business interests. Key individuals drawn from these bodies have become the chairs of the Government Authorities of three key third level institutions. The chair of NUI Maynooth (NUIM), for example, is Dan Flinter, a former CEO of Forbairt, and also director of IDA and board member of Forfas. The chair of Dublin Institute of Technology is Sean Dorgan, who is the CEO of the IDA and a board member of Forfas. The chair of UCD is Kieran McGowan, the former CEO of the IDA and director of a host of other firms. This very narrow stratum of Irish society sees the universities as sites where the culture of entrepreneurship needs to take a stronger hold. They view education as a 'product offering' and demand that universities 'change like a business'.[36] The blunt statement of the NUIM chair summed up this philosophy when he asserted that 'it is imperative that the educational requirements of future entrepreneurs be addressed in more innovative ways'.[37]

An elite consensus has also emerged at the top of the Higher Education Authority that sees government under-funding as an opportunity rather than a threat because it opens the way for privatization. The preferred model is a variation of the US system where the state would set up an educational market and then encourage different agencies to contract in to provide services. One HEA submission proposed

> A financial and strategic framework for a process which would allow the individual 'public institution' to evolve into private institutions, where appropriate, with essentially contractual obligations with the state along the lines of some of the leading research-based universities in the US and elsewhere.[38]

This position was supported by the then Education Minister Noel Dempsey, who stated that he had 'no objection ... to a college ... going out of the public system and becoming private'.[39]

This, then, is the end goal which the political elite would like to 'roll out' in the coming years. The process is underway already as market mechanisms are driven deeper into the universities so that they can function like a corporation. Schools or departments have been transformed into 'cost centres' and encouraged to compete against each other to become 'centres of excellence'. As Bill Readings pointed out in his classic book *The University in Ruins*, 'nearly all departments can be urged to strive for excellence, since the general applicability of the notion is in direct relation to its emptiness'.[40] Words like 'excellence' and 'centres of excellence' have become part of a banal 'business speak' whose main function is to grade different units against one another on one common, vacuous yardstick. It is linked to an organizational philosophy that treats university departments as small business enterprises that compete for funds. When university departments internalize this culture and conform to the 'realities' of the market place, they are 'incentivised' with the awarding of greater funding. When they don't, they are 'starved' and put out of business.

The effect on genuine education is deeply destructive. Instead of different intellectual disciplines cooperating in a real intellectual engagement, they compete with each other to possess postgraduate students. Internally, the schools start to follow the money trail when it comes to research topics. Instead of critical research inquiring into hidden power structures, they are allocated set problems for resolution from state or corporate funding agencies. There are vast resources to inquire in the best psychometric tests to recruit the most adaptable employees, but few seek to look at the psychological damage caused by managerial bullying. Funds are available to study 'stake holder participation in EU water directives' but not to explore how the EU uses fake consultation exercises to legitimize water charges. The health sector encourages 'policy orientated' research on decisions by triage nurses on entry to A&E units, but does not invite any research applications on the manner in which privatized health care sucks resources from the public sector. What starts out as a market mechanism to justify 'economic realities' becomes a form of social engineering to produce a compliant intelligentsia.

Where markets cannot be created, pseudo markets are formed, but this can only occur where activities are divorced from their context and measured in an arbitrary fashion. This occurs in many spheres of modern life where 'benchmarks' are set up to audit white-collar employees against each other. In universities, it works by reducing intellectual inquiry to a set of research 'outputs', which are then measured through Research Assessment Exercises (RAE). The RAE is a British system for measuring the number of articles in peer-reviewed journals, rating academic departments on a common index against each other for funds. The exercise is inspired by market fundamentalists such as R.H. Cose, who argued in a polemic in the 1980s entitled 'The Market for Goods and the Market for Ideas' that, 'I do not believe that this distinction between the market for goods and the market for ideas is valid'.[41] Since then, the movement to measure research outputs has accelerated and been exported to Ireland.

The RAE system is an intrinsically absurd exercise because you cannot measure ideas with numbers. The absurdity does not, however, stop there. To meet the strange demand for articles in 'international peer reviewed journals', a new market has emerged, with publishers such as Reed Elsevier producing ever more specialized journals – they currently run a stable of 1,800 such journals.[42] The average readership (a commercial secret but reputedly standing at less than ten per article) is absurdly low, but the average cost of the journal is absurdly high because publishers know their market is publicly funded libraries.[43] One result is that libraries are cutting back on books in order to buy journals which contain more poor quality material. As Lindsay Waters put it, 'there is a causal connection between the corporatist demand for increased productivity and draining of all publications of any significance other than a number'.[44]

Even as the traditional university is hollowed out from inside, corporations still want to make use of its reputation for objective research. In the past, rulers acquired their legitimacy by being blessed by the church, but in a secular society this no longer applies. Instead, corporations sometimes justify their action by claiming it is supported by independent research. One has only to think how governments commission reports from their favourite consultants or 'pet academics'. The corporations have also understood this and, under the guise of philanthropy, are commissioning research projects and sponsoring professorial chairs.

The drinks company Diageo, for example, has sponsored a €1.5 million research project on drinking by young adults from UCD Geary's institute. McDonald's are sponsoring a postgraduate scholarship on the management of diversity in the services sector from DCU. Fujitsu, Diajeo, and the Bank of Ireland are also sponsoring other scholars from the same university. In Trinity College, Peter Sutherland, chairman of Goldman Sachs International, is sponsoring an Institute for International Integration Studies housed in a building bearing his name. The centre's mission statement claims that there has been 'insufficient understanding' of globalization and that 'basic academic research has the potential to narrow the differences between different sides of the debate'.[45] Yet the International Advisory Council for the institute reads like a 'who's who' of the pro-corporate globalization camp. It includes Peter Sutherland who was former director of the WTO; Klaus Schwab, the chair of the World Economic Forum; Gerhard Bruckermann, chair of Depfa bank and Jacques Delors, former President of the EU Commission. Despite aspirations to 'narrow the differences' between the different sides of the debate, there is not one figure associated with the anti-corporate globalization movement on the council.

Like schools, universities also provide a captive audience to corporations who are eager to reach a youth market and their tactics can range from the crude to the more subtle. In the former camp belongs the case of Third Year Mechanical and Engineering students in UCD who were required to attend a workshop hosted by Exxon Mobil and asked to take part in a business simulation exercise.[46] At the other end of the spectrum is Heineken, which targets the student market through both university events and music festivals such as Oxegen and the Green Energy festival. A lesser-known policy is that of corporations using colleges to recruit future employees and gain an input into their training. Thus, the biotechnology company Centocor has a partnership with UCC to ensure that the 'critical human resource infrastructure to support high technology investments' is maintained.[47]

In the US, where the corporate university has developed at a faster pace, decision-making powers have shifted from academics to a managerial layer. Such powers promote courses with more 'market potential'; shift resources within the university to 'strategic areas' defined by the needs of business and monitor the performance of academics.[48] Under the guise of restructuring, the same elements are starting to develop in Ireland. With them come a new differentiation of the academic community into entrepreneurs, 'stars' and house-trained intellectuals who parrot the neo-liberal line on one side; and teachers and researchers who are under growing pressure to perform on the other. The pay scales of the 'stars' will be subsidized by the casualization of other staff. Currently in the US, 60 per cent of academics are 'non-tenured' compared to a mere 3.3 per cent in 1969.[49] In the immediate firing line are academics in the Arts and Humanities who, in the words of *Business Week*, must demonstrate that 'Chaucer pays the bill as effectively as engineering or business'.[50]

The managerial elite of the universities sometimes make an appeal to students to be their allies, claiming to give them more 'choice' under a modularized system where students select their own package of courses. In reality, students are receiving a form of education that does not engage with their full human capacity but treats them as customers buying a product. There is a growing emphasis on textbook delivery and courses packaged in terms of definite 'learning outcomes'. Essay writing is discouraged as a mode of assessment in favour of 'exciting' new alternatives such as multiple choice questionnaires. While the former require some thought, the latter technique of 'learning off' will get you by. As the corporate university expands, students will find themselves interacting more with the casualized staff rather than the full-time academics who have been sent off to generate more research 'outputs'.

The corporate university's educational philosophy is to produce a student population adaptable to the needs of modern capitalism. And it makes little attempt to hide these ambitions. A recent document from the heads of the Irish universities states that, 'through a reformed, innovative 3rd level, the universities will produce a new breed of entrepreneurial 3rd level graduates entering and improving the workplace and the wider society'.[51]

In the new 'knowledge economy', particularly as it is imported from the US, in-depth knowledge of particular subjects is not required. 'Generic competences', which allow the future worker to be flexible, will instead be privileged. The modern workforce has already experienced 'qualification inflation', with many holding degrees and diplomas. Many graduates assumed that this entitled them to decent jobs and a level of participation in decision-making. But in modern capitalism, most white collar employees are not paid to think, and their jobs require information processing rather than evaluation. They may require periodic re-skilling, but this is a matter of individual responsibility, and they will be required to recycle themselves at their own expense onto courses for 'life long' learning.[52] The corporate university that sent them out with generic, bite-size competencies will, however, again be at hand for these 'deliverables'. In North America, the universities are already turning courses into 'courseware', copyrighted videos and CDs through distance education.[53]

Despite all the talk about commercializing research and university-industry links, the irony is that universities in Ireland will continue to rely on public funds. They are funded by taxpayers who want decent, quality education for their sons and daughters – taxpayers who also want universities to give a contribution back to society as a whole. For all the talk of 'partnerships with industry', the corporate contribution to education and research remains low. In the US, for example, industry contributions to academic research run at approximately 7.7 per cent per year of total funds, and only a small number of institutions are able to earn serious money from 'commercializing' their research.[54] Yet despite these low contributions, the corporations want to shape university research to fit with their needs and to relegate the need of society for genuine education to second place. Nowhere is this more in evidence than in the sciences.

THE CORRUPTION OF SCIENCE

In the twentieth century, science shifted from being the pursuit of gentlemanly amateurs to becoming 'Big Science' conducted in large-scale institutions by teams of investigators who worked on projects in a strategic way. In Europe, this occurred predominantly in universities, while, in the US, large corporations ran their own research centres or sometimes funded a small amount of research fellowships in universities. Everywhere it was assumed that the university conducted 'basic' upstream research that was made freely available to society, and Merton's norms prevailed. If corporations wanted more 'applied' research, they could dip in the general pool of basic knowledge to develop it in particular directions to suit their purposes.

This began to change with the discovery of recombinant DNA technology and the subsequent revolution in molecular biology, which allowed scientists to rearrange the basic structure of living things by transplanting genes. The cutting and splicing of genes offered immediate or quicker applications in therapeutic drugs, agriculture and food science. This in turn led to the breaking down of older barriers between 'basic' and 'applied' science, as their immediate commercial usage became apparent.

In the US, the response was to privatize and deepen capitalist relations within science after a landmark Diamond v. Chakrabarty case where the US Supreme Court ruled that living things could be patented. In other words, the genetic structure of plants, animals and eventually human beings could become the private property of owners who could then sell licences for their use. The scale of change might, at first sight, appear difficult to grasp, but it had enormous implications. In the nineteenth century, Karl Marx became a socialist as he watched how the traditional feudal rights of the peasantry to collect firewood were removed under the new laws of private property. Yet this trenchant critic of capitalism could hardly imagine a future scenario that occurred to a certain John Moore.

One day he went to the University of California, Los Angeles hospital for treatment for an enlarged spleen and was diagnosed with hairy cell leukaemia. His physician, however, quickly realized the commercial potential of his rather rare cells and decided to patent them.[55] Repeated withdrawals of blood, skin, bone marrow and sperm were performed on the unfortunate Mr Moore. After he was cured he was asked to attend for annual rechecks when further withdrawals of his 'valuable' body fluids took place. Henceforth his relatively rare cells became the property of medical entrepreneurs who were determined to profit by selling them on to Sandoz Laboratories. This extraordinary incident could only occur because of the US Supreme Court's decision to uproot the 'commons of knowledge' and set off a gold rush for commercially minded scientists. Unfortunately, this decision by five elderly men was also imposed on the rest of the world through international trade agreements such as Trade Related Intellectual Property agreement.

By the 1980s, the US had developed an elaborate structure to harvest university research for commercial purposes. After the Diamond v. Chakrabarty judgement came the Bayh-Dole Act of 1980 that allowed universities to get into the market of selling patents. Then the US government promoted Cooperative Research and Developments Agreements (CRADAs) to foster collaborative work between government and industry. Under the Reagan regime, US corporations were encouraged to directly sponsor entire university departments. In 1982, for example, Monsanto signed a five-year agreement with Washington University that gave it first call on the patenting of the results of its biomedical research.[56] Within universities, 'Technology Transfer Offices' were established to quickly turn over the results of scientific research to corporations. Meanwhile, individual scientists were legally bound to 'non-disclosure' and 'exclusivity agreements' with sponsoring corporations. The very notion of a 'republic of science' where knowledge was evenly shared within the one university began to disappear. In 1998, for example, only 14 per cent of US experimental biologists said they were willing to talk openly about their current research.[57]

This elaborate structure for corrupting the 'scientific commons' has been imported into Ireland through Enterprise Ireland and the IDA. These agencies have helped to draw up a set of 'requirements and guidelines' which are being imposed on Irish 'research performing organizations' by state funding agencies.[58] Under its terms:

• Universities have to appropriate the ownership title of every idea or piece of writing from their staff or post-graduate students that comes from their intellectual activity in the institution. In other words, they claim ownership of their thoughts.
• Oblige staff to 'submit timely reports of discoveries' to the commercialization office within thirty days.

- Allow these offices to draw up legal agreements with corporations to give them first option to patent the research or come to an agreement on licence fees from the patent.
- Give these corporations the right to review the publication of research articles and require 'the removal of confidential, propriety or commercial information before publication'.

The emerging framework has encouraged the corporations to colonize science departments. The most dramatic case is Bristol Myers Squib that has set up a Centre in Bioanalytic Sciences involving both DCU and UCG. The company will help pay for thirty researchers and two professors who will, among other things, be selected on the basis of 'their high level interaction with the biopharma industry'.[59] The other major pharmaceutical company targeting Irish universities is Wyeth who sponsor a biotherapeutic drug discovery research facility at the Conway Institute in UCD. UCD is also involved with Sigmoid Biotechnologies to develop drug delivery systems. The Royal College of Surgeons has 'spun out' a number of companies involved in clinical research for the drug companies such as SurGen and Biosys. The latter claims to 'work closely with renowned pharmaceutical research companies' and has 'acquired unique expertise in successfully finding innovative solutions to clients' requests'.[60] UCC has probably developed the closest connections to the pharmaceutical corporations and its Analytical and Biological Chemistry Research Faculty has links with Pfizer, Novartis, Roche, Eli Lilly, Merck, Janssen and GlaxoSmithKline. UCC's Alimentary Pharmabiotic Centre has also teamed up with Procter and Gamble to research 'functional foods' to target intestinal bacteria. In the area of harder technology, Intel have joined with Trinity College to sponsor the Centre for Research on Adaptive Nanostructures and Nanodevices, while Hewlett Packard have joined up with the Digital Enterprise Research Institute in UCG.

On a more general level, the food industry, which is facing growing criticism over its use of salt levels and other ingredients which increase obesity, has set up a Nutrition and Health Foundation, to provide 'evidence based information' to consumers. The foundation brings together a number of business representatives and university scientists, some of whom have consultancy contracts with particular food companies. Its ethos and its organizational structure is rather unusual for a foundation claiming to offer objective research. It is explicitly stated that 'the Foundation will be led by the food and drinks industry through IBEC's food division, Food and Drink Industry Ireland (FDII)'.[61] The executive board of the foundation is composed entirely of representatives of GlaxoSmithKline, Nestle Ireland, Tayto, Dawn Farm Foods, Greencore Sugar, Kellogg's and PepsiCo. A Scientific Advisory Committee which is responsible for ensuring that all the foundations communications are 'evidence based' is composed of a mixture of university scientists and those employed by the food industry.

This wider academic-industrial complex, which is embracing many areas of research, claims to be a partnership that can forward both objective science and still allow corporations to benefit from commercial opportunities. However, the international literature indicates that there are major problems.

There are clear conflicts of interest between the scientific search for truth and commercial pressures. The history of the tobacco industry, for example, indicates that corporations try to manipulate science by suppressing data they control, or by generating reports to 'cast doubt' on links between smoking and cancer.[62] Today the pharmaceutical industry has replaced tobacco as the main target of complaint. A number of celebrated cases have already emerged, revealing attempts to silence critics.

One such case is David Healy, a well-known psychiatrist who accepted a post as director at the University of Toronto's Centre for Addiction and Mental Health. After giving a critical lecture about the use of Prozac and anti-depressants, his contract was suddenly withdrawn. It transpired that the centre had received a €1.5 million gift from Eli Lilly, the manufacturer of Prozac. Later, Healy settled a €9.4 million lawsuit against the university. Another case was that of Nancy Oliveri who voiced her concern about an iron chelation agent while working on a university programme sponsored by its manufacturer, Apotex. Not only was funding withdrawn, but she was dismissed from her position as director of the programme on Haemoglobinopathy, and had a gagging order imposed on her by her own university.[63]

There is considerable evidence that research scientists who

are sponsored by pharmaceutical companies tend to write research papers more favourable to the drugs under examination. The most disturbing case concerns the Wyeth corporation and its diet drug, Redux. The company hired a company called Excerpta Medica to draft manuscripts and pay doctors to review and sign the articles. One of those who agreed to sign was Richard Atkinson, the renowned obesity expert at the University of Wisconsin-Madison. To combat growing fears that the drug was linked to pulmonary hypertension, 'the company packed a Food and Drink Agency hearing room with a who's who list of the nation's top academic obesity experts, all of whom were paid consultants of Wyeth-Ayerst or other companies involved in the sale of Redux'.[64] Even after the withdrawal of the drug, Wyeth doggedly spent $80 million dollars paying scientists to do research that might cast doubt on the drug's side effects.[65] The corporation has now found itself embroiled in a multi-billion law suit, but of far greater concern is the integrity of science itself.

The infamous case of Wyeth and Redux alone makes it all the more incredible that Irish university authorities could blandly claim that they have never heard of a link between corporate sponsorship of research and problems with the outcomes. But unfortunately there is much wider evidence. An evaluation of conflicts of interests in new drugs used in oncology found that studies funded by pharmaceutical companies were nearly eight times less likely to reach unfavourable qualitative conclusions'.[66] A comprehensive study by a team of Canadian researchers which looked at academic reports on one particular class of drugs, calcium channel antagonists (CCAs), found that 96 per cent of the authors identified as supportive of these drugs had relationships with the manufacturers.[67]

The colonization of the academy has become so serious that the editors of two leading medical journals, *The Lancet* and *New England Journal of Medicine*, have sounded the alarm. Richard Horton, editor of the former, has observed that academic 'journals have devolved into information-laundering operations for the pharmaceutical industry'.[68] Marcia Angell, the former editor of the latter, was so appalled by her own experience that she wrote the book *The Truth About Drug Companies* and concluded that:

Until the 1980s, researchers were largely independent of companies that sponsored their work. Drug companies would give a grant to an academic medical centre, then step back and wait for faculty researcher to produce the results. Now, however, companies are involved in every detail of the research – from design of the study through analysis of the data to the decision whether to publish the results. That involvement has made bias not only possible but extremely likely. Researchers don't control clinical trials any more; sponsors do.[69]

Pharmaceutical corporations can bias research design in a host of ways. They can select younger rather than older patients for testing; they can look at shorter rather than longer time frames to minimize side effects of their drugs; they can compare their branded drugs with older drugs of a lower dosage.[70]

However, their most crucial weapon is the right to censor research findings. Typically, this occurs when some of their intellectual property is used in the research. This can either be actual material like cell tissue, or just technical 'know how'. Most contracts between universities and companies contain clauses that allow companies to remove the 'propriety information' they supplied before publication. If they don't like the scientist's results, they can suddenly exercise that right and demand that any reference to the material they supplied be removed. But this, in turn, makes the publication of the results meaningless as some of them will be based on the material the company supplied. This 'non-disclosure clause' is repeatedly used to censor research results or to pressurize scientists to self censor themselves.

In a celebrated case, Professor Betty Dong, a pharmacologist at the University of California at San Francisco, submitted an article to the prestigious *Journal of the American Medical Association* which revealed that there was no significant difference in the effectiveness of a branded drug and four similar generic drugs in the treatment of hypothyroidism. The article, which was peer reviewed by five individuals, was accepted, but prior to publication Dong's corporate sponsor warned her that she could not publish because of the restrictive clause in the contract she had signed. Fearing costly litigation, Dong withdrew her article. The case only eventually came to light when attorneys for thirty-seven US states filed a class action against the company, Flint Laboratories, for disseminating misleading information. The company was forced to pay $98 million in damages.

Unfortunately, this was not an isolated case. The *New York Times* has revealed that Merck overruled one of its own scientists after he suggested that a patient had died of a heart attack during a clinical trial of Vioxx.[71] A survey by the *Boston Globe* showed that 28 per cent of the 410 scientists who held back publication of articles for more than six months did so because of undesirable results.[72] An article in the *Lancet* compared published and unpublished trials of serotonin reuptake inhibitors or anti-depressants. It found that the unpublished trials showed an unfavourable risk/benefit ratio compared to the published trials.[73]

This damning evidence is barely acknowledged by the political elite. If concerns are expressed, it may even be whispered that 'he who pays the piper, calls the tune'. But who exactly is paying the piper? Corporations already gain huge subsidies from the Irish state through generous tax reliefs. It seems extraordinary, then, that the public sector must also subsidize their research. Research by its very nature needs to build up long-term competencies and cannot be organized effectively if there are pressures for immediate returns. This is why corporations sometimes prefer to outsource their research requirements, provided they can keep control over its design. Far from corporations 'helping' universities, it is in fact universities who will be subsidizing business. They do so by placing skills that have been developed through long-term state spending at their disposal, and giving them access to cutting-edge knowledge which they would otherwise not get.

Bristol Myers Squibb, for example, may seem to be generous in its funding of DCU but, in reality, some of the huge fortune has already come from ripping off publicly-funded research. One of its best selling drugs, Taxol, an anti-cancer drug, was developed from the Pacific Yew tree even though the company did not own the land where the tree grew, nor did it discover, develop or carry out the main tests on the drug. The drug was developed by a public agency of the US state, the National Cancer Institute, and then handed over to Bristol Myers Squibb through one of the CRADAs formed in the Reagan era.[74]

Corporations deal with universities through one central prin-ciple – you socialize the risk involved in research, we privatize the rewards. It is the price we pay for the corporate take over of our world.

NOTES

1. J. Bowen, *A History of Western Education Vol.2* (London: Methuen, 1975), p.42.
2. Ibid., p.57.
3. Ibid., p.97.
4. For a modern defence of this idea see H.A. Giroux and S. Giroux, *Take Back Higher Education* (New York: Palgrave Macmillan, 2006).
5. K. Polanyi, 'The Republic of Science', in P. Mirowski and E. Mirjam Sent (Eds), *Science: Bought and Sold* (Chicago: University of Chicago Press, 2002).
6. R. Merton, 'The Normative Structure of Science', in R. Merton, *The Sociology of Science* (Chicago: University of Chicago Press, 1973), pp.267–78.
7. World Bank, *World Development Report: Knowledge for Development* (New York: Oxford University Press, 1999).
8. 'Interview with James Wolfensohn'. *Far Eastern Economic Review*, 27 June 2002.
9. D. Bell, *The Coming of the Post Industrial Society* (New York: Basic Books, 1973).
10. See S. Collins, *The Race to Commercialize BioTechnology: Molecules, Markets and the State in the United States and Japan* (London: Routledge, 2004).
11. J. Washburn, *University Inc: The Corporate Corruption of American Higher Education* (New York: Basic Books, 2005), p.63.
12. S. Slaughter and G. Roades, 'The Emergence of a Competitiveness Research and Development Policy Coalition and the Commercialization of Academic Science and Technology', in P. Mirowski and E. Mirjam Sent (Eds), *Science: Bought and Sold* (Chicago: University of Chicago Press, 2002), p.70.
13. Quoted in J. Rutherford, 'Cultural Studies in the Corporate University'. *Cultural Studies*, 19, 3 (May 2005), pp.297–317.
14. B. Trench, 'Representations of Science in the Knowledge Society'. Paper presented to 8th International Conference of Public Communication of Science Network, Barcelona, June 2004.
15. Forfas, *Science Foundation Ireland: The First Years 2001-2005 Report of an International Evaluation panel* (Dublin: Forfas, 2005).
16. D. Greenberg, *Science, Money and Politics* (Chicago: University of Chicago Press, 2001), pp.445–6.
17. Forfas, *Science Foundation Ireland*, Paragraph 2.1.
18. Department of Enterprise, Trade and Employment, Press Release, 5 July 2006.
19. L.G. Zucker, M.R. Darby and M.B. Brewer, 'Intellectual Human Capital and the Birth of US Biotechnology Enterprises'. *American Economic Review*, 88, I (March 1998), pp.290–306.
20. Enterprise Strategy Group, *Ahead of the Curve: Ireland's Place in the Global Economy* (Forfas: Dublin, 2004), p.76.
21. Ibid., p.62 Table 2.1.
22. Ibid., p.65.
23. *Building Ireland's Knowledge Economy. Report to Inter Departmental Committee on Science, Technology and Innovation* (Dublin: Government Publications, 2004), p.1.
24. Ibid., Paragraph 2.8.
25. N. Rosenberg and R. Nelson, 'American Universities and Technical Advance in Industry'. *Research Policy*, 23, 3 (1994), pp.323–48.
26. 'Irish subsidiary lets Microsoft off the hook'. *Wall Street Journal*, 7 November 2005.
27. Collaboration to Commercialisation http://www.amcham.ie/c2c/slides/connolly/

connolly5.html.
28. Ibid http://www.amcham.ie/c2c/slides/cennis.html.
29. 'Careering Towards the Knowledge Society'. Proceedings of a Joint IUA/IBEC Conference, Dublin City University, 30 November 2005, pp.15–16.
30. R. Geiger, *Knowledge and Money: Research Universities and the Paradox of the Marketplace* (Palo Alto, CA: Stanford University Press, 2004), p.185.
31. D. Noble, *Digital Diploma Mills: The Automation of Higher Education* (New York: Monthly Review Press, 2002).
32. Minutes of University Council Trinity College, 12 April 2006.
33. P. Colgan, 'Campus Commander'. *Sunday Business Post*, 27 February 2005.
34. K. Fitzgerald, 'Grim View from the Ivory Tower'. *Irish Examiner*, 22 March 2002.
35. Washburn, *University Inc.*, p.108.
36. Kieran McGowan Interview, *UCD News*, February 2005.
37. Dan Flinter, 'Commercialising Research Boosts Entrepreneurial Activity'. Galway Chamber of Commerce lunch, 29 April 2003 http://www.galway.net/galwayguide-news/2003/04/gcci20030429/.
38. HEA, *Creating Ireland's Knowledge Society: Proposals for Higher Education Reform* (Dublin: HEA, 2004), p.15.
39. E. Oliver, 'Minister backs idea of private college'. *Irish Times*, 4 February 2005.
40. B. Readings, *The University in Ruins* (Harvard: Harvard University Press, 1996), p.23.
41. Quoted in L. Waters, *Enemies of Promise: Publishing, Perishing and the Eclipse of Scholarship* (Chicago: Prickly Paradigm Press, 2004), p.9.
42. B. Wysocki, 'Web cuts Scholarly Journals Status'. *Wall Street Journal*, 24 May 2005.
43. T. Bergstrom, 'Free Labour for Costly Journals', March 20 2001 www.econ.ucsb.edu-tedb/journals/jeprevised.pdf.
44. Waters, *Enemies of Promise*, p.6.
45. Institute for Integration Studies http://www.tcd.ie/iiis/.
46. N. Courtney, 'Compulsory Exxon Seminar Replaces Labs in Engineering'. *University Observer*, 24 February 2005.
47. UCC Press Release, 'UCC/Centocor Biologics Partnership', 23 June 2006.
48. See D. Kirp, *Shakespeare, Einstein and the Bottom Line* (Harvard: Harvard University Press, 2003).
49. Washburn, *University Inc.*, p.204.
50. Quoted in ibid., p.215.
51. Irish Universities Association, *Reform of 3rd Level and Creation of 4th Level Ireland: Securing Competitive Advantage in the 21st Century* (Dublin: IUA, 2005), p.3.
52. L. Levidow, 'Marketing Higher Education: Neo-liberal Strategies and Counter Strategies'. *Education and Social Justice*, 3, 2 (2001), pp.12–21.
53. D. Noble, 'Digital Diploma Mills: The Automation of Higher Education'. Firstmonday www.firstmonday.org/issues3_1noble.
54. Geiger, *Knowledge and Money*, pp.181 and 219–20.
55. S. Krimsky, 'The Temptations of Corporate Funding'. *Trusteeship: Journal of Association of Governing Boards of Universities and Colleges*, March/April 2004, pp.18–23.
56. S. Krimsky, 'The Profit of Scientific Discovery and Its Normative Effects'. *Chicago-Kent Law Review*, 75, I, (1999) pp.15–39.
57. J.P. Walsh and W. Hong, 'Secrecy Increasing in Step with Competition'. *Nature*, 422 (24 April 2003), pp.801–2.
58. Commercialisation Steering Group, 'Funding Agency Requirements and Guidelines for Managing Research-Generated Intellectual Property', December 2005.
59. Personnel Advertisement www.dcu.ie/vacancies/080705a.p.
60. Royal College of Surgeons website www.rcsi.ie/research2/campsu/index.htm.
61. IBEC Press Release, 'NHF to Provide Science-based Information to Consumers', 6 January 2005.
62. World Health Organisation, *Tobacco Company Strategies to Undermine Tobacco Control Activities* (WHO, 2000) available at http://www.who.int/tobacco/en/who inquiry.pdf.

63. J. Thompson, P. Baird and J. Downie, *Report of the Committee of Inquiry on the case involving Dr Nancy Olivieri, the Hospital for Sick Children, the University of Toronto and Apotex Inc*(Ottawa: Canadian Association of University Teachers, 2001).

64. J. Washburn, 'Hired Education'. *The American Prospect*, 4 February 2005, p.5.

65. R. Lenzer and M. Maiello, 'The 22 billion gold rush'. *Forbes*, 10 April 2006.

66. M. Frieberg, B. Saffran, T. Stinson, W. Nelson and C. Bennett, 'Evaluation of Conflict of Interest in Economic Analysis on New Drugs in Oncology'. *Journal of American Medical Association*, 282, 15 (20 October 1999), pp.1453–7.

67. H. Stelfox, G. Chua, K. O Rourke, A. Detsky, ' Conflict of Interest in the Debate Over Calcium Channel Antagonists', *New England Journal of Medicine* Vol. 338 No. 2 pp 101-106 8 January 1998.

68. Washburn, *University Inc.*, p.112.

69. M. Angell, *The Truth about Drug Companies* (New York: Random House, 2004), p.100.

70. J. Abramson, *Overdosed America* (New York: Harper Perennial, 2004), Chap. 7.

71. A. Berenson, 'Evidence in Vioxx suits intervention by Merck officials'. *New York Times*, 24 April 2005.

72. R. Knox, 'Biomedical Results often are withheld', *Boston Globe*, 16 April 1997.

73. G.J. Whittington, T. Kendall, P. Fonagy, D. Cottrell, A. Cotgrove and E. Boddington, 'Selective Serotin Re-uptake Inhibitors in Childhood Depression: Systematic Review of Published versus Unpublished Data'. *The Lancet*, 363, 9418 (24 April 2004), pp.1341–5.

74. D. Newman, 'The Great Taxol Giveaway'. *Multinational Monitor*, 5 May 1992.

Chapter Seven

The Silver Lining in Health

What if Irish hospitals were a source of illness rather than places of cure? This frightening prospect arises as the number of patients contracting the MRSA superbug has grown from 553 in 2004 to 592 in 2005.[1] MRSA is a type of bacteria that has become resistant to most antibiotics and, while usually harmless, can become fatal if it gets into the bloodstream as septicaemia. If contracted by a patient who has undergone extensive surgery, it is extremely dangerous because their immune system has already been weakened.

MRSA is one of the great scandals of the Irish health system. According to a report from the Irish Patients Association, the number of cases of MRSA per million of the population in Ireland is the highest of all the twenty-five European countries.[2] The situation has become so sensitive that the chief executive of the Health Services Executive (HSE) has said that, 'To give the figure of how many people died with MRSA to the public would be almost unfair and would frighten people'.[3] Unlike Britain, MRSA information is not included in hospital death certificates and sometimes relatives are not even told about the infection.

The Irish health authorities originally defined MRSA as primarily a problem of individual hygiene. 'It is quite incredible that we still have to operate in an environment where doctors and nurses have to be reminded of the importance of hand hygiene', said Health Minister Mary Harney, who launched a 'Clean Hands' campaign.[4] Health staff should, of course, adhere to basic medical principles by washing their hands, and improvements in this area would no doubt help. But blaming individuals can also be a convenient way of blind-siding any questioning of wider structural problems.

Most international evidence shows a connection between the spread of MRSA and bed occupancy rates. MRSA infection rates start to rise when these rates go over 85 per cent – even when the most stringent hygiene regime is in place. An eighteen-month survey in London, for example, looked at the effect of adding a fifth bed to a four bedded bay in three acute medical wards and found that it heightened the risk of infection with MRSA.[5] A study in Malta over a twenty-four month period found a similar connection, even in non-intensive settings.[6] A study published in the *British Journal of Nursing* noted that high bed occupancy rates meant that turnover times could be as little as 15 minutes – even though the minimum time for cleaning a bed to an acceptable level could be 75 minutes.[7] Yet, despite this overwhelming evidence, bed occupancy rates in some Irish hospitals approaches 100 per cent – and sometimes exceeds that figure due to the widespread use of trolleys.[8]

There are other structural problems. Caps on employment in the health service have meant significant delays in hiring much-needed infection control staff. Hospitals need scores more microbiologists, infection control nurses and laboratory scientists, but 'budgetary constraints' stand in the way. The contracting out of cleaning and long waits by people in A&E wards who bring in take-away food has led to filthy hospitals. After a particularly bad cleanliness audit, the Fine Gael politician, Dr Liam Twomey, said that half of the state's hospitals would be 'closed down in the morning if the standards applied to restaurants and meat factories were applied to them'.[9] There are not enough beds in single rooms so that patients can be isolated and beds are not kept the desired 2.5 metres apart. One consultant microbiologist in the National Maternity Hospital in Holles St where five babies were infected with MRSA says that, 'It is a major problem that we have a total lack of isolation facilities in the neonatal intensive care ward. There is just one room in the unit.'[10] In brief, MRSA is both a consequence and a dramatic symbol of a wider crisis at the heart of the Irish health system.

The immediate cause has been a systematic under-funding for more than a decade. The situation deteriorated dramatically during the reign of the millionaire Taoiseach, Charles J.

Haughey, who had come to power under an election slogan 'Health cuts hurt the old, the sick and the handicapped'. Once in office he introduced savage cuts with the connivance of both the official opposition and a trade union leadership who desperately wanted to get into social partnership. Between 1987 and 1990, the overall number of hospital beds decreased by 6,377 or nearly 15 per cent.[11] During the subsequent Celtic Tiger boom, the Irish state never replaced those beds, even though it has since acknowledged a shortfall of 3,000 beds. In 1988, health spending also declined to 58 per cent of the EU average and throughout most of the 1990s remained below three quarters of that average. Even when the figures appeared to improve after 2000, closer scrutiny revealed that the government was overstating its health spending.[12] The dark side of tax cutting is that Ireland has a Third World health service in a First World economy. There is no direct link between health spending and MRSA, but the rundown of the health service created structural problems which made eradicating the infection much more difficult.

The rot at the heart of the Irish health system goes even deeper because, historically, it denied the principle of equality of access and equity in treatment. The contrast with Britain is instructive here. In 1946, after the sacrifices of war and the threat of working-class militancy, a free universal health care service was instituted. Aneurin Bevan summed up the underlying philosophy of the National Health Service in the simple statement, 'the resources of medical skills and apparatus of healing shall be ... made available to rich and poor alike'.[13] More than half a century later, the NHS system has been hollowed out, but its underlying philosophy that healthcare should be organized according to need and not income is still a powerful feature of the British political landscape. The roots of the Irish health system, by contrast, go back to the defeat of Noel Browne's Mother and Child Scheme in 1951.[14] This had proposed a very limited edition of Bevan's philosophy by introducing free medical care for mothers and children up to the age of 16. However, an alliance of the Catholic Church and the medical elite used the fear of socialism and 'totalitarianism' to defeat the plans. When greater access to healthcare was finally granted, it came with a highly unusual contract for hospital consultants.

The contract allowed them to work, unsupervised, in public

hospitals for 33 hours a week, and then engage in unlimited private practice from which they could earn a huge income. As Maev Ann Wren put it,

Consultants would receive a state salary to treat the majority of patients, yet retained a financial incentive – payment of extra fees – to devote more time to private patients than their unmonitored public commitments.[15]

In practice, this instituted a two-tier system where those with little money got inadequate treatment while growing numbers, from raw fear, took out private insurance to ensure they would be seen by a hospital consultant. Currently one half of the Irish population have private health insurance. The Irish health system is thus founded on what Wren has called 'an expression of Victorian values in which health care is a commodity to be purchased or, when it is unaffordable, to be given as a charity, never a right'.[16]

The state also subsidizes private insurance and thus encourages its citizens to leave the public system. Insurance premiums receive a tax relief which costs the state €94 million a year. Moreover, to earn much needed cash, public hospitals take in private patients but do not charge their insurance companies the full cost. In 2004, private patients accounted for one quarter of the cases in public hospitals. In other words, resources that could be going into tackling MRSA or the wider A&E crisis is used to subsidize the very insurance schemes that people take out because of fear of inadequate facilities. It is truly an absurd arrangement.

There is universal acknowledgement that the Irish health care system is crying out for reform. The question is, which direction will the reforms take? Unfortunately, all indications are that they are ideologically driven to suit the interests of private corporations.

THE CREDO

Political elites have a major problem with health service reform. After adopting a neo-liberal framework, they need to reduce spending on the health service. These cuts can, in turn, deliver opportunities for private 'service providers' to enter the arena. Yet the broader population does not accept that health should be treated simply as another commodity. It demands a quality health service and wants the latest advances in medical technology to be made available to all, rather than just a select few. Caught between these conflicting pressures, governments look to a broad menu of 'reform' that has been developed in global elite networks in the past two decades. One overarching strategy is to turn health into a tradeable commodity, and the impetus for this has come from the General Agreement on Trade in Services (GATS).[17]

However, before health can be defined as a commodity, a number of deeper ideological changes need to occur. Sometimes, because of their unpopularity, these are not expressed explicitly but appear as dense organizational prescriptions. Behind the sometimes-impenetrable jargon that surrounds much business-speak, important social choices and meaning are imposed. Like the Jesuits of old, the elite assume that if people accept organizational practices that derive from a business culture, their mentalities will soon adjust to the new 'realities'.

Two key concepts structure the thinking of the political elite on health care. One is the notion of the New Public Management that seeks to introduce market principles and new management techniques into the public sector. The goal is a slim, minimal state where key decision makers are not involved in detailed administration but are 'steering rather than rowing'. Under the guise of cutting down bureaucracy, New Public Management advocated greater monitoring and surveillance by the central executive 'steering agencies' and more regulation and reduced public spending for the 'rowing agencies'.[18]

As part of this philosophy, governments are merely supposed to ensure the provision of services but the actual delivery is passed over to separate organizations. Sometimes this involves outsourcing to private providers. At other times, it means the 'marketization' of state run services where the desired goal of 'efficiency' is to be achieved by creating quasi markets made up of different centres competing for performance targets. All of this can only work if there is a high degree of quantification, so measurements and prices are imposed on everything from surgical operations to nursing care.

This, in turn, brings important changes in health care. Instead of a wider, more holistic, concept of care, there is a set of treatments that can be measured as deliverable outputs. These treatments are then standardized and a list of 'reference costs' are established.[19] The aim is to identify 'outliers' – medical service providers whose costs are above the average. Cost centres that meet 'key performance indicators' are rewarded with incentives while those who fail are penalized. Cost-watching, in turn, lays the basis for cost-cutting through, for example, greater use of day surgery which has become more technologically possible. While day surgery may be better for some patients, for others it may mean that the burden of care is shifted onto families and friends. These overall changes are often promoted through a language that sees patients as customers who 'shop around' for treatments from different providers. The public service is supposed to respond 'flexibly' to their individual choices and also to get their costs in order. The new patients/customers can thus be mobilized by the senior administrators to undermine professional medical hierarchies.

The other key idea that arose in elite circles is that of 'managed competition' which originated with Alain Enthoven. A Stanford health economist, Enthoven began his career at the Pentagon in the 1960s as Robert McNamara's chief 'Whiz Kid', where he helped tabulate figures on everything from nuclear warfare strategies to body counts during the Vietnam War.[20] The same obsession with cold quantification in the name of a spurious efficiency permeates his writings on health economics. Enthoven recognized that the neo-liberal dream of a fully privatized, market-based health system is an impossibility for a number of reasons. There is a profound information imbalance between the 'buyers'/patients and 'sellers'/doctors and so the patients end up doing the last thing that a proper buyer should do: they trust their 'seller' to order the best treatments. The doctors who prescribe drugs for patients are not disciplined by self-interest because they do not have to pay for the drugs themselves. To make matters even worse, there are too many buyers and only a limited number of suppliers in the form of local doctors or hospital facilities. The result, according to Enthoven, is that a pure market system like the US produces profound and multifaceted market failure.

The solution, he argued, is managed competition between different providers by means of transparent pricing, quality control and limitations on patients' choice. Enthoven's ideas were originally applied to the Health Management Organizations (HMOs) of the US and a concerted effort was made to export these to Latin America.[21] In Europe, Enthoven's work became particularly popular in Britain and the notion of managed competition was translated into the idea of 'purchaser-provider' splits, where health authorities buy in services from a variety of suppliers. Later this evolved into Public-Private Partnerships (PPPs), where the public sector made long-term arrangements with private corporations for the supply of health care. These partnership arrangements gave neo-liberals the best of both worlds. They could talk about the market and business methods but rely on the regular supply of captive patients for their profit-making ventures.

Despite the popularity of these ideas in ruling circles, there is little empirical evidence that they have brought improvements because there are huge problems with the abstract concept of efficiency when applied to human health. How does one measure the efficiency of doctors who use intuition and experience to make a sharp diagnosis? Or what performance indicator will capture subtle patient-nurse interactions? In reality, accountants and health managers often assign crude ad hoc measurements. However, even if quantifiable indicators are used there is little evidence of rising efficiency, and the new credo has instead led to a growth of excess paper work and administration. In the language of economists, it has pushed up 'transaction costs'.

A non-market, planned system of health care can be far more efficient because, instead of floors of administrators working in billing departments, resources can be devoted to looking after patients. The administrative costs of the Canadian public system, for example, are about one third of the US system.[22] Before the reform era, management costs in the British NHS ran at 5 per cent of its budget compared to 15 per cent in the US.[23] However, with the growth of quasi markets and new billing requirements, management costs have soared. Between 1981 and 1991, the number of people classified as general or senior managers grew from 1,000 in 1986 to 26,000 in 1995,[24] and vast sums were spent on the information requirements of the new business managers.

Despite these problems, the ideas of New Public Management and Enthoven's 'managed competition' offered a number of attractions to governments. 'Steering not rowing' meant that they could pull back from health administration and not take responsibility for health failures. Health could thus be depoliticized and regarded as a matter of technical organization carried out by business-style executives. In the name of 'managed competition' governments could also hide behind a wall of complexity and create divisions between potential opponents. Moreover, in the name of diversity and customer choice, they could promote partnerships between the public sector and private health corporations. This would enable them to both reduce health spending and create more openings for private corporations. It should be clear by now why the Irish state was so enthusiastic to embrace these reforms.

FROM BUSINESS SPEAK TO CORPORATE BOARDS

During the Celtic Tiger years, the medical and political elites engaged more actively with these arguments. The problem with the Irish system was defined not as a lack of funding or the rigid, hierarchical structures that had been inherited from the Church, but instead it was supposed to be the lack of competition and over-politicization. Professor Muiris Fitzgerald, for example, summed up this emerging elite consensus when he called for more 'competitiveness' and 'incentives' within the system. If these were 'responsible for our national Celtic Tiger economy [they should have] a place within the most conspicuous consumer of these benefits – namely, the Health Service'.[25]

One of the first attempts to impose competitiveness was the casemix system of budgeting. This was a technique to partially fund hospitals on the basis of a fee per discharged patient. Each patient was assigned a Diagnosis-Related Group (DRG) and the hospital was paid according to a standard price for the DRGs it treated. Hospitals do not put the same time and effort into every patient they care for, but the casemix system forced such comparisons to be made. Hospitals who performed 'efficiently' were allocated extra resources, which were drawn from a common pot to cover all hospitals within the system. This pot was filled regularly from annual cuts of around 2 per cent imposed on those hospitals which performed 'inefficiently'. By staying budget neutral, the casemix system thus forced hospitals to compete against each other. In 2006, for example, the Department of Health and Children published a league table on this 'performance related funding' which showed that 15 positive performers gained extra money while 22 'underperformers' had been penalized.[26] By 2007, half of a hospital's budget will come from the casemix system.

The new business ethos took a further qualitative leap forward with two reports published in 2003. The first was commissioned from a consultancy consortium led by Prospectus Consultancy and Watson Wyatt entitled *Audit of Structures and Functions in the Health System 2003*. Prospectus Consultancy has a very particular profile within the elite decision-making process in Ireland. Its chairperson is Sean Donnelly, who was a former director of the IDA and is a board member of several other companies, including Donnelly's Fruit and Vegetables. The managing director is David Duffy, who is a member of the Dublin regional committee of IBEC. The firm has won many consultancy contracts from public sector bodies but it has also been able to hop over the fence and work for the private sector as well. It did a major report, for example, on the opportunities for private health care for a private health care insurer. Its particular corporate ethos meant there was little likelihood that it would recommend universal free health care or any extension of democratic decision-making.

The Prospectus report advocated the formation of a Health Service Executive (HSE), modelled on a corporate board, to take charge of all executive functions pertaining to the health system. This entailed the abolition of local health boards where elected representatives sat, and their replacement with a centralized apparatus. Prospectus claimed the new board would enjoy 'arms length' accountability and so could develop an organizational culture that could focus on 'delivery with a strong managerial and performance ethos'.[27] It also recommended a divisional structure for the HSE with a National Hospital Office being responsible for allocating funding to hospitals and, significantly, 'managing the interface with private acute providers'.[28] The report represented a fundamental attack on any notion of democratic involvement in day to day health decision-making. Like other consultancy reports, it was written in a peculiar business-speak that covered this over by references to 'consumer' empowerment and 'stakeholder' involvement. The threadbare nature of such 'stakeholder' involvement, however, was revealed in one particular proposal. The composition of the National Consultative Forum was to be at the discretion of the Minister and to adhere to the admonition that it 'was not intended in any way to interfere with the clear executive role of the HSE'.[29]

With the threat of democratic involvement in decision-making removed, the neo-liberals were free to carry though even more decisive changes. Another key landmark was the Brennan Commission on *Financial Management and Control System in the Health Service*. Once again, the composition of the Brennan Commission was drawn from a very particular elite strata of Irish society. The chairperson, Niamh Brennan, is a chartered accountant and academic director of the Institute of Directors Centre for Corporate Governance in UCD, and is also the wife of the Justice Minister Michael McDowell. The Institute of Directors is an organization of senior executives, CEOs, and directors of leading corporations who are affiliated to similar organizations in Britain and elsewhere. The commission also included, among others: George Mansfield, chairman of Ark Life Assurance Co Ltd and a director of AIB Finance and Leasing Ltd; Donal de Buitleir, a general manager at the office of the chief executive of the AIB Group; John Greely, a former director of Smurfit Finance; Maurice Tempany, a former president of the Institute of Chartered Accountants in Ireland and Sean Barrett, a well known economist with strong neo-liberal views. He recently addressed the Progressive Democrat conference where he told delegates that 'the vital reforms in Irish society require the Progressive Democrats to drive them'.[30] There was no representative of a trade union or any health advocacy group or any campaigner for democratic health reform, with the possible exception of RTE's Tommie Gorman. As the title of the report indicates, the report was written in a style of tedious banality that rivalled the literature which emanated from the former Soviet politburo. Behind the near-impenetrable walls of boredom, however, lay further important changes.

The report acknowledged that the consultants' contracts and the subsidies offered to private patients in Irish hospitals did not conform to any rational model for allocating resources. However, while media attention focussed on the proposal that future contracts for hospital consultants ensured that they worked exclusively for the public sector, the main thrust behind the report lay elsewhere. It advocated nothing less than that the health service should be run like any other business, with 'a corporate board with responsibilities and accountabilities that are consistent with those of a normal corporate/commercial board'.[31] It proposed: to appoint a CEO by means of a standard 'international search and selection process' and an executive board who would devise indicators to monitor performance, productivity, quality of care and value for money. It suggested regional CEOs who would draw up 'service plans' to contract in health services from a variety of providers, and better information systems to support financial management and control systems. A series of abstract, detailed structures were suggested to align the health service to an ideal business model. Despite the focus on cost control, however, there was little by way of concrete proposals for actually controlling costs. One of the largest costs, for example, is the way the pharmaceutical industry rips off the health system by charging high prices for branded drugs. Yet there was little discussion on possibilities for more generic drugs and the report merely suggested that agreements with the Irish Pharmaceutical Healthcare Association (IPHA) be 'evaluated against international experience' and these evaluations be taken into account in new negotiations.[32]

These proposals found a determined backer in Mary Harney, who took up the position of Minister for Health in 2004. She named Kevin Kelly, a former Managing Director of AIB and President of the Irish Bankers Federation, as interim head of the HSE. PricewaterhouseCoopers were then hired at the cost of €36,000 to recruit the permanent CEO of the new body.[33] Terms and condition were the most generous in the Irish public sector with a starting salary of €330,000; a €40,000 relocation allowance; a €15,000 car allowance; pension provision of €25 per cent and a performance bonus with a maximum of €80,000.[34] The job eventually went to Professor Brendan Drumm, a consultant and professor of paediatrics. The new HSE board was also dominated by people from a business background. Its chairperson was Liam Downey, the former chief executive of Becton Dickson, a medical technology company and a member of the National Executive of IBEC. It also included Joe Macri, the Managing Director of Microsoft Ireland and also a member of the National Executive of IBEC; Eugene McCague, a partner with the solicitors firm Arthur Cox and council member of Dublin Chamber of Commerce; Donal de Buitleir, a General Manager with AIB; Professor John Murray, President of the Marketing Institute of Ireland and Niamh Brennan, among others.

If the cure for the health service is a business culture, then it followed logically that business people should be appointed to all sorts of health bodies, and Mary Harney embraced it with some gusto. A direct representative of the Irish Pharmaceutical Health Care Association was appointed to the Health Research Board, which is responsible for commissioning research of many areas linked to health. The IPHA is an organization that is run by local executives of the largest pharmaceutical companies in the world, and is quite explicit that its aim is 'to shape health-care policy in Ireland'.[35] The board of the Health Information and Quality Authority also includes the key account manager for Abbott Laboratories but, once again, no representative of any lobby group for the poor or labour movement.

It is sometimes claimed that a 'partnership' with business brings a dynamic, cost-saving culture to a sluggish public sector. But, it might be equally argued that business can look on the public sector as a prey for easy pickings. Public sector executives who have embraced a pro-business ethos will be less critical of attempts by private firms to milk the system for easy profit. Even before the new corporate colonization got underway, there was considerable evidence that this is a major danger. In 1998, Beaumont hospital decided to earn extra money by charging their patients to park and entered a partnership arrangement with National Car Parks to provide a multi-story car park. The deal, however, meant that the public finances were worse off by somewhere between €9 million and €13 million because of the choice of a PPP option rather than having the car park built themselves.[36] After local hospital incinerators were closed in the late 1980s due to environmental considerations, hospitals entered into commercial relations with private firms to dispose of risk waste. Once again, however, there is evidence of a 'rip-off' as they were charged €1,430 a ton to dispose of such waste even though the vast bulk of it could be treated with disinfection at the service provider's plant.[37]

Ironically, the greatest rip-off came from installing the very information system that the Brennan Commission thought would support more efficient financial management. PPARs was a human resource management and payroll information system intended to bring business culture into the hospitals. The initial project was for €9 million but the final bill came to €131 million before it was scrapped. The shocking element to the whole saga was the ruthless way that businesses avoided risk. The initial contract went to Bull Information Systems Ltd (BISL) to install sophisticated software. But when the costs grew beyond their initial estimates, BISL simply pulled out of their 'fixed price contract' and faced no legal punishment. Incredibly, they were then re-hired on a 'time and materials' basis whereby they could bill the hospitals for every day they worked and every ounce of material they used.[38] The hospitals hired external consultants for 'project advice' and the contract went to Deloitte and Touche. Between that and its rather ill-defined role as a 'strategic implementation partner', it managed to clock up a staggering €41 million.[39] Deloitte ensured that they too worked on a 'time and materials basis' with no over-arching contract and sometimes with no prior agreement on the number of staff who would be employed.[40] On one element of the project Deloitte charged for 19,200 days at an average daily fee rate of €1,520 exclusive of expenses and VAT.[41] In the dry words of the Comptroller and Auditor General, 'the arrangements with Deloitte did not incorporate an appropriate sharing of risk. In practice, the State carried all the risk.'[42] Deloitte and Touche had previously been hired by the Department of Health and Children to conduct a 'value for money audit of the Irish Health system' and so, clearly, they had some appreciation of the weakness of its financial controls! As if to compound this bizarre Alice in Wonderland saga, a number of other consultancy firms were hired on five occasions to assess the project. These firms included such well-known names as Hay Management Consultants, ReedSmith Healthcare Consulting and IBM. However, not one of them challenged the continuation of the project despite the widening costs, the reduced scope and the risks to its coherence.

Nothing better symbolizes the absurdity of corporate ethos than PPARS. But it may well be asked, what is the alternative for cost control? Despite its love of hierarchy, modern medicine has one great cultural achievement – it progresses through evidence-based research. By carefully testing hypotheses, doctors and health administrators generate predictions that can be subsequently adjusted if necessary. This ethos has allowed for important advances in public health medicine and epidemiology – the study of the social patterns of illness and disease. Prevalence of many common diseases and infection can be predicted from past patterns. Using this data, it is perfectly possible to allocate budgets to a health service on an area basis. This would be even more effective if the relevant medical units were engaged in longer-term preventative medicine in their areas. Clearly, this means acknowledging that poorer areas with older populations need more resources than those in more affluent areas. It is not a matter of competing for resources but matching them to human need. It is clearly inefficient not to allocate the most qualified doctors to the most complex cases and under a planned system this could be done. The poorest patients who had complex cases would have a better chance of seeing consultants than the present system, whereby money, rather than the difficulty of cases, determine the allocation of consultant time. If this type of planning were combined with democratic structures that engaged with the civic, humanitarian spirit of health staff, even more cost controls could be developed. Medical staff know far more about the relative effectiveness of branded or non-branded drugs than accountants. They understand that care is about more than just a set of treatments, and that, sometimes, keeping someone in hospital is more 'cost-effective' than an early discharge that leads to complications.

But wouldn't they use such decision-making power to promote their self-interest? This bleak vision underlines the neo-liberal case for financial penalties and wasteful paperwork – but it misses one central point: If healthcare staff were employed directly on public contracts, and if private contracts were banned, there would be no incentive to push up costs. Costs would reduce because there would be no need for all the paper work and legal contracts that goes with mixing a public and private system. There would be no need to take resources out of the health system to fund the profits of private individuals. There would be no need to duplicate items like MRI scanners, as staff would have an interest in sharing such equipment. Moreover, hospital staff are often motivated by something more than money, and where there is a culture which sustains their civic, humanitarian instincts, this can produce sound healthcare. By corrupting the medical profession with the lure of gold, however, the neo-liberals produce a worse service – and a more costly one as well.[43]

AMERICANIZATION

On 5 March 2003, in the most casual manner imaginable, a decisive event occurred which could change the Irish health system forever. In the final stages of the Finance Bill, Charlie McCreevy sprung an amendment to make it easier to get tax relief to build private hospitals. The rationale he offered was that, over Christmas, he had been approached by a GP in his constituency who wanted to build a private hospital and he just wanted to help. Henceforth, anyone building a private acute hospital could have the cost of construction written off over a seven-year period against their rental income. The debate on the proposal took less than five minutes and consumed no more than 441 words.[44]

The implications of McCreevy's proposal only became apparent when his long-time ally, Mary Harney, dropped a bombshell in July 2005. Private hospitals were henceforth to be allowed to build on the land previously owned by public hospitals. This would create 1,000 more beds, she claimed, and would free up beds for public patients. The proposal was not preceded by any evidence-based research and no documentation was produced on how this might affect wider planning in the health system. Instead, Prospectus Management Consulting was once again engaged to draw up 'investment appraisal frameworks for the development of private facilities on public hospital sites'.[45] Interestingly, they would later go on to organize the sale of Mount Carmel Hospital to Harlequin Healthcare Ltd. Their proposals specified that there should be 'service level agreements' covering quotas and priority status of patients transferred from public hospitals to the private hospitals. There should also be a sharing of clinical and support services between both types of hospitals. Harney was quite explicit, however, that the public hospitals would continue to deal with the 'high complexity cases'.[46]

The two measures that McCreevy and Harney introduced started a goldrush among investors because it gave them two key prerequisites they had sought – tax reliefs and a guaranteed supply of 'customers'. Paul Higgins of Goodbody Corporate Finance explained the importance of tax reliefs by noting that the first private clinic, the Blackrock Clinic, had opened in 1984 but that the second, stand-alone, private hospital was not built until twenty years later. He noted that 'if it wasn't for tax incentives it might have been 40 years'.[47] The sheer generosity of the state meant that 'for every €1 million of qualifying expenditure, investors are able to reduce their tax bill over a seven-year period by €470,000'.[48] Moreover, developers could 'sell the capital allowances to external investors' and so attract financiers in to take their cut.[49] The second factor – the guarantee of 'customers' – was another form of state subsidy. The practice had already begun with The National Treatment Purchase Fund (NTPF) that transferred patients who had been on waiting lists for a year (or six months in the case of children) to private clinics mainly. In 2004, for example, the NTPF paid the Mater Private hospital €14.3 million for treating patients. This represented 10 per cent of its total income and allowed it to make an estimated €2.2 million in profit from this one source. With co-location, investors could assume that this type of subsidy to the private sector would expand even more dramatically.

Later, Jerome Mansman, the CEO of Nation Healthcare Ltd, told the first conference of private health care investors that the Irish market had three main advantages over Britain. It had a higher percentage of people who had private health insurance. Its hospital consultants were more 'entrepreneurial'. And it was more receptive to change because it did not face strong opposition from the unions or a parliamentary opposition.[50] The high number insured is probably the key. The decades-long deterioration of the health service created a US-style insurance market that, it is now thought, can sustain a US form of medical apartheid. Private patients who pay costly insurance premiums will be able to avail themselves of high-tech equipment and hospital wards with flowers, flat-screen TVs and computer terminals. The rest will continue to queue and pray.

Typically, three different groupings have come together to build private hospitals – builders, hospital consultants and financiers. The Irish rich have a passion for property and many of the funds that created hotels or holiday homes in the past are flowing into private hospitals today. Two different networks are driving the process.

There is, first, the older Catholic-based network such as the Mater Private, the Bons Secours and the Blackrock Clinic. Nuns who forged a close relationship with local businessmen originally established the first two. In 2000, however, the Mater Private was taken over in a management buy-out for €33 million and quickly grew in value to €100 million. It is controlled by a holding company, Copperway Limited, which is owned by figures closely associated with the former owners, the Sisters of Mercy. These include Brian Joyce and Eamonn Walsh, both former CIE chairmen, and Mark Moran. Subsequently other directors such as Paul Haran, a former top civil servant, who is also the Principal of the UCD Business School, joined them.

The Bons Secours Group, which was the largest network at one time, is an example of an organization in transition. It still proclaims itself to be a not-for-profit organization and has four religious sisters on its board alongside the chairperson, Sister Margaret Hanafin. However, increasingly, the business executives play a greater role and it declares a profit.

Jimmy Sheehan, a hospital consultant with strong Catholic views, set up the Blackrock Clinic in 1984 along with his brother Joe and another hospital consultant. He had originally teamed up with BUPA, but its stake was subsequently sold off to the meat baron, Larry Goodman, for €25 million. Goodman has had a chequered history and appeared before the Mahon tribunal for making payments to the former FF politician, Liam Lawlor. He seems to favour markets with high entry costs and public sector contracts. So the transition, from selling meat into EU intervention stock to providing private health care, may not have been so unusual. The Blackrock clinic group hit the expansion trail recently by first opening the Galway Clinic, but this got into difficulties when it did not receive the expected number of patients from the NTPF. They then teamed up with the property developer Sean Mulryan to open the 125-bed Hermitage Clinic in Dublin West. Mulryan is one of the largest property tycoons in the country and the owner of Ballymore Properties. The company made payments to the disgraced, former FF TD, Liam Lawlor and to the lobbyist, Frank Dunlop. Mulryan is also a frequent visitor to the Fianna Fail tent at the Galway races.[51]

The second private hospital network comes from the new wealth accumulated during the Celtic Tiger. It tends to be more developer-led and is establishing closer links with the US multi-nationals. The key corporations here are the Beacon Medical Group, Harlequin Healthcare and Euro Care International.

The Beacon brings together the three main elements of private healthcare – a hospital consultant, Mark Redmond, a property developer, Paddy Shovelin, and a businessman, Michel Cullen, a former car dealer who sold Porsches and Ferraris. Goodbody Corporate Finance, who produced a special report on opportunities in the private healthcare market, is involved in raising investment. Beacon runs a hospital, a renal clinic, and a medical mall and is situated near the Beacon South apartment complex built by Landmark Developments, which is owned by Shovelin. They have teamed up with the giant US corporation Triad to manage their hospital and this is seen as the first step to a wider involvement in the Irish market. 'Put it this way: Triad did not come to Ireland to manage one hospital' a Beacon spokesperson said.[52] Triad has an interesting history. It was spun off from the larger Colombia HCA after it was forced to pay fines of €1.7 billion for bribes and kickbacks. Many of the top executives of Triad were on the board of Colombia HCA during this period. The CEO of Triad is paid a salary of $2 million a year and gets stock options worth $12 million.

The Kildare property developer, Jerry Conlon, who made a fortune by selling land in Kildare, founded Harlequin Healthcare Holdings. Other prominent directors include Richard Conroy, a staunch Fianna Fail supporter, who runs a number of oil, gold and diamond exploration companies; David Martin, former financial controller of the agribusiness firm, IAWS; Colm Gunne, originally from the family-owned auctioneering firm and Joe Kelly, a prominent health administrator. Harlequin began life running St Joseph's Hospital in Sligo and Aut Even Hospital in Kilkenny, and is now building a private healthcare empire. It took over Mount Carmel, the exclusive private maternity hospital, and is now focussed on areas such as dialysis, diagnostics and radiography.

Euro Care International is the brainchild of another property developer, Mary Madden and her dentist husband Jim. They
have teamed up with the owner of Miltown Engineering to build
private clinics in Waterford and Carlow. Behind them is the
giant US operator, University of Pittsburgh Medical Centre,
which describes itself as the leader in cancer care in the US.

The involvement of the US private health care industry in the
second network is interesting. The industry experienced a decline
in profits in the US after the end of the stock market boom and
has reached saturation point in its home markets. It is, therefore,
determined to spread abroad and is using the GATS agreement to
do so. One feature of healthcare reform programmes generally
has been the appearance of these US healthcare providers in Latin
American and, increasingly, European systems.[53]

These, then, are some of the main players who are shaping the
private Irish health industry. But alongside them, in virtually every
major town, the same alliance of property developers, hospital
consultants and financiers is in evidence. In Letterkenny, the former boss of the local health board is leading the effort. In
Dundalk, a former prominent Progressive Democrat supporter,
who is a medical doctor, is to the fore. In Limerick, the multi-
millionaire owner of the luxury hotel, Adare Manor, is building a
hospital on its grounds. In Tullamore, a builder and Fianna Fail
councillor, who already has contracts with the HSE to lease his
property, leads the effort. Gradually a US-style health system is
developing in an apparently unplanned way. In reality, it is driven
by powerful corporate interests. If this were simply a matter of
individual investors taking a risk it might not be of major public
concern. But the whole process is being subsidized by diverting
funds that could be used for the public system into tax breaks for
these investors. Moreover, the evidence from North America
shows there will be even deeper consequences in future.

In general, private hospitals cost more than public hospitals
for similar work, so if they get contracts from the public sector,
this can only mean a drain of funds from the latter. A major US
study of eight comparable hospitals in a number of US states
found that private hospitals employed more aggressive pricing
practices. The average per day charge was higher than in non-
profit institutions and the main reason for this was that ancillary
costs were 36 per cent higher, as they charged more for drugs and

medical supplies.[54] A study in California also found a tendency 'to engage in aggressive marketing and pricing strategies to generate high profitability'.[55] It found that while 'loss leader' treatments might first be employed, afterwards large mark-ups were made on complimentary ancillary services. A study of charges made to Medicare, the US government- sponsored insurance programme for the over-65s, found that the bills went up significantly when not-for-profit hospitals changed their status and sought profits.[56]

The international literature also shows that private hospitals do not always give better care than not-for-profit equivalents. A major Canadian review of the evidence found that there is a higher risk of death in for-profit hospitals. This is despite the fact that not-for-profit hospitals tend to serve poorer patients with a greater disease severity.[57] Another US study which compared investor-owned hospitals with not-for-profit hospitals on fourteen quality of care indicators found that the investor-owned had lower scores on all of them.[58] The private sector tends to cherry-pick the more profitable aspects of medicine and leaves chronic (long-term) care treatment to the public sector. It focuses on areas such as radiotherapy, dialysis or more generally day-care treatments where complications are less likely. Private hospitals tend to employ highly paid doctors but use a lower proportion of nursing staff because they are not interested in longer-term care.

These findings are relevant to future health care plans in Ireland. Contrary to popular mythology, the US health system is not fully privatized. The US spends more on health care than any other industrialized country, but just over half of that spending comes from the state through insurance programmes such as Medicare and Medicaid. In 2002, for example, the US spent $5,269 per capita on health compared to $2,730 in France or $2,160 in Britain. The spending is not reflected in a better quality of medical care because the private sector exerts such leverage by wasting money on higher transaction costs and milking the system for profit. The US, however, has one fine example of health care – that provided by the Veteran's Association, which gives a better quality medical care to its members at a lower cost than the private hospitals. It forces drug companies to give large discounts on their prices and has taken the lead on electronic medical record keeping because patients stay with it for decades.

It invests heavily in preventative care, knowing that its patients do not 'shop around' but stay with its services for decades. In brief, it is an example of planned, socialized medicine.

Ireland, unfortunately, is getting the worst American option. The private healthcare industry is being encouraged to siphon off the most profitable cases and leave the 'high complexity cases' to the public sector. Its bills to the HSE for services will be high and these will cause funding cuts elsewhere. There will be a US-style system of insiders and outsiders, where the poor subsidize the wealthy's access to high tech medicine. In the words of Paul Krugman, it will mean 'robbing Peter of basic care in order to pay for Paul's state-of-the-art treatment'.[59]

SOCIAL ENGINEERING FOR PROFIT

The plans to restructure the hospital sector are the central plank in a wider agenda to change how people think about healthcare. The neo-liberals want to indoctrinate people with the notion that 'personal responsibility' means they must pay individually for their health. They want to expunge any memory that well-being is a social right of citizens. Goodbody Stockbrokers, which is an arm of the Allied Irish Banks, have produced a special report on 'Opportunities in the Irish Healthcare Sector', where they identified two other crucial areas for corporate expansion – primary healthcare and care homes.[60] There is little doubt that the privatization agenda is receiving tacit support from the HSE as the agency joined Goodbody's in sponsoring the first private healthcare industry conference in Ireland.

Traditionally, Irish primary care was built around a General Practitioner who ran a surgery from his or her own home and provided an out-of-hours service for patients. Few GPs are now willing to do this and the service is in somewhat of a mess. Ireland has only 2,750 GPs, which means just 0.6 doctors for every thousand people – one of the lowest ratios in Europe.[61] To make matters worse, the payment system for GPs has encouraged many to leave large working-class areas to cater for wealthier suburbs where they can earn more. One result is that more sick people have to present themselves at A&E units.

The time when the GP could both run a small business and

be the first point of contact for the wider population appears to be running out. An obvious solution might be to revamp the whole service so that free universal primary care is provided through the state itself. The advantage of such a strategy is that it could lay the basis for sophisticated preventative care that keeps people out of hospitals. By allowing doctors to work together in primary healthcare centres, they would be able to organize proper rostering arrangements and this might help overcome the unwillingness of many doctors to enter this area of practice. The absurd situation whereby more money is made by treating patients in wealthier areas could also be scrapped.

In 2001, two influential reports appeared which took a few small, tentative steps in this direction. The Irish Medical Organisation and the Irish College of General Practitioners produced a joint report on *A Vision for General Practice – Priorities 2001–2006* and the Department of Health produced *Primary care – A New Direction*. Both reports agreed on developing a service that went beyond diagnosis and treatment and embraced the ideas of prevention and health promotion. This in turn necessitated more teamwork, whereby doctors would work in primary care centres with administrative backup, and a team of physiotherapists, nurses, home helps and other health professionals. Such centres might also help to develop electronic recording of a patient's history and monitor wider patterns of illness in the area. All of this could only develop with expanded resources and a value being placed on public health.

However, it did not happen. A few impressive pilot projects were built, such as that in Dublin's Ballymun, but thereafter the proposals were simply scrapped. No sustained arguments were produced for a change of strategy and no evidence-based research appeared. Instead it was replaced with a for-profit business model that is once again modelled on the American way.

Health Minister, Mary Harney, signalled the change when she opened Touchstone's first medical centre in Mulhuddart in Dublin in October 2005. Touchstone is the brainchild of Fergus Hoban who sold his interest in the pharmacy chain, Unicare, for over €100 million. His new business strategy is to construct up to sixty centres where GPs are housed in a retail shopping environment with pharmacists. Instead of a doctor remaining totally independent from the pharmacist who is selling drugs, they will now operate under the same roof and possibly develop closer relationships in the future. The board of Touchstone includes Mark Redmond who is a director of the Beacon Medical Group. Like Beacon, Touchstone is backed by big corporate financial interests – in this case IBI Corporate Finance – and it is modelling itself on a US model, Touchstone New York, which organizes one of the largest chains of doctors in the city.

The other big gold rush is in care of the elderly. Ireland has an aging population and the state wants to reduce its involvement in their care. The Irish political elite has always tried to get away with the lowest possible level of state provision and used the Catholic ethos of duty to shift responsibility onto individual families. Social expenditure on the over-65s is only 61 per cent of the average of the original EU 15.

Many older people want to stay at home, especially if they can get some assistance with cleaning, housework or even some conversation. Traditionally, an unseen and unpaid army of 150,000, mainly middle-aged women carers, looked after relatives.[62] About 40,000 of them spend over 43 hours a week working, but they received no legal rights to respite care.

Care by relatives was traditionally either supplemented or replaced by care from Home Helps who were often recruited by voluntary organizations in local areas. Until 1998, these women were also invisible, and paid a pittance. But a major union recruitment drive which began in Cork, and then spread to Dublin, changed all that. Mass rallies and demonstrations by home helps succeeded in winning better pay and establishing overtime rates. By 2004, SIPTU had concluded an agreement with the Department of Health to give proper contracts to home helps rather than the 'zero hour' contracts that were used to keep them in the dark about whether they were working or not.[63] However, powerful corporate interests were once again at work behind the scenes to promote a different agenda.

Instead of enjoying their victory, the home helps found that their hours were decreasing rather than increasing. Between 2002 and 2004, the number of home help hours was cut by 737,484 hours.[64] And suddenly on to the scene appeared yet another US healthcare provider. This time it was Comfort Keepers, a chain of franchises that had been founded in Dayton Ohio and ran 508 centres in the US. It brashly claimed that it could sell comfort and 'fill the void' left by busy families.[65] Ray Hays, the international director, summed up the company's motivation for arriving: 'Ireland is an excellent location to establish an early European presence because of the commonalities with the US in its approach to business. It is a good proving ground for American franchise brands.'[66] Comfort Keepers needed an Irish partner and they found it in the Elder Care Group, a small Irish company that ran nursing homes in the mid-west. A more significant backer was Health Minister, Mary Harney, who gave the new entrant a contract for providing home care packages. In a most unusual move, she also obliged by officially launching the company.

Comfort Keepers charge over €20 an hour for its service, but just under half of that will go to the actual staff it hires. This will probably undercut the going union rate that has been negotiated with other companies and voluntary agencies. There appears to be no agreement on overtime payments nor holiday and sick pay benefits but, instead, the zero hour contracts will return. This may well be why the agreement that was negotiated with SIPTU in 2004 has not been implemented. Comfort Keepers is also gearing itself to the upper middle-class market by advertising the fact that customers or their relatives can claim 42 per cent tax relief on their service (the relief for higher earners). Instead of a properly funded home care scheme the Irish state is again giving tax reliefs which disproportionately benefit the wealthier sections of society.

A similar pattern is evident in long-stay care for the elderly. Even though the vast majority want to stay at home, about 4 or 5 per cent of the population need a different option. The absence of 'step down' facilities in the Irish health service has meant that many stay longer in hospitals than are needed. This has led to a rather nasty focus by the press on 'bedblockers', which implies that older people are responsible for the A&E crisis. That crisis, however, has also focused state attention on the issue, but instead of developing a quality public service for the elderly it is once more resorting to the neo-liberal solution.

Over the past decades there has been an unspoken assumption in state circles that publicly-run long-stay facilities should not be expanded, but instead a greater reliance should be placed on the private sector.[67] Provision of public nursing home beds has fallen from 42 beds per thousand in 1968 to 23 beds per

TABLE 7.1
BEDS BY CATEGORIES OF LONG STAY ACCOMMODATION: VARIOUS YEARS

Year	Health Board/HSE Geriatric Homes	Health Board/HSE Welfare Homes	Health Board/HSE District	Voluntary Geriatric Homes/Hospitals Community Hospitals	Private Nursing Homes	Total
1985	7,275	1,506	N/a	3,197	3,091	15,069
1996	6,126	1,056	2,391	3,786	6,209	19,568
2000	5,646	740	2,415	2,236	7,272	18,309
2003	5,340	866	2,567	2,717	11,269	22,759
2004	6,135	1,280	N/a	2,954	9,042	19,411

Source: Department of Health, Health Statistics, various years.

thousand in 2001.[68] Some of this was due to the closure of large psychiatric institutions but there is also a wider state policy at work. Table 7.1 illustrates the pattern whereby the provision of public beds has declined while the number of beds in private nursing homes has trebled. Tax changes brought about a new surge of interest in this sector, because new tax reliefs allowed the capital costs of nursing homes to be written off over a seven-year period. Nursing homes started to sprout up all over the country – regardless of whether they served areas of urgent need or how they integrated with local health systems.

In the US, the private nursing homes are seen as big business. William Floyd, chair of the largest US chain, Beverly Enterprises, claims that providing nursing care is not all that different from selling at Taco Bell, a fast food chain where he was previously an executive.[69] Both rely on low paid employees, and as a consequence experience high staff turnover. The nursing home 'industry', however, also has its unique set of problems because it often relies on public service contracts and sometimes shows an over-enthusiastic urge to milk them dry. Beverly Enterprises itself had to pay the federal government €175 million to settle a fraud allegation.

The evidence from Britain, Australia and the US indicates that care in private nursing homes is an inferior service in a host of areas. Overall, about one fifth of residents die in nursing homes in the US, but patients in private homes receive less palliative care and experience higher levels of untreated pain.[70] One of the reasons is that the homes do not employ a range of specialist medical staff with diverse skills but often rely on one general nurse. A US study which analyzed the inspection reports of 13,693 nursing facilities showed those owned by investors had a 47 per cent higher level of measurable deficiencies than non-profit homes.[71] Staffing levels in for-profit care tend to be about 20 per cent less than in not-for-profit institutions, and there is typically one nurse for every thirty-two patients and one care assistant for every twelve.[72] Patients in for-profit homes experience a higher risk of infection and one review of the literature even suggested that care in as many as one third of US for-profit homes could jeopardize health.[73] Studies in Britain indicate that drug therapies in private nursing homes are not subject to adequate scrutiny and there may also be an overuse of pyschotropic drugs and an inferior medication review[74] In Australia, Braithwaite found that the quality of care was lower in private for-profit nursing homes because of pressures to generate profit.[75]

In these three countries (US, UK and Australia), there are strong neo-liberal currents, but pressure from the wider society had produced a more transparent regulatory regime. In Ireland, however, there is neo-liberalism and a weak regulatory regime. So weak in fact that one dedicated Fine Gael TD, Fergus O' Dowd, has had to send in freedom of information requests on a regular basis just to get inspection reports. By the time he overcame objections to disclosure, the reports are as much as four years old.

Inspections are supposed to take place once every two years, but sometimes the visits only occur once a year. There appear to be no inspections at night-time or at weekends, and the focus tends to be on the physical layout, basic hygiene and fire regulations. There are few reported conversations with the elderly residents themselves to ascertain their views about the quality of care. Despite the limited nature of the regulations, there are breaches, particularly in relations to contracts of care and the maintenance of medical records. Yet few sanctions are taken against the operators. Between 2000 and 2005, for example, there were 126 breaches of medical and nursing regulations and 32 breaches of contracts of care regulations at Galway's nursing homes. Yet in every one of the cases, the follow-up action was reported to be 'verbal advice at inspection followed up by written report'. The worst sanction that any home received was an extra inspection.[76]

Up to now the nursing home sector appears as a small cottage industry. The largest is Mowlan Healthcare, which currently has ten properties and had one of its newest facilities in Moate, Co Westmeath opened by Finance Minister Brian Cowen. Two property developers, who previously benefited from tax breaks on holiday homes, own the company. The other main operator is Silver Stream Health, which has six homes and appears to offer a more holistic approach to care. However, in other countries this fragmented cottage industry tends to give way to larger corporate chains. Waiting in the wings is the large Barchester group controlled by Dermot Desmond, J.P. McManus and John Magnier. This company is already the third largest operator in Britain with a chain of over 170 homes. Its founders made their fortunes in property and horses and benefited considerably from tax breaks. When companies like Barchester finally start buying up other nursing homes, the corporate takeover of the aged will have begun in earnest. The scandalous treatment of older people was dramatically highlighted by the Leas Cross report. In a scathing indictment of state policy, Professor Des O'Neill pointed to 'institutional abuse' at the North Dublin nursing home but warned that

> it would be a very major error to presume that the deficits in care shown in Leas Cross represent an isolated incident. Rather given the lack of structure, funding, standards and oversight, they are likely to be replicated to a greater or lesser extent in institutions throughout the long term care system in the county.[77]

He noted that a policy of privatising the residential care sector had occurred without any public debate, even though it 'may have important consequences for the health of older people in residential care'.[78] One of the reasons was that the levels of qualified nursing staff in private nursing homes was approximately half that of the public sector.[79]

NOTES

1. E. Donnellan, 'No Drop in MRSA Infection Rates in Hospitals'. *Irish Times*, 5 July 2006.

2. E. Donnelan, 'Call for Mandatory Reporting of Hospital Infections'. *Irish Times*, 7 June 2005.
3. Donnelan, 'No drop in MRSA Infection Rates in Hospitals'.
4. C. Newman, 'MRSA raises Concerns about Basic Standards says Minister'. *Irish Times*, 7 December 2004.
5. C.C. Kibber, A.Quick and A.M. O Neill, 'The Effects of Increased Bed Numbers on MRSA Transmission in Acute Medical Wards'. *Journal of Hospital Infection*, 39, 3 (July 1998), pp.213–19.
6. M.A. Borg, 'Bed Occupancy and Overcrowding as Determinant Factors in the Incidence of MRSA Infections within General Ward Settings'. *Journal of Hospital Infection*, 54, 4 (August 2003), pp.316–18.
7. J.B. Cunningham, W.G. Kernohan and T. Rush, 'Bed Occupancy, Turnover Intervals and MRSA in English Hospitals'. *British Journal of Nursing*, 15, 12 (12 June 2006), pp.656–62.
8. A. Dale Tussing and M. Wren, *How Ireland Cares: The Case for Health Care Reform* (Dublin: New Island, 2006), p.85.
9. E. Donnellan, 'Hygiene Standards Inadequate in 91% of Hospitals'. *Irish Times*, 4 November 2005.
10. Press Release of Liz McManus TD on 'Harney Presiding over Deterioration of Health Services', 25 October 2005.
11. M. Wren, *Unhealthy State* (Dublin: New Island, 2003), p.77.
12. M. Wren, 'Health Spending and the Black Hole'. *ESRI Quarterly Economic Commentary*, Autumn 2004, pp.1–23.
13. Quoted in M. Draekord, *Privatisation and Social Policy* (Harlow: Longman, 2000), p.118.
14. R. Barrington, *Health Medicine and Politics* (Dublin: Institute of Public Administration, 1987), Chap.9.
15. Wren, *Unhealthy State*, p.61.
16. Wren, *Unhealthy State*, p.11.
17. See *Trading Health Care Away? GATS, Public Services and Privatisation*, (Dorset: Corner House publications, 2001), p.19.
18. D. Osborne and T. Gaebler, *Reinventing Government* (Boston, MA: Addison-Wesley, 1992).
19. C. Leys, *Market Driven Politics* (London: Verso, 2001), pp.189–90.
20. P. Yamin and R. Dreyfus, 'The Godfather of Managed Competition'. *Mother Jones*, May–June 1993, pp.8–10.
21. H. Waitzkin and C. Iriart, 'How the United States Exports Managed Care to Developing Countries', in V. Navarro and C. Muntaner (Eds), *Political and Economic Determinants of Population Health and Well Being: Controversaries and Developments* (New York: Baywood, 2004), pp.147–54.
22. S. Wollhandler, T. Campbell and D. Himmelstein, 'Costs of Health Care Administration in the United States and Canada'. *New England Journal of Medicine*, 349, 8 (21 August 2003), pp.768–75.
23. A. Maynard, 'Reforming the NHS', in M. Bishop, J. Kay and C. Mayers (eds), *The Regulatory Challenge* (Oxford: Oxford University Press, 1995), pp.67–83.
24. C. Webster, *The National Health Service: A Political History* (Oxford: Oxford University Press, 1998), p.203.
25. M. Fitzgerald, 'The Lack of Competition and its Impact on the Supply of Acute Healthcare', in R. Kinsella (ed.), *Acute Healthcare in Transition in Ireland* (Dublin: Oak Tree, 2003), p.57.
26. DOHC Press Release, 'Casemix Budget Adjustments', 16 January 2006.
27. Prospectus, *Audit of Structures and Functions in the Health System* (Dublin: Stationary Office, 2003), p.80.
28. Ibid., p.87.
29. Ibid., p.97.
30. Address by Sean Barrett to Progressive Democrat Conference, 2005.
31. *Commission on Financial Management and Control Systems in the Health Service*

(Dublin: Government Publications, 2003), p.49.
32. Ibid., p.84.
33. 'Health Service gets sick feeling as Halligan takes tonic away'. *Irish Examiner*, 16 November 2004.
34. Ibid.
35. IPHA, 'The Benefits of IPHA Membership', www.ipha.ie.
36. Comptroller and Auditor General, *Car Parking at Beaumont Hospital* (Dublin: Government Publications, 2002), p.2.
37. Comptroller and Auditor, *General Waste Management in Hospitals* (Dublin: Government Publications, 2005), p.9.
38. Comptroller and Auditor, *Development of a Human Resource Management System for the Health Service* (Dublin: Government Publications, 2005), pp.47–8.
39. Ibid., p.47.
40. Ibid., p.55.
41. Ibid., p.54.
42. Ibid., p.12.
43. P. O Grady, *Why is the Irish Health Service in Crisis?* (Dublin: Bookmarks, 2005).
44. Dáil Debates, Vol. 562, 5 March 2003.
45. Letter from Mary Harney to Liam Downey, Chairperson of HSE, 14 July 2005.
46. Ibid.
47. P. Higgins, 'Tax Breaks attract Healthcare Investors'. *Sunday Business Post*, 24 July 2005.
48. Ibid.
49. Ibid.
50. J. Mansman, 'Private Healthcare Opportunities for Ireland'. Powerpoint Presentation, National Private Health Care Conference, 5 April 2006 www.privatehealth.ie.
51. N. Callanan, 'Building Kingpin looks East'. *Sunday Business Post*, 15 June 2003.
52. 'Beacon Plan Four More Hospitals'. *Sunday Business Post*, 5 December 2005.
53. D. Price, A. Pollock and J. Shaoul, 'How the World Trade Organisation is Shaping Domestic Policies in Health Care'. *The Lancet*, 354, 9193 (27 November 1999), pp.1889–92.
54. J.M. Watt, R. Derzon, S. Renn, C. Schram, J. Hahn and G. Pillari, 'The Comparative Economic Performance of Investor Owned Chain and Not-For Profit Hospitals'. *New England Journal of Medicine*, 314, 2 (1986), pp.89–96.
55. R. Pattison and H. Katz, 'Investor Owned and Not-For Profit Hospitals'. *New England Journal of Medicine*, 309, 6 (1983), pp.347–53.
56. E. Silverman, J. Skinner and E. Fisher, 'The Association between For Profit Hospital Ownership and Increased Medicare Spending'. *New England Journal of Medicine*, 341, 6 (August 1999), pp.420–5.
57. P.J. Devereaux, P. Choi, C. Lacchetti, B. Weaver, H. Schunemann, T. Haines, J. Lavis, B. Grant, D. Haslam, M. Bhandari, T. Sullivan, D. Cook, S. Walyer, M. Meade, H. Khan, N. Bhatnagar and G. Guyatt, 'A Systematic Review and Meta-analysis of Studies Comparing Mortality Rates of Private For Profit and Private Not For Profit Hospitals'. *Canadian Medical Association Journal*, 166, 11 (28 May 2002), pp.1399–1406.
58. D. Himmelstein, S. Wollhandler, I. Hellander and S. Wolfe, 'Quality of care in Investor-Owned vs Not-for-Profit HMOs'. *Journal of American Medical Association*, 282, 2 (14 July 1999), pp.59–163.
59. P. Krugman and R. Wells, 'The Health Care Crisis and What to do About It'. *New York Review of Books*, 53, 5 (23 March 2006).
60. Goodbody Stockbrokers, Opportunities for Private Investment in the Irish Healthcare Sector: Presentation to the IPHA 12th Annual Members Meeting, September 2005.
61. Tussing and Wren, *How Ireland Cares*, p.157.
62. P. Murphy, 'This is no Country for old men: Older People in the Republic of Ireland'. Age Action Briefing paper, 2 June 2004.
63. SIPTU Press Release, 23 March 2006.

64. Written reply to Parliamentary Question from HSE to Liz McManus, 4 October 2005.
65. 'Comfort Keepers bring "Comfort" to Ireland'. *Bizjournals*, 19 December 2005.
66. 'Master Your Future as a Brand Builder'. *Irish Franchise*, May 2006.
67. I. Mangan, *Older People in Long Stay Care* (Dublin: Irish Human Rights Commission, 2003), p.3.
68. IMO position paper, 'Care of the Elderly' (Dublin: IMO, 2006), p.4.
69. R. Abelson, 'Bringing Discipline (and Scorecards) to Nursing Homes'. *New York Times*, 7 July 2002.
70. J. Zerzan, S. Stearns and L. Hanson, 'Access to Palliative Care and Hospice in Nursing Homes', *Journal of American Medical Association*, 284, 19 (15 November 2000), pp.2489–94.
71. C. Harrington, S. Woolhandler, J. Mullan, H. Carrillo and D. Himmelstein, 'Does Investor-Ownership of Nursing Homes compromise the Quality of Care'. *International Journal of Health Sciences*, 32, 2 (2002), pp.315–25.
72. C. Harrington, C. Kovner, M. Mezey, J. Kayser-Jones, S. Burger and M. Mohler, 'Experts Recommend Minimum Nurse Staffing Standards for Nursing Facilities in the United States'. *Gerontologist*, 40, 1 (2000), pp.5–16.
73. C. Harrington, 'Residential Nursing Facilities in the United States'. *British Journal of Medicine*, 323, 7311 (1 September 2001), pp.507–10.
74. See A. Turrell, 'Nursing Homes: A Suitable Alternative to Hospital Care for Older People in the UK'. *Age and Aging*, 30, S3, pp.24–32.
75. J. Braithwaite, 'Regulating Nursing Homes: The Challenge of Regulating Care for Older People in Australia'. *British Journal of Medicine*, 323, 7310 (25 August 2001), pp.443–6.
76. Written reply to Parliamentary Question by Fergus O'Dowd, Ref Q2005-4440.
77. D. O'Neill, *A Review of the Deaths at Leas Cross Nursing Home 2002–2005* (Dublin: HSE 2006), pp.5–6.
78. Ibid., p.22.
79. Ibid., p.64.

Chapter Eight

Green or Gold

Ireland has a wonderful green landscape. Its climate, while occasionally wet, is warmed by the Gulf Stream and has a particular mildness. In one of those cunning tricks of history, its environment benefited from missing out on the Industrial Revolution. There are few decaying smoke stacks, and past underdevelopment has given rural areas a low population density. You can still drive for miles in parts of east Galway or south Leitrim and see nothing but green foliage and the occasional passer-by. What more could a country want for when it came to the environment!

Yet the political elite are blowing it. Between 1998 and 2003, Ireland had the second highest level of complaints brought against any country by the EU Commission for breaches of environmental directives.[1] One of the most common complaints related to water quality. E coli has been found in some group water systems, and in one appalling case an animal burial plot was located near a source of groundwater in Mayo. In a terrible indictment, the normally mild mannered EU Commission noted that

> Many Irish water supplies are contaminated by bacteria, the principal cause of which are land spreading of animal wastes and leaking domestic water treatment systems. Ireland is attempting to deal with the public health risk by devoting community and Irish tax payer resources to investments in chlorination and other forms of disinfection of contaminated water sources. However, more needs to be done to protect these sources from becoming polluted in the first place.[2]

Nine separate European Court of Justice judgements were registered against Ireland between 1993 and 2004. The following are an example of the types of judgements: a lack of proper procedures for major accident hazards concerning dangerous substances; a failure to monitor the pollution of shellfish – there are hundreds of commercial shellfish operations but only a minority had been designated under EU directives; a failure to tackle illegal dumping of waste; the non-provision of proper information on the transport of waste abroad. Ireland, according to the court, was guilty of 'general and persistent' flouting of EU rules on waste disposal.[3]

One issue in particular shows the Irish government's callous approach – its attitude to global warming. Despite the best efforts of George Bush and US business interests, few now doubt the dangers that global warming pose to the planet. The unusually hot summers and the more common occurrence of extreme weather conditions bear adequate testimony to the phenomenon. While the response of international governments has been painfully slow, they finally, against enormous opposition from US energy interests, agreed a Kyoto protocol that promises to reduce emissions to defined targets. For the EU as a whole, the target was set at a modest 8 per cent below 1990 levels to be achieved between 2008–12. While these figures were being negotiated, Ireland was regarded as an underdeveloped country and so the EU allowed it to increase its emissions to 13 per cent *above* its 1990 level. This was done in an effort to overcome regional disparities in industrial growth.

Ireland, however, has failed abysmally to meet its target, overshooting it so dramatically that, on current estimates, greenhouse gas emissions are 23 per cent over the 1990 baseline level.[4] It has the highest level of emissions of green-house gases per head of the population in the EU.[5] Closer inspection of the figures show that the increases are mainly attributable to transport and industry, while emissions from residential homes and farms have actually declined.

Ireland went 'car crazy' during the Celtic Tiger years. The number of cars virtually doubled from 1 million in 1990 to just under 2 million in 2003 – as did the amount of C02 emissions. This little island became the most car dependent country on the planet, overtaking even the US for the average number of kilometres clocked up each year. Only 8.5 per cent of the population took a bus, a train or a DART to work and two thirds went by car.[6] Most, however, didn't do so from choice. Who, in their right mind, would want to sit in Ireland's notorious traffic jams? Or join a queue to contribute generously to the fortunes of National Toll Roads? The majority of people were forced into cars by the systematic under-funding of public transport. In a survey conducted by the Central Statistics Office, 80 per cent said they took a car because public transport was either not available, impractical or did not go to their destination.[7] Very few people said they preferred private cars. One group, however, who might possibly have expressed a preference for transport by private car were the owners of the gas guzzling SUVs that spew out 300,000 tons of emissions each year.

The Irish government did little to counter these trends. In October 2000 it drew up a document on a National Climate Change Strategy that proposed a number of measures to tackle the problem,[8] before moving to abandon virtually every one. The document proposed taxes on carbon emissions – but that was scrapped because it might affect business 'competitiveness'. It proposed a higher motor tax on fuel inefficient cars – but the government dropped that and then resisted an EU proposal to encourage more energy-efficient fuels. It could not even bring itself to tax SUVs because it claims that they are too hard to define for tax purposes.[9]

The original climate change strategy document suggested the introduction of regulations for better insulated houses from 2002. However, in deference to the Irish cement industry, these regulations were relaxed to allow the use of hollow blocks to continue for some time longer. The result was that nearly 300,000 more houses were built according to older, less efficient standards.[10] The only measure accepted by the state was an emission trading system that allows Ireland to buy pollution slots from poorer countries that cannot use their own quotas. It is a non-solution which will cost the Irish people €1 billion over five years. Valuable resources that could have alleviated, for example, the bed crisis in hospitals will literally go up in smoke.

It is sometimes assumed that environmental concerns are incompatible with 'modernity' and industrialization. Proponents of this view often see nature in spiritual terms and criticize modern society for turning its back on emotion and the soul. However, starting from this premise, you can do little except advocate personal choice. So a 'change of lifestyle' is recommended whereby the individual becomes an 'ethical consumer' or assumes personal responsibility by not taking airplanes or eating agricultural produce imported from thousands of miles away. While one can respect such individual decisions, the danger is that they simply dovetail with the dominant neo-liberal strategy to deflect the blame onto the individual. Instead of focussing on societal structures, it is assumed that individuals always have 'choices', and should be castigated for not being moral enough to exercise them. However, as we have seen in the survey about cars, some people simply do not have these much-vaunted choices. No matter how many moral admonitions are administered, people who need to get to work, or parents who need to get children to crèches, will take cars simply because they have to. The moralist, therefore, paints him or herself into a circle of despair.

Instead of blaming 'modernity' or 'industrialization', it may be more fruitful to look at how our society is unique in its irrational drive to accumulate for the sake of accumulation. To survive in the marketplace, large corporations have to make profits in order to reinvest to make more profits in order to reinvest and so on. The whole process is coincidental with, rather than dependent on, human need. The unplanned nature of the market means that resources are grabbed quickly with little thought for sustainability. Individual corporations are not obliged to pay much attention to the harmful environmental side effects of their products, as they do not always pay the cost.[11] Calls for more controls are resisted because each corporation can imagine a rival who can escape regulation and so undercut them.

In newly industrializing economies, these larger processes are compacted into a much shorter timeframe. The result is, as writers have remarked about the Asian Tigers, that 'export industrialisation has telescoped into three decades processes of environmental destruction that took many more years to unfold in earlier industrialising countries'.[12] It could have been a description of the Celtic Tiger, albeit with a slightly quicker timescale. The decade-long boom produced a rush for raw materials, infrastructure and labour that were sourced in ways that showed little concern for the environment. Talk of sustainability and heritage is the last thing that the Irish construction boss wants to hear when there is money to be made from a property boom. The state's ethos of 'lite' regulation meant that nothing has been allowed to stand in the way of 'competitiveness'. On the surface, of course, there was a show of compliance to EU environmental standards as the presentation of development plans were cloaked in the rhetoric of sustainability and environmental sensitivity but the underlying ethos remained the cutting of corners and the minimization of pressure on business.

However the core question still remains unanswered. How exactly did those officially charged with protecting the environment fail? What exactly was the Environmental Protection Agency doing?

THE ENVIRONMENTAL PROTECTION AGENCY

The EPA was formed in 1993 in response to a wave of disillusionment with the pharmaceutical corporations. These corporations had come to Ireland from the 1970s onwards to benefit not only from low taxes, but also to enjoy the large quantities of unpolluted groundwater and lax environmental controls. The country was seen as a 'pollution haven' because IDA officials could hold meetings with local officials to suggest a relaxation of environmental controls.[13] However, a backlash had set in by the late 1980s. In 1988, the Supreme Court found that Merck, Sharp and Dohme were responsible for the deaths of 200 cattle at the farm of John Hanrahan at Ballydine in Co. Tipperary. A year later a protracted campaign of street protests and planning appeals forced Merrell Dow to abandon plans to open a site in Killeagh in East Cork. Complaints about ill health and ecological damage grew around the Cork harbour area where many pharmaceutical corporations had located. A promise to conduct an epidemiological study was granted by the Minister for Health, but then subsequently withdrawn.[14] The growing controversies threatened to drive multinationals away. The Environment Minister, Mary Harney, decided to act.

Harney was also aware of the growing avalanche of EU directives designed to clean up the environment. Her strategy was to depoliticize the conflicts by making concerted efforts to eclipse the contentious political issues at stake with a purely administrative response through the establishment of a new agency, the Environmental Protection Agency. It was a strategy that would be repeated ten years later with the formation of the Health Services Executive. The 'independent' nature of such agencies creates a shield for politicians and shifts discussion onto a highly technical realm.[15] If there was any doubt about Harney's intention, it should have been dispelled when she gave Merck, Sharp and Dohme a 'good environmental management award' in 1992 – the same year in which she brought in legislation to set up the EPA.[16]

The particular mandate and function ascribed to the EPA ensured that corporations had little to fear. The agency is not explicitly required to accept full responsibility for pollution impacts on human health. A proposal in 2002 from the Department of Health, that Environmental Health Impact Assessments should be submitted for new projects, was never accepted.[17] The agency has no medical or epidemiological expertise to make decisions relating to public health, and instead relies on general standards issued by the EU or the World Health Organisation. Corporate lobbyists, and scientists sponsored by them, however, play a major role in negotiations on these standards.[18]

The agency receives a modest grant – €24 million from the state in 2004 – that represents 75 per cent of its income. The remaining funds come from fees earned from issuing Integrated Pollution Prevention Control (IPPC) and waste licences. These meagre resources mean that it often relies on self-monitoring of emissions by corporations. It can make its own unannounced visits, but these can be quite limited. The data on regular discharges from a particular factory often comes from monitoring machines maintained by its owners. The ethos of the EPA is, therefore, to encourage voluntary compliance rather than strict enforcement of regulations.

Some environmentalists originally welcomed the Integrated Pollution Prevention Control licence system because it seemed to offer a more holistic approach to pollution.[19] However, it soon became apparent that a different agenda was at work. By using site-specific licences, the EPA did not have to promulgate absolute standards or emissions levels for many items. Instead, they could take the economic circumstances of the operator into account in deciding acceptable levels of emissions at particular sites. Before a licence is issued, the EPA also engages in a dialogue with the applicant. The content of these discussions is, by and large, not available to the public. Once a licence has been granted, there is no independent process for appeal and the EPA sits in judgement on itself.

The agency is the sole body entitled to initiate criminal prosecutions. But it is only entitled itself to bring cases to the District Court and in other cases it must refer matters to the DPP. This is particularly important because the fines that can be imposed by the District Court are quite small for any substantial business. This explains why the EPA fines on companies who breach their regulations are so derisory.

One of the stranger characteristics of the Irish system is the phenomenon of project splitting. An Bord Pleanála is responsible for adjudicating on planning permissions, but is not supposed to take potential environmental pollution into account. So a large project like Masonite in Leitrim, where there were huge concerns about pollution, can first secure planning permission to build the facility by bracketing off the question of a pollution licence until later. However, once the pollution issue has been removed from the equation, it is easier to get planning permission and this, in turn, puts pressure on the EPA to grant some sort of IPCC licence. There are very few projects, if any, which have received planning permission and then have been refused a pollution control licence from the EPA.

Most of these institutional processes help to produce a soft regulatory approach to business. However, in an extraordinary move, the state has gone one step further and appointed individuals who have had close ties with business to the five-person board of the EPA. In 2002, Dr Mary Kelly, the former assistant director of IBEC's environmental unit, was appointed director general of the EPA. The IBEC environmental unit played a key role in lobbying for measures favoured by business interests. Dr Kelly worked for seven years with IBEC and played an active role in these lobbying practices. She was involved in the organization of the IBEC 'excellence awards' for green practices where companies such as Intel, Masonite and Merck, Sharp and Dohme won prizes.[20]

Two years after Dr Mary Kelly's appointment, Laura Burke,

who had worked as a project manager for Indaver, was appointed to the EPA board. She had played a key role in seeking permission for incinerators in Carranstown and Ringaskiddy. As part of her job to promote the benefits of incineration, she presented a powerpoint presentation where she claimed that less than 15 per cent of ash from incinerators is 'mildly hazardous'.[21] She also quoted the World Health Organisation's claim that 'it is perfectly possible to locate plants near densely populated areas'.[22] Laura Burke was appointed to the EPA while the agency was considering an application from her former company to build an incinerator in Ringaskiddy. The conflict of interest appeared so blatant that she absented herself from that particular decision.

Statistics on the EPA's activity also indicate an extremely soft attitude to business. A small number of audits are conducted, but they show a fairly high level of non-compliance. One reason for low compliance rates may be located in the fact that companies have little to fear from prosecutions or the tiny fines issued on conviction. Between 2001 and 2005, Irish industry paid less than €50,000 in total in fines in any one year, as Table 8.1 indicates. The average fines received by individual companies were less than €3,000 and that was for all sorts of offences. Yet during this same period Ireland developed an appalling record on pollution.

One particular case illustrates very clearly the leniency shown to large corporations. In 2002, the Belgium authorities notified their Irish counterparts that a hormone product, medroxyprogesterone acetate (MPA), had contaminated pig food. The source of the infection was traced to a Wyeth facility in Newbridge, Co. Kildare. The EPA sent inspectors on site and the individual inspectors did a thorough job.[23] They showed that, since November 1999, Wyeth and a waste management company,

TABLE 8.1: EPA AUDITS, COMPLIANCE RECORD AND PROSECUTIONS

	Number of Audits	Number of Prosecutions	Total Fines on all Industry	Average Fine Imposed
2005	173	17	€44,000	€2,588
2004	271	16	€32768	€2,048
2003	191	18	€40285	€2,238
2002	126	17	€40285	€2,370
2001	59	40	£64775	£1,619

Source: EPA Annual Reports and website list of prosecution various years.

Cara Environmental Technology, had been shipping wastewater from the Kildare plant to a Belgian company, Bioland. Bioland produced animal feed and used the sugary substance to fatten the pigs. The waste, however, was wrongly labelled 'green waste' when it should have been either 'amber' or 'red'. If it had belonged to either of the latter two categories, it would have had to be notified to the EPA.

From July 2000, the hazardous substance MPA was added to the wastewater stream and the shipments continued under the 'green' label. The hormone found its way into the pig feed that was distributed throughout Europe, giving rise to concerns about infertility in human beings. If ever a company had broken the terms of its IPPC licence, then this was it. But what was done? According to the EPA, the matter was 'referred to the Director of Public Prosecutions' but their subsequent records do not indicate any prosecutions.[24] It was only in January 2007 that newspaper reports indicate that Wyeth was asked to appear in Naas District court, but the company sought an injunction to stop the charges.

The pattern of light regulation on corporations can be illustrated in three other cases. In 2005, the EPA tested water near Leap castle in Co. Offaly and found that it contained a potentially cancerous chemical that was 50 times over the allowable limit. The chemical was chromium, a toxic substance used to treat timber, and the source of the discharge was Standish Sawmills.[25] A similar substance had featured in the film, Erin Brockovich, that told of one woman's fight against the pollution of groundwater in California. It was not the first time that such discharges had occurred in Co. Offaly, much to the consternation of the sawmill's neighbours. Yet, even though the EPA prosecuted the firm in Roscrea District Court, it simultaneously decided to grant the company a new pollution control licence. Its own technical committee advised against granting a renewed licence because of a history of non-compliance, but the Board of the EPA decided otherwise.[26] As if to compound matters, An Bord Pleanála also granted planning permission for the sawmill even though one of its own inspectors had also recommended against it. Some residents drew a fairly dark conclusion about the role of the state authorities, concluding that 'the law, particularly its enforcement side, took a negative attitude to us, to say the least'.[27]

The highest fine ever imposed on a firm was on Schwarz

Pharma, whom the EPA took to court in February 2006. The firm pleaded guilty to discharging emissions of a cancer-causing substance, dichloromethane (DCM), that were thirty-five times over the legal limit. It was fined €110,000 and forced to pay costs of €42,359, after the EPA carried out an investigation.[28] The judge had refused to hear the case in the district court and it was referred upwards to the circuit court because of the company's history of non-compliance. In 2003, the same company had also been fined because of emissions that left a strong powerful odour in the area. It took 450 people to issue separate complaints for legal action to be mounted.[29] In 2000, seven employees were injured in three separate explosions at the same plant.[30] The case raised questions about why the company was able to get away with this type of activity for so long. Many residents also wanted the agency to conduct epidemiological studies to ascertain the effect on people's health. The state's response amounted to nothing more than rapping the knuckles of a repeat offender.

The other case concerns Intel, one of the largest multinationals in Ireland and one that assiduously promotes a green image. Despite such images, however, the high tech industry uses highly toxic and hazardous substances in production. One leading industrial analyst, Jan Mazurek, noted that 'chip plants use, emit and transport a host of constantly shifting substances that are known to be among the most toxic used in contemporary industrial production'.[31] These plants also require a high intensity of water usage that can have implications for the surrounding area. As Intel expanded operations in New Mexico, for example, water tables dropped by as much as 10 feet per year in some areas as a result of over-pumping.[32] Given this background, it might be assumed that the EPA would employ a strong regulatory hand.

Unfortunately, the evidence suggests otherwise. An in-depth comprehensive study by Eoghan Meagher on Intel's compliance record with its pollution control licence raises important questions about the role of the EPA. Meagher started by investigating why the town of Leixlip had twice the concentration of sulphur dioxide in its atmosphere compared to similar towns such as Athy, Celbridge, Naas or Newbridge in the period between 1994 and 2000. The level of SO2 in the atmosphere breached EU limits on several occasions but no satisfactory explanation was given as to why. Matters improved after 2000 but the town still experiences higher levels than neighbouring towns. Meagher concentrated his investigations on two years, 1996 and 1998, and examined the official explanations offered by authorities. Kildare County Council explicitly claimed that there was no evidence to link these concentrations to the Intel plant, and suggested that increased traffic was to blame. However, the highest levels of emissions tended to be in the summer months when traffic was lower. The EPA suggested that the results might be attributed to faulty monitoring equipment, but tests carried out on the equipment failed to specify the faults. Despite lack of cooperation from Intel, the EPA and Kildare County Council, Meagher conducted a detailed examination of wind patterns in the area and examined the precise Integrated Pollution Control licence that Intel held.

He found that the most potent substance that Intel emitted was hydrogen fluoride gas (HF), but the company claims that it could not measure these emissions because no monitoring equipment was available at reasonable cost. The result was that neither the EPA nor Intel held data on such emissions. HF is five times stronger than SO_2, and could be confused with it. The EPA had allowed Intel to build new emission points that had the cumulative effect of increasing HF emissions. Looking at the wind patterns in the area at the times of high recorded emissions, Meagher suggested that the monitoring equipment in Leixlip might be picking up both SO_2 and HF emissions, and this might account for the higher levels.[33]

Meagher's study also pointed to another vital gap in the Irish system of pollution control – the absence of data that would allow for full-scale examination of emissions on public health. Morbidity data on respiratory illness is only provided on a county basis rather than at the level of small area statistics that might cover all or part of Leixlip. Using the available data, Meagher detected a rise in respiratory illnesses in Kildare that went against the national trends for the particular years at issue in his study. But as he was unable to access smaller area data he could not explore the issue further. All of which, however, raises questions about the role of the EPA. If it is to be about more than reconciling people's concern for the environment with the demands of business for greater 'competitiveness', then surely it needs to conduct epidemiological research in the locations where pollutions licences are granted. That, however, would imply a major change of direction. It would mean unequivocally establishing human health as the agency's first priority and developing an ethos of organized distrust about firms seeking pollution control licences.

THE WASTE MOUNTAIN

The political elite's attitude to environmental concerns came back to haunt them in the waste crisis that hit the Celtic Tiger. Up to 1996, waste was mainly disposed of in poorly regulated landfill sites. There were approximately 120 such sites dotted around the country, many of them receiving relatively small amounts of waste. A survey conducted by the EU Commission in 1994, found that only 40 per cent of the sites had liners underneath them or leachate collection systems.[34] Leachate is the toxic liquid that is formed when the rubbish comes in contact with water and, if not siphoned off, it can leak into nearby groundwater.[35] The fact that the Irish state did not, however, monitor public health patterns in areas where the poorly regulated landfill sites were situated, ensured that such a major problem would never be made manifest.

In 1996, a new law was passed in response to EU directives, the Waste Management Act. This required the owners of landfill sites to obtain a licence and bring all sites up to a minimum standard. However, the vast majority of owners – including public authorities – decided that cost of upgrading was prohibitive and closed sites instead. Over the next six years, a 70 per cent reduction in the number of landfills took place, leaving only thirty functioning by 2004.[36] By that time, however, the amount of waste being produced was also growing dramatically as the construction industry boomed and many more people were buying consumer goods. In a market driven economy, the only response to high demand and declining supply is a major hike in prices. And this is precisely what happened. The cost of landfill gate charges jumped from €10 per tonne in 1996 to €240 in 2004.[37]

Given this extraordinary development, a rational response might be to adopt a strategy of reduction and recycling. 70 per cent of all waste is agricultural waste and the bulk of non-agricultural waste comes from construction. The state could have pressurized these sectors to reduce their output by adopting different production and disposal methods. The technology of segregating stone and concrete from construction waste, for example, is well established and the material can be re-used in roads, drainage and other building projects.

The state, however, focused on individual households as if they were the main producers of waste. Contrary to popular perception, however, only a tiny proportion of Ireland's waste comes from households. In 2004, for example, household waste accounted for only 1.7 million tonnes of the 85 million tonne waste mountain.[38] Yet, even here, there could have been improvements if there had been a strong policy to force retailers to cut back on unnecessary packaging. Ireland generates the highest level of packaging waste per head of population in the EU – producing, for example, 214 kilograms per head of the population compared to 100 kg per head in Greece.[39]

Even in the absence of such policies, there was huge scope for recycling. In 1995, for example, Ireland was only recycling 15 per cent of its waste compared to the Netherlands which recycled 73 per cent.[40] This low recycling rate may be attributed in significant part to the dearth of recycling facilities. Since then there have been improvements, but it is still totally inadequate. A serious recycling system would require investment in the necessary infrastructure in order to facilitate the reuse of much of the material. At a minimum, that would require the provision of waste units in housing estates for tin, paper, plastics and organic waste. Some of this investment could be recovered if local authorities collected the segregated waste, such as paper, and resold it. But this would still have required an expansion of local authority employment and a reversal of those policies intended to effect a much diminished public services sector.

The Irish political elite, however, took the opposite approach. They first turned a blind eye to wholesale illegal dumping by business. They then used the waste crisis to legitimate the imposition of bin charges on individual households, creating, in the process, a new market for private operators.

They adopted a hypocritical moral stance about recycling as a way of blaming the individual – but created no serious infrastructure to enable meaningful recycling. As their final quick-fix solution, they pushed the discredited technology of incineration. In summary, they bowed once again to the corporate agenda.

ONE LAW FOR THE RICH

The first response of many businesses to the waste crisis was to engage in illegal dumping to avoid paying increased landfill prices. The biggest culprit, according to an EPA study, was the construction industry, but there was also significant dumping by wider commercial and industrial sectors between 1997 and 2002.[41] In 1998, one million tonnes of Dublin's 2.3 million tonnes of waste went missing. Even as late as 2004, sources within the industry told the *Irish Times* that between 500,000 and 750,000 tonnes of waste, or more than 10 per cent of the waste generated that year, had been disposed of illegally.[42] A number of different illegal methods were commonly used.

Illegal sites were initially operated within the Republic of Ireland, principally in Wicklow, where 100 sites were eventually identified. The first of these dumps was discovered at Coolnamadra, and then two further dumps were discovered at Whitestown. The former contained 8,000 tons of waste, including a significant quantity of hospital waste, while the latter two sites contained a staggering 480,000 tonnes of waste between them.[43] One of the extraordinary features of the Wicklow situation was the casualness with which council officials dealt with complaints. In 1998, for example, Wicklow County Council officials received a complaint from a Mr and Mrs Bailey about illegal dumping activity at Whitestown, but the council gave no response.[44] The Baileys then reported the matter to a local TD and an inspection was carried out, but nothing was found. Their letter, which purportedly contained the registration numbers of trucks using the site, was lost, and no other inspection was carried out for three and half years, even though the illegal activity continued throughout this time.

The failure of the EPA to act on hospital waste is particularly puzzling because, as Frank Corcoran of An Taisce explained:

I asked the senior person [in the EPA] why hazardous clinical waste can go missing when there is a fool-proof method in place called a C1 form – to track it. The form is filled out by the hospitals, the contractor and the local authority. It says where the waste is going, and the receipt goes there. The local authority that receives the C1 form, sends it away, every 28 February, to the EPA. I asked the EPA what it does when they see from the return from the local authority that hazardous waste has gone missing. They answered that they do not read the form.[45]

Given this type of carelessness, it is hardly surprising that business followed the lure of easy money. The gate fee for accepting 20 tonnes of hospital waste for deep burial in Fingal County Council in North Dublin was approximately €2,400 in 2001, whereas only €90 was charged at the illegal sites.[46]

One of the Ireland's largest corporations was implicated in illegal dumping activity in Wicklow when 110,000 tonnes of illegal waste was found at a Roadstone site in Blessington. The company, which is a subsidiary of Cement Roadstone Holdings (CRH), denied all knowledge but could not tell a Dáil committee exactly how it monitored traffic to and from its site. The Kerry TD, Jackie Healy Rae, who is not normally known as a scourge of large corporations, could hardly believe his ears.

It appears there are 650 acres involved here in Wicklow, and I am bamboozled to think that we have not been told clearly how many entrances there are to these sites. Is there a gateway at every entrance? Are they manned, as they are in remote parts of Kerry? I know the people manning the gates in Kerry. There are watchmen in place all day and night.[47]

CRH denied that the waste had contaminated the local water supply and received some support from the local council for this claim. The council refused to release records of water tests to the Irish Doctors' Environmental Group – a decision which even Dick Roche, the Minister for Environment and local TD, found 'totally unacceptable'.[48] An Taisce, however, persisted in making the connection and argued that simply adding chlorine to the water was not a solution. Eventually the EPA's Dr Mary Kelly acknowledged the problem, albeit in the most cautious of tones, when she said that 'the evidence we have is that there is contamination beginning to occur into the ground water from the site. However, it's moving at a very slow pace.'[49]

A three-year investigation was also conducted by members of the National Bureau of Criminal Investigation into dumping at the Roadstone site. It reported to the Director of Public Prosecutions, who decided not to press charges against the company, claiming that only those who 'knowingly' allowed illegal waste to be dumped on their land could be prosecuted. As the company did not 'knowingly' do so, it followed that it must be innocent. So despite evidence that public health had been endangered, not a single company director was arraigned before the courts. Coincidently, CRH had used the same 'we know nothing' defence about payments to the Ansbacher account organized from its head office, and faced no charges on that occasion either. In a belated move to impose some small sanction on this occasion, Environment Minister Dick Roche wrote to the local council, urging them not to buy land from Roadstone at another location while the company had outstanding planning issues. The council, however, cheekily replied that his own department had already approved the plan to buy Roadstone land.[50] It was a small symbolic indication of where the power really lay.

Having escaped prosecution, Roadstone somewhat incredibly then applied to the EPA for a licence to open a legal dump on the very site of its illegal activity. It argued that this was a more cost effective way to deal with the problem and engaged in extensive discussions with the EPA and Wicklow Council on the proposal. For a period it even looked as if they might get the licence. However, the revelations about the threat posed by their previous activities to water supplies, and a huge public campaign of opposition, eventually forced the hand of the EPA. The licence was not granted and the company was ordered to remove the waste. It seemed like a rare victory for local people until it was later revealed that the EPA had, in fact, permitted Roadstone to retain some of the waste on the site.

After the discovery of the illegal dumps in Wicklow, the focus of activity shifted to Northern Ireland. Some of the Republic's waste went to illegal sites within the six counties while, in other cases, the province was used as a transit point to take waste to

Scotland where landfill charges are one fifth of those in Ireland. About twenty illegal sites were discovered in Northern Ireland. At one stage during February and March 2004, the NI Department of Environment was finding between one and two illegal dumps every week near the border.[51] One site in Cookstown was found to have had waste from thirteen different southern counties, including Cork, 260 miles away. However, even after information was passed onto the relevant Southern authorities, no prosecutions ensued. An *Irish Times* investigation revealed that hauliers from Northern Ireland had lobbied waste contractors in the Republic for regular business and up to eight contractors in the Greater Dublin area had entered these arrangements.[52]

The EPA were aware of this activity but again did very little to stop it, claiming that 'the responsibility is mainly on the destination – it is up to them to refuse acceptance of the waste'.[53] Eventually it took a case against the Waterford Utilities Services company, who were fined €600 on seven counts and ordered to pay costs. Once again, however, this was a rather exceptional case. The Northern owner of the site, Tyrone Waste Re-Cycling, which had been used by the Waterford company, had already been convicted in the North on thirty-six separate counts of importing waste from the Republic. Local residents could not stand the plague of flies arising from the mounds of waste and pressurized the authorities to take action.[54]

'Waste tourism' is a term used to describe unscrupulous companies who dump hazardous waste on poorer African or Asian countries. The practice was made illegal under the Basel Convention in 1987. Under the EU's 'proximity principle', it was acknowledged that states should ensure that waste is treated, recycled or disposed of as close to the place of origin as possible. However, as the Irish authorities took a rather casual attitude to illegal dumps within their own boundaries, it is hardly surprising that they often turned a blind eye to dumping outside those boundaries.

Typically, the issue only came to light when other states found Irish waste being transited within their borders. In 2004, for example, the Dutch sent back fifty-nine containers of Irish waste that had been discovered at Rotherham. A few months after that, the Belgian authorities sent back containers from Antwerp. In all, about 2,000 tonnes of waste had been discovered, with the final destination for disposal being either India or Indonesia, or possibly even the seabed itself. The EPA named the nine companies involved but only warned of future prosecutions. The names do not appear on their list of prosecutions for the next two years.

AND ONE FOR THE POOR

The resort to wide-scale illegality by private corporations was a short-term response to the crisis, and it soon became apparent that there was a wider neo-liberal framework proposed to deal with the problem. The various elements of this strategy began to emerge in discussion papers produced by the Department of the Environment, Forfas and private consultancy firms such as the RPS group. The latter grouping is particularly interesting, as they appear to have had an inordinate influence on Irish environmental policy.

One of their component firms, the engineering group MC O'Sullivan, won a major consultancy contract to draw up a waste management strategy for Dublin's four local authorities in 1997. Then after the government split the whole country into a number of regions, MC O'Sullivan was awarded the consultancy contracts in many of the regions. These reports tended to pay lip service to the idea of recycling, but they also advocated incinerators as the classic 'end of the pipe' solution. The senior local authority officials tended to accept the company's proposals uncritically, but the elected councillors came under considerable pressure to reject incinerators. MC O'Sullivan also went beyond offering merely engineering solutions and proposed forms of consultation that would win legitimacy for its waste projects. The firm subsequently merged with the British-based RPS Group that boasted revenues of $327.3 million dollars in 2004.

The neo-liberal framework for waste management stressed two elements – bin charges and incineration. Bin charges were the archetypal solution because the individual was held responsible via their purse strings for their own waste. Forfas, the Department of the Environment and the engineering consultancy firms also assumed, however, that incinerators and super-dumps would be needed. The country was divided into seven different regional groupings and at one stage it was thought that each of these would house an incinerator.[55] The political elite expected considerable opposition, but assumed that this could be diffused and contained through sophisticated strategies of consultation and co-option along the lines that MC O'Sullivan had suggested. We shall look at each element in turn.

Bin Charges

After 1997, the structure of local government finances changed. Central government reduced the rates support grant and gave greater powers to the local authorities to charge for services.[56] In practice, this was an invitation to local authorities to impose bin charges and to move away from providing a free public service for waste collection. The move would eventually overthrow one of the cornerstones of public health policy – the Public Health Act of 1875. This act was enacted in response to an outbreak of cholera in London, and had charged local authorities with the duty to arrange the removal and disposal of waste. Citizens were obliged to store their waste in a 'moveable receptacle' – henceforth known as a dustbin – and the council had to take it away each week. The act had helped to improve public health immensely for over one hundred years, but in an era which redefined citizens as consumers, it was effectively abolished. Henceforth the disposal or recycling of waste would be seen as an individual responsibility.

Bin charges offered three advantages to local councils. First, under the slogan 'polluter pay principle' a new form of indirect or stealth tax could be imposed. They gained extra revenue from a new 'double tax' even though PAYE taxes were already supposed to pay for public services such as waste collection. Second, by using the rhetoric of individual responsibility, councils could off load the issue of recycling onto households. Instead of the local authorities investing in the necessary infrastructure to recycle, individuals could segregate and pay for the disposal of their own waste. Third, once waste was being treated as any other commodity, new opportunities for the private sector could be created. Forfas assumed that €571 million, out of the necessary €825 million to develop a waste management infrastructure, would come from the private sector by 2005.[57]

The state, however, faced a huge problem, as enormous protest meetings were called in working-class areas in Drogheda, Cork, Dublin, Waterford and Limerick. Active resistance continued for the longest time in Dublin, where areas like Crumlin and Ballyfermot saw regular well-attended meetings of 600 and 300 respectively. These meetings agreed not to pay the bin charges and to take mass direct action to ensure that bins were collected. The state responded with a combination of propaganda and repression to try to win what was, in effect, a cultural war. A 'public information' campaign was organized by RPS-MC O'Sullivan engineering consultants in conjunction with a number of public relations experts. These included Monica Leech, a fundraiser for the Minister for the Environment, who was paid €1,200 a day. The 'Race Against Waste' campaign took the moral high ground by claiming to be about 'reduction and recycling'. Repression came in the form of extensive jailings. This had started in Cork in 2001, when seven campaigners were jailed for dumping refuse on the steps of City Hall in protest at non-collection. It then spread to Dublin when the Socialist Party TD, Joe Higgins, and twenty-three others, were jailed for breaking court injunctions. The severity of sentencing stood in sharp contrast to the leniency meted out to polluting firms.

However, it soon became clear that there were major problems with the wider state strategy. First, while there was a show of recycling, there was little substance to it. Nor did recycling go much beyond very basic segregation of waste. By 2006, Forfas itself exposed the problem when it noted that

> Ireland has only one glass, one paper and one plastic reprocessing facility in operation. The lack of facilities indicates that the vast majority of Ireland's recyclable materials are exported for further treatment. The transport costs alone add an estimated €25 to €50 per tonne, depending on the material, to the waste costs of the enterprise sector. Scotland, New Zealand and Denmark are comparable countries to Ireland in terms of population and waste generation, but have developed a wider range of indigenous reprocessing.[58]

Foras was complaining because companies themselves were being caught in the failure by the state to invest in public services. They knew that bigger companies were even being forced to landfill a significant amount of waste on site.[59] But all of this was occurring because of neo-liberal policies which agencies such as Forfas had long advocated.

Second, bin charges placed further pressure on the poor and many responded by pulling out of the waste collection system itself. Most local authorities have a waiver system for low income families, but it is not an automatic entitlement and the procedure for applying is complicated. The result is that many people experienced difficulty in meeting the escalating costs of bin charges. In the six-year period between 1997 and 2000, bin charges grew by 223 per cent, or by an average of 37 per cent a year.[60]

Households who faced difficulties paying the charges resorted to other ways of disposing of waste, with four out of five local authorities claiming that backyard burning has become a significant issue, particularly in rural areas. In poorer parts of cities, black bags stuffed full of waste are discarded on side streets. There has also been an increase in sink macerating units, as waste is being washed down into the already overloaded sewerage system.[61] Nearly a quarter of Irish households – 23 per cent – have withdrawn from the waste collection service and the situation is set to worsen as charges rise further.[62] Currently, large city councils such as Dublin are only charging two thirds of the full economic costs of waste disposal as they try to break resistance to the charges and coax non-payers into compliance. The assistant city manager has claimed that Dublin's four local authorities are 'subsidizing' the service to the tune of €60 million a year, and that 'this will change bit by bit'.[63] However, if the full cost is charged, it is likely that even more people will leave the service, with incalculable effects on public health.

Third, private sector investment has failed to materialize on the expected scale. The main company that has entered the market is Greenstar, a subsidiary of National Toll Road, which concentrates on getting public contracts to 'plug infrastructure deficits'.[64] Its current strategy is to buy up waste disposal units to gain greater control over the market. It currently has four landfill sites and thirteen recycling plants. The other major firms in the sector are Thorntons, and AES, which has been bought by Bill McCabe, the former chief executive of Smartforce. There are also a number of specialist firms such as Sita, the hazardous chemical waste firm owned by Denis O'Brien and Oxigen, which has made significant profits after Dublin City Council awarded it the franchise to collect waste paper.[65] But although €571 million was supposed to be raised from the private sector, by the end of 2005 there was only €250 million of combined government and private investment.[66]

The waste industry was once seen as the Klondike of the new millennium. But the scale of popular resistance, and difficulties in securing planning, has dissuaded many big corporations from entering this new market place. At present, the market is fragmented and dominated by smaller firms who, by creating local monopolies, are able to charge high prices. Table 8.2 illustrates the pattern with one company in Northeast Wicklow. The future, however, promises greater consolidation and Greenstar are determined to be ahead of the game. As their chief executive, Stephen Cowman puts it 'Big is going to be beautiful'.[67] It also might mean that Ireland will continue to have high waste charges.

TABLE 8.2
GREENSTAR'S PRICES FOR HOUSEHOLD WASTE IN NORTHEAST WICKLOW

Year	240 litre bin	% Increase	Annual % in Consumer Price Index
2000	€198		
2001	€228.55	15.4	4.87
2002	€310	35.6	2.7
2003	€350	13	3.5
2004	€372	6.3	2.16

Source: Competition Authority Enforcement Decision 1/05/2002.

Incineration

The corporate agenda also favoured incinerators because they appear to offer a short-cut solution. Currently there are proposals for three incinerators which the EPA has supported with claims that 'research studies of possible health outcomes in populations living close to incinerators have not given clear indications of the presence or absence of an effect'.[68] However, international evidence is far more ambiguous and the Irish authorities have only a limited capacity to monitor health outcomes.

A Health Research Board study on incinerators in 2003 stated that 'Ireland presently has insufficient resources to carry out risk assessments for proposed waste management facilities'. It also acknowledged that 'Irish health information systems cannot support routine monitoring of the health of people, living near waste areas'.[69] The objectors to the siting of an incinerator in Ringaskidy, Co Cork, were shocked to discover that neither the Departments of Health nor the Environment would take responsibility for monitoring human health if the incinerator were built. Nor was the EPA, which suggested that the Department of Health was responsible. No official party would, it appeared, be accountable for the consequences of this supposed panacea to the Irish waste crisis.

Typically, consultancy firms like MC O'Sullivan justify incinerators by asserting that it is unrealistic to expect high levels of recycling. In their Connaught Waste Management Plan, for example, they claimed that it was unrealistic to expect that 50 per cent of household waste could be recycled.[70] Yet, after Galway City Council was pressurized into rejecting their plan for an incinerator by an enormous mass movement, the city went on to recycle 56 per cent of its waste – the highest in the country![71] The so called 'realistic' option was based on a false assumption which was disproved by the greater wisdom evident in the popular mobilization.

The authorities initially tried to deal with opposition to incinerators though exercises in 'stakeholder consultation'. This technique has grown in popularity in business circles, as it allows them to employ the rhetoric of 'empowerment' while obscuring the fact that decisions have already been made in advance by the powerful. The very term 'stakeholder' is sufficiently vague to give corporations or public authorities power to decide who should be invited to sit at 'the table'. This, in turn, means that there is no question of a democratic conclusion arriving from whatever deliberations take place around these same tables. The threadbare nature of 'stakeholder consultation' has failed to convince many – and this has led to even more draconian measures.

In the Waste Management (Amendment) Act 2001, the power to adopt or reject a local waste management plan was removed from elected councillors and transferred to city or county managers. Henceforth managers could overrule objections to bin charges or incinerators. It was one of the most serious attacks on the democratic rights of the majority of citizens which the state has ever imposed. Its purpose, however, was to give councillors from the ruling political parties a certain shelter, as they could henceforth claim to be powerless. They could even safely engage in a form of posturing, knowing that decisions would be made by unelected officials. Few of their more left-wing opponents dared to advocate mass civil disobedience as the only feasible alternative to a withdrawal of democracy.

One of the first effects of the new measure was seen when elected councillors on Dublin City Council voted to have all refuse – including that of non-payers – collected in the interests of public health. However, in line with the new Waste Management Act, the councillors were simply told by unelected officials that 'The vote means nothing. We're going to continue on as we have been.'[72] A new arrogance was already in evidence as little attempt was made to hide the contempt which senior officials had for democratic involvement

Emboldened by the manner in which local democracy had been uprooted, the state went one step further and introduced a Strategic Infrastructure Act 2006. In the case of a number of 'strategic' amenities such as incinerators or other waste disposal units, scrutiny by local planning officials was removed. Instead, An Bord Pleanála was to enter a consultation process with developers and other interested parties in advance of the submission of any planning applications. It would then assume the role of adjudicator on all ensuing applications. As the Irish Planning Institute put it, 'there is a concern that the perception of An Bord Pleanála as an independent quasi judicial body may suffer from the proposed introduction of special procedures of "consulting with parties"'.[73]

Business interests often advocate a reduction in local democracy when it stands in their way, and ist appears that the political elite now shares this same antipathy to local democracy. Speaking in far distant China, Bertie Ahern gave vent to what was actually on his mind,

> Naturally enough, I would like to have the power of the mayor (of Shanghai) when he decides he wants to do a highway and if he wants to bypass an area, he just goes straight

up and over. I know that that is not going to happen at home. I would just like when I am trying to put it on the ground that we can put it through the consultation process as quick as possible.[74]

Ahern's syntax might not be totally clear but it should not obscure his intent. In China, the builder can ring up the mayor and the highway just goes ahead. In Ireland, Ahern wishes to move through all perfunctory consultative procedures as quickly as possible in order to get to the real business of construction. Either way the builders are pleased.

NOTES

1. P. McKenna, *Ireland's Compliance with EU Law* (Dublin: Green Party, 2004).
2. D. Staunton, 'Ireland Accused of Breaching EU Rules on Health'. *Irish Times*, 12 April 2005.
3. Ibid.
4. Central Statistics Office, *Environmental Accounts for Ireland 1997–2004* (Dublin: CSO, 2006), p.14.
5. European Environment Agency, *The European Environment: State and Outlook 2005* (Brussels: EEA, 2005), p.414.
6. CSO, *Quarterly National Household Survey: Travel to Work Module Q1 2000* (Dublin: CSO, 2000), Table 1.
7. Ibid., Table 8a.
8. Department of Environment, *National Climate Change Strategy* (Dublin: Government Publications, 2000).
9. D. Clerkin, 'Special Tax on SUVs Rejected'. *Sunday Business Post*, 23 July 2006.
10. L. Reid, 'Taxpayers will Pay High Price for Broken Promises on Kyoto'. *Irish Times*, 3 April 2006.
11. J. Bellamy Foster, *Marx's Ecology* (New York: Monthly Review Press, 2000).
12. W. Bello and R. Rosenfield, *Dragons in Distress: Asia's Miracle Economies in Crises* (San Francisco: Institute for Food and Development Policy, 2000), p.12.
13. H.J. Leonard, *Pollution and the Struggle for World Product: Multinational Corporations, Environment and International Comparative Advantage* (Cambridge: Cambridge University Press, 1988), p.127.
14. D. Chambers, *Protection or Pollution: An Evaluation of the Environmental Protection Agency* (Cork: Cork Environmental Alliance, no date), p.9.
15. For discussion see C. Shipan, *Independence and the Irish Environmental Agency: A Comparative Assessment* (Dublin: Policy Institute, TCD, 2003).
16. R. Allen, *No Global: The People of Ireland versus the Multinationals* (London: Pluto Press, 2004), p.17.
17. I. Pocock, 'Department of Environment Resists Health Clause in Planning Reform'. *Irish Times*, 30 December 2002.
18. K. Buse and K. Lee, 'Business and Global Health Governance'. Discussion Paper No.5, Centre on Global Change and Health, London School of Hygiene and Tropical Medicine, December 2005.
19. G. Taylor, *Conserving the Emerald Tiger* (Galway: Arlen House, 2001), p.44.
20. IBEC Press Release, 'IBEC Endorses Environmental Innovators', 24 January 2002.
21. Laura Burke, 'Integrated Waste Management'. Power Point Presentation to Dundalk Chamber of Commerce, Fourth National Environment Conference, 8–9

October 2002.
22. Ibid.
23. EPA, *Report on IPC Licensing and Control 2002* (Dublin: EPA, 2002), p.17.
24. Ibid.
25. E. Hogan, 'Sawmill Firm Fined for Toxic Chemical Discharges'. *Irish Independent*, 6 December 2005.
26. EPA, Report of Technical Committee on IPPC reg. 706, 30 January 2006.
27. Ciaran Damery at Oireachtas Joint Committee on Environment and Local Government, Dáil Debates, Vol.71, 15 February 2006.
28. G. Deegan, 'Investigation urged into Health Patterns after Firm is Fined'. *Irish Times*, 16 February 2006.
29. G. Deegan, 'Drugs Firm in Shannon admits to Causing Smell'. *Irish Times*, 28 November 2003
30. E. Mulqueen, 'Workers Injured in Blast at Factory'. *Irish Times*, 13 April 2000.
31. California Global Corporate Accountability Project, *Dodging Dilemmas? Environmental and Social Accountability in Global Operations of California-Based High Tech Companies* (San Francisco, CA: Global Accountability Project, 2002), p.11.
32. Ibid., p.15.
33. E. Meagher, 'Compliance of Intel with Integration Pollution Prevention Control licence' (MA Thesis, Department of Geography, National University of Ireland, Maynooth, 2005).
34. European Environment Agency, *Environment in the European Union at the turn of the Century* (Brussels: EEA, 1999), p.222.
35. For problems involved see 'Leachate Collection Systems: The Achilles's Heel of Landfills'. *Rachel's Hazardous Waste News*, 119 (7 March 1989), http://www.ejnet.org/rachel/rh'vn119.htm.
36. EPA, *The Nature and Extent of Unauthorised Waste Activity in Ireland* (Dublin: EPA, 2005), p.4.
37. Ibid., p.viii.
38. EPA, *National Waste Report 2004* (Dublin: EPA, 2005), pp.3 and 7.
39. European Environment Agency, *Effectiveness of Packaging Waste Management Systems in Selected Countries: An EEA Pilot Study* (Brussels: EEA, 2005), p.6.
40. EEA, *Environment in the European Union*, p.220.
41. EPA, *The Nature and Extent of Unauthorised Waste Activity in Ireland*, p.ix.
42. L. Reid, 'A Dirt Business'. *Irish Times*, 27 March 2004.
43. Edward Sheehy, Wicklow Country Manager, at Joint Committee on Environment and Local Government hearing on Dumping in County Wicklow, 5 February 2003, pp.17–18.
44. Liz McManus, ibid., p.29.
45. Frank Corcoran, Chair of An Taisce, ibid., p.50.
46. Edward Sheedy, ibid., pp.18–19.
47. Jackie Healy Rae TD, ibid., p.9.
48. T. O'Brien, 'Council Refuses to Release Pollution Data'. *Irish Times*, 29 May 2004.
49. J. Humprey, 'EPA says Wicklow Dump now Polluting Local Water'. *Irish Times*, 20 July 2005.
50. T. O'Brien, 'Council says Roadstone Purchase is already Approved'. *Irish Times*, 21 November 2005.
51. J. O'Sullivan, 'Towards Zero Waste? Sustainable Waste Management in the Enlarged European Union'. Paper to Alternative Environment Summit, Waterford, 14–15 May 2004.
52. K. Hanlon, 'Waste from Dublin dumped Illegally in North'. *Irish Times*, 10 February 2003.
53. Ibid.
54. A. McCabe, 'Waterford Waste Contractor Convicted'. *Sunday Business Post*, 28 December 2003.

55. M. Boyle, 'Cleaning up after the Celtic Tiger: Scalar 'fixes' in the Political Ecology of Tiger Economies'. *Transactions of the Institute of British Geographers*, 27, 2 (2002), pp.172–94.
56. E. Morgenroth, 'Waste Collection, Double Taxation and Local Finance', in T. Callan and A. Doris (eds), *Budget Perspective 2006* (Dublin: ESRI, 2005).
57. Forfas, *Waste Management Benchmarking Study* (Dublin: Forfas, 2006), p.2.
58. Ibid., p.20.
59. Ibid., p.3.
60. Combat Poverty Agency, *Waste Collection Charges and Low Income Households* (Dublin: CPA, 2003), p.14.
61. P.J. Rudden, 'Lessons from Integrated Waste Management in Europe: Case Study Ireland'. Paper delivered to Conference of Waste Management Association of Australia, 2006.
62. EPA, *National Waste Report 2004*, pp.13–14.
63. T. Brien, 'Waste Charges set to rise due to EU Waste Management Directive'. *Irish Times*, 19 April 2005.
64. B. Carey, 'Waste not Want Lots'. *Sunday Times*, 3 April 2005.
65. Ibid.
66. Forfas, *Waste Management Benchmarking Study*, p.2.
67. Carey, 'Waste not Want Lots'.
68. EPA, *Municipal Solid Waste Incineration as part of Ireland's Integrated Waste Management Strategy* (Dublin: EPA, no date), p.7.
69. D. Crowley, A. Staines, C. Collins, J. Bracken, M. Bruen, J. Fry, V. Hrymak, D. Malone, B. Magette, M. Ryan and C. Thunhurst, *Health and Environmental Effects of Landfilling and Incineration of Waste – A Literature Review* (Dublin: Health Research Board, 2003), p.8.
70. Submission by Galway for a Safe Environment to the Connaught Draft Waste Management Plan, http://homepage.eircom.net/-galsafenv/gse/debate/subgse.htm.
71. 'Incinerator not Required if other Local Authorities follow Galway, says O Brolachan'. *Galway Advertiser*, 16 February 2006.
72. O'Kelly, 'City Ruling on Refuse Dismissed'. *Irish Times*, 2 March 2005.
73. Irish Planning Institute, 'Submission on Planning and Development (Strategic Infrastructure) Bill 2006', p.1.
74. M. Hennessy, 'Taoiseach Indicates Incinerator Route must be taken'. *Irish Times*, 21 January 2005.

Chapter Nine

Under New Ownership

In 1987, Charles Haughey wrote to the unions to inform them that Fianna Fail was opposed to the privatization of semi-state companies.[1] The union leaders duly accepted the assurance and agreed to enter the first social partnership deal with his government. Like much else during the Haughey years, however, the letter was a little economical with the truth. Within four years two major state owned companies, Irish Sugar and Irish Life, were sold off. Since then the record on privatization has gotten worse.

In the ten year period between 1991 and 2001, €8.2 billion of state assets were sold to private corporations, bringing little benefit to Irish society at large. The costs of organizing the privatization amounted to €2.2 billion, or 27 per cent of the proceeds.[2] In 1992, Irish Steel was sold to ISPAT for £1, and debts of £27.5 million were also written off on a promise that the new company would invest in the plant. ISPAT, however, broke its promises to invest and sold off valuable company land prior to closure. It then left behind a huge mountain of debts. In 1996, B&I was sold off to Irish Ferries, the company which later tried to replace its workforce with migrants who were to receive less than the minimum wage. In 1999, it was the turn of Telecom, which was initially marketed to small shareholders, but then taken over by a series of venture capitalists who did little to build up its infrastructure. In 2001, the Irish National Petroleum Company was sold to Tosco, a US company with a poor environmental and safety record.[3] The purchase price was €100 million, but the state had invested the equivalent of that figure in the company just before the sale. In the same year, three state banks, ACC Bank, ICC Bank and the Trustee Savings Bank, were sold off.

The remarkable thing about this wave of privatization was the lack of sustained opposition. Dublin bus workers went on strike to oppose attempts to franchise out their company, but few others followed suit. Workers were willing to ballot for industrial action, when asked, but the union leaders showed little desire to fight. They argued that if an elected government made political decisions, they could not challenge them.[4] By way of contrast, the large corporations rarely accept No for an answer, no matter how elected representatives oppose them.

One of the reasons why unions showed little willingness to fight was that they had dropped their 'ideological' opposition to privatization, and some even sought to transform workers into shareholders. In the late 1980s, the ICTU embraced the idea of a 'social market' economy, claiming that it was not 'opposed to the declared aim of a shareholding democracy'.[5] This mirrored the Thatcherite rhetoric of the time, which justified privatization by claiming that it would extend share-ownership. Initially, the ambiguities in the unions' position remained at a rhetorical level but, as the process of social partnership deepened, important changes occurred. The unions shifted from believing there was a conflict of interest between capital and labour to viewing business as its actual partner.

The change was illustrated most dramatically in telecommunications. In 1992, the Communication Workers Union produced a campaign pack that trenchantly opposed the privatization of Telecom. 'Don't let the Fat Cats Get their Claws on Telecom' it proclaimed.[6] Yet by 1996, the union did an about face and dropped its opposition in return for a government agreement to an Employee Share Ownership Plan. Its General Secretary, David Begg, explained

> Significant employee ownership is a radical concept which challenges the status quo. It has the potential to alter the balance of power in a capitalist society towards employees and to transform the relationship within companies between management and workers to one of co-operation and consensus.[7]

If workers became capitalists, it appears, they could give the corporations a human face.

The roots of this remarkable idea go back to the US lawyer, Louis Kelso, who developed the concept of Employee Share Ownership Plans as a way to 'build support for the capitalist system'.[8] Kelso argued that the governments should give tax breaks to allow employees to buy shares in their own company and this would lessen industrial conflict. In a pun on Marx, he wrote a book in 1958 called *The Capitalist Manifesto*.[9] By 1994, his ideas had some impact when workers at United Airlines appeared to take ownership of the company through an ESOP scheme which controlled 55 per cent of shares. Behind the seemingly rosy picture, however, there was a much grimmer reality. The United Airline workers took a 15 per cent cut in their wages and accepted further cost cutting measures. Union consciousness in the 'worker owned' firm declined and management pushed through even more concessions, including the halting of pension payments.[10] The relentless drive to put profit over human need took its toll.

Begg took Kelso's ideas extremely seriously, and engaged the Wall Street bankers, Keilin and Co, to secure an equity stake in Telecom. 'Investment bankers are needed now in America as when (workers) needed lawyers to fight injunctions', he told his membership.[11] The dawn of the new era of worker capitalists and popular shareholding democracy was to come with the selloff of Telecom, or Eircom, as it became known in June 1999.

The Fianna Fail Minister who was responsible for the sale, Mary O'Rourke, agreed. 'I have no time for fat cats', she claimed, as she promised that privatization would mean a 'company that is literally owned by the people through the widest possible share ownership'.[12] Dan McLoughlin, the well-known stockbroker economist, predicted that the sale would be 'like a mini-budget, increasing people's wealth by hundreds of millions'.[13] A huge advertising campaign, modelled on the 'Tell Sid' campaign which had been run in Britain, persuaded 1.2 million people to register for shares and 575,000 eventually subscribed. Prior to the sale, Eircom workers had accepted thousands of redundancies so that the remaining workforce could become shareholders.

The dream of popular capitalism, however, quickly turned sour when tens of thousands lost their savings in a share price slump. The original consortium of KPN/Telia, which David Begg predicted would have a long term commitment to the work-force, disappeared. Their place was taken by the ubiquitous Sir Anthony O'Reilly, who forged an alliance with the financier George Soros, Goldman Sachs and Providence Private Equity firm, a group of Wall Street vulture capitalists, to take over the company. It soon emerged that their aim was to asset strip as much as possible by selling off prime sites and cutting back on investment in necessary infrastructure. Between 2001 and 2004, this combined group managed to make a gain of €950 million.[14] The four top managers who presided over the company were also paid €29 million between them.[15]

Far from worker share ownership restraining the ethos of greed, the Employee Share Ownership Trust joined in the orgy. In 2004, at the time of a new floatation, it was revealed that the CWU union leader, Con Scanlon, who became the vice-president of Eircom, received shares worth €562,000, pension payments worth over €1 million and a lump sum payment of €230,000.[16] The trust no longer even represented current employees, as half of its shareholders had retired from the firm, and new employees did not join the trust on the same terms. The composition of the trust began to reflect a strong managerial ethos that diverged from the broader workforce. In 2006, there were four union representatives in the trust, but one of them had become a middle manager and another was a full time 'partnership coordinator'. There were also two direct representatives of management, including Cathal Magee, who had earned €5.8 million in payments to top managers.

The Eircom experience was a salutary lesson in how populist rhetoric can be used by corporations to further their own interests. It provides a baseline from which to examine the wider implications of privatization.

FOUR STEPS TO PRIVATIZATION

A host of commentators promote privatization as the only realistic and viable option for society. Right wing economists present their argument for privatisation as if they were pronouncing on a simple fact of nature, while some newspaper columnists often assume that it brings victory to the common man. The theme of these arguments is that privatization is inevitable – part of a new 'reality' that everyone has to adjust to. Like colonial armies, corporate interests promote a message that 'resistance is futile'. However, the so called reality is carefully constructed as the road to privatization tends to follow four key steps.

First, there is an investment strike from the state. The Irish state has systematically held back on investment in semi-state companies in order to force them down the privatization route. Aer Lingus provides a classic case of this tactic. Since 2001, the company has added over fifty new routes and funded its short-haul replacement fleet from its own resources. Against all odds, its pre-tax profits jumped to €82.6 million in 2005, and the number of passengers it carried increased to eight million. Its senior management, however, argued that it needed a further €2 billion to expand, principally on the North Atlantic route which they expect will open up after 2007. The company is highly profitable, having accumulated profits of €340 million in the past four years, but clearly does not have the resources to raise €2 billion by itself. The management may either be right or wrong about the new possibilities, but the key point is that the Irish state refused to invest in the company it owned. Transport Minister Martin Cullen asserted that 'investment could not and should not come from the government'.[17]

Why should this be the case? The Irish state already invests in companies – but only those it does not own. The National Pensions Reserve Fund is a multi-billion investment fund designed to generate income for future pensions. Its fund managers scour the world for investment opportunities and have invested 80 per cent of its total in companies listed on stock exchanges.[18] It has reputedly even invested €27 million in airlines all over the world, including Aer Lingus's rivals, British Airways and Ryanair.[19] Why, therefore was one agency of the state – the Aer Lingus management – looking for more funds – while another, NPRF – not only refused to oblige, but instead backed its rivals?

Politicians respond to this type of question by claiming the EU ties their hands. Under EU competition rules and directives that limit state subsidies, they claim they are not supposed to invest in companies like Aer Lingus. The EU, as we have seen, has become an arena whereby lobbyists, funded by giant corporations, can exercise a significant influence over policies. These, in turn, give shelter to local politicians, who claim that privatization is 'inevitable'. However, in the case of Aer Lingus, the Irish state has gone one step further, and deliberately confused investment with subsidy. Even within the limited neo-liberal structures of the EU , there is nothing to stop the Irish state investing in a profitable state company like Aer Lingus, as long as it adhered to the 'market investor principle' – that it was not operating any less rationally than a prudent investor.[20]

The Irish state, however, pursued an investment strike in order to force Aer Lingus into the ownership of large global corporations. The sale of a majority of the state's 85 per cent stake in the company raised just over €500 million, but this will only purchase a handful of wide-bodied jets and still leaves an extra €1.6 billion to be raised elsewhere to pursue the current management strategy. The whole proposition made little sense on many levels because Ireland is hugely dependent on the movement of freight and passengers. Privatization means that the state will have no control over how this will be done in the future.

The second step to privatisation is the introduction of consultants. The big players in the consultancy business are the four big accountancy firms – PricewaterhouseCoopers, KPMG, Deloitte Touche and Ernst and Young – who have gained an unparalleled influence over policy making in the global economy. They have been joined by a number of stock broking firms who have also developed consultancy wings. Governments often turn to such firms for expert advice on privatization, but they can hardly be regarded as neutral because the same firms that give the advice also benefit considerably from the policy of privatization itself. In 1999, PricewaterhouseCoopers, for example, held a total of 193 privatization mandates worldwide, and KPMG held 153.[21] A year later, PWC handled 222 privatization deals for international clients valued at $5.1 billion and described itself as 'the market leader in project finance and privatization'.[22] The consultancy firms are also closely tied in with the bigger corporations and, as Enron showed, sometimes develop an extremely unhealthy symbiotic relationship.

The notion that advice is for sale is a profoundly neo-liberal concept and it has only grown with the hegemony of these policies in global elite circles. Governments use consultants when they want to create politics free zones around decision making. By claiming to adhere to independent consultants reports, they remove the elements of political choice and create a shelter for themselves. This is why, in the ten years after 1988, fee income from consultancy service for the nine largest firms has grown ten- fold.[23] A company such as PricewaterhouseCoopers, which combines accountancy and consultancy, now has a total net global revenue of $14.7 billion, which is greater than any country in sub-Saharan Africa bar Nigeria and South Africa.[24]

The Irish state has followed this global pattern of calling in the consultants when it wants to privatize a semi state company. In the case of Aer Lingus, they issued a contract to Goldman Sachs to take a 'fresh look' at the ownership structure and paid a fee of €30,000 to get their report. Due to political sensitivities, Goldman Sachs was not asked to provide a specific recommendation but, rather, a framework for decision making. However, they left little doubt that they favoured the sale of a majority stake of the state holding, and suggested that any 'introduction of a new investor should be viewed as the first step towards the eventual exit by that investor and, likely, the state'.[25]

The incredible element of this process, however, was that, while one wing of Goldman Sachs was making these suggestions, another wing was profiting by €14 million from its part in asset striping Eircom after it had been privatized.[26] Similar conflicts of interest pervade the wider practice of this particular firm. The year before it issued its report on Aer Lingus, Goldman Sachs made a €110,000,000 settlement with the Security and Exchange Commission in the US for, among other things, 'publishing research reports that do not provide a sound basis for evaluation facts, are not properly balanced, and/or contain exaggerated or unwarranted claims and/or opinion for which there is no reasonable basis'.[27]

The settlement arose because the firm had issued investor reports that had misled shareholders. However, if Goldman Sachs can mislead individual shareholders, there are even more grounds to question its objectivity when there is a conflict of interest between wealthy shareholders and the wider public interest.

The firm chosen to recommend on the future of the ESB

was Deloitte and Touche. Nobody thought to ask if this was appropriate, since the same company had cost the state €131 million in the PPARS debacle. Nor was there any concern expressed about Deloitte's rather uncritical attitude to private business. The company is currently facing a major law suit because of its failure to blow the whistle on the Italian firm Parmalat, which collapsed amidst huge debts. Individual Deloitte accountants who tried to raise concerns about fraudulent activities in Parmalat were either reprimanded or taken off the case.[28] The company makes little secret of its full support for privatization and its stated aim is to 'organize initial public offerings of state owned energy assets as an indicator of a mature merger and acquisition environment'.[29] Expecting such a firm, therefore, to recommend against de-regulation and privatisation is like expecting an army general to embrace peace and universal love.

The third step to privatization is taken when senior managers of semi-state companies openly voice a desire to become private entrepreneurs. Managers in the past were often driven by a robust statist outlook and saw themselves as serving the public interest. The model here was Todd Andrews, the former chair of CIE, who titled his autobiography *Man of No Property*, and often made caustic remarks about the failures of private enterprise. His reign at CIE was not known for a fondness to trade unionism, and he closed many rail lines on the spurious grounds of inefficiency. However, his income was modest by today's standards and he saw his primary duty as serving a state rather than purely corporate interests. This attitude, however, has been undermined in an era when state managers caught the privatization virus. They seek to transform themselves from being functionaries in a state capitalist sector to become fully fledged private owners.

One of the most dramatic examples of this occurred in Irish Sugar, privatized in 1991. Even before it was privatized, four directors bought half of a subsidiary for £1.67 million and then sold it back to their own board of Irish Sugar for £12.4 million, making a profit of £10.73 million in just fifteen months. When the state company was privatized, the salary of the chief executive, Chris Comerford, trebled overnight. Sometimes the process of turning state managers into private entrepreneurs can be accelerated by putting private business people onto the boards of state companies. The first suggestion for the privatization of Telecom, for example, came from Michael Smurfit, the prominent businessman appointed as chair of its board. He later had to resign when it was discovered that Telecom was paying inflated prices to buy a site in which he had an interest.

The fourth step to privatization is slimming down of the state company through redundancies and out sourcing. Semi-state companies in Ireland traditionally combined a certain social ethos with a ruthless, internal hierarchical structure. Although they often had rigid, authoritarian managements, firms like the ESB, CIE and Telecom provided services to isolated rural areas that were inherently unprofitable. This meant that they often carried high numbers of staff and were targeted as 'inefficient' by right-wing commentators who claimed that the taxpayer was burdened with too many public employees. In 1980, for example, 8 per cent of all those at work were employed by semi-state companies. The route to privatization could only be opened if staff numbers were reduced and flexible labour practices imposed.

In Aer Lingus, the offensive against staff numbers began after the September 11th attacks on the World Trade Centre in 2001. The downturn in passengers was used by many airlines to restructure their operations, often with government support. In the four years between 2001 and 2005, Aer Lingus cut its workforce from just under 7,000 to just over 3,000.[30] Some of the methods used by management to pressurize workers to leave were pretty extreme. One confidential memo, for example, recommended a number of 'environmental push factors' such as introducing 'tacky' uniforms to demoralize staff; sending pilots on tedious training programmes; changing shift patterns to make life uncomfortable.[31] In the ESB, the reduction in numbers took place through a partnership approach. Numbers were first cut from 11,500 in 1997 to 8,750 in 2002, and then reduced further through an agreed programme that gave extra payments in return for an acceptance of outsourcing. In both cases, many workers believed that they were making sacrifices in order to ward off the threat of privatization. In reality, the sacrifices merely paved the way for it.

MYTHS OF PRIVATIZATION

The push to win public acceptance of privatization has relied on the repetition of a number of myths about low prices and efficiency of service. The icon of the myth makers is Ryanair's boss, Michael O'Leary, who has become a virtual symbol of private enterprise. According to one rather over-enthusiastic journalist, 'we should be erecting statues in his honour all over the country'.[32] He is credited with single-handedly showing how private enterprise can survive without state support and bringing low fares to its customers. O'Leary is a strong supporter of the Progressive Democrats and he once made a €50,000 donation to their cause.[33] They in turn have become the political mouthpieces of the 'Ryanair way' and argue that if privatization is followed elsewhere it can slash prices and give the public a better service. Twenty years ago they were the only party advocating privatization, but today their position has become the consensus among the political elite.

The Ryanair argument for privatization starts with a number of half-truths about the success story of the company itself. Contrary to impressions, the company did not grow because it was led by rugged individualists who scorned any state support. Quite the opposite. The success of Ryanair depended on direct state support and state restrictions being placed on Aer Lingus. In 1989, competition from Aer Lingus had brought Ryanair to the brink of collapse, and O'Leary had even begun to put the wheels in motion to wind up the company.[34] The company was only saved by the political intervention of its founder, Tony Ryan, who held direct meetings with Fianna Fail's Transport Minister Seamus Brennan. Ryan demanded that Aer Lingus be expelled from the cheaper landing slots which it had recently acquired at London's Stansted airport, and that Ryanair be given the exclusive access instead. Against the advice of his department, Brennan acceded to this request. Aer Rianta, the state-owned airport company, was also told to write off £1 million in debts from Ryanair, and to supply it with duty-free products on very generous terms.[35] In 1998, Aer Rianta revealed that it had given Ryanair €35 million in rebates in the previous four years, foregoing landing fees and passenger load fees.[36] When asked about why he made the original decision to save Ryanair,

Brennan refused to deny that company directors had made donations to Fianna Fail.

The equation of privatization and cheaper prices arose out of the Ryanair experience, but there is in fact no necessary connection. Ryanair operates a particular business model which sells no frills, point-to-point flights. It certainly was innovative in adopting this model in an era when snobbish concepts prevailed about airline travel being a luxury experience. However, there is absolutely no reason why a state-owned service could not adopt a similar model, as Aer Lingus proved when it successfully moved over to this model while still a state company. Aer Lingus managed to successfully move over to this business model even while it remained a state company.

Ryanair has, however, given that model a special twist by imposing a particularly harsh regime on its staff. Long hours and temporary contracts are used to squeeze the maximum of productivity out of cabin crews, while pilots have faced major intimidation for trying to join a union.[37] Some of the low prices have, therefore, been borne by the mistreatment of staff. Nor should the low fares experience be exaggerated as both firms use the advertising of baseline fares to disguise the full cost of flying. In July 2006, for example, Ryanair offered flights to Krakow in Poland for as little as 99 cents, while Aer Lingus promised to charge €49. However, the *Sunday Tribune* has shown that if a family of four, including an infant, were to make that journey, their actual costs would come to €889.12 with Ryanair and €904.88 with Aer Lingus.[38]

However if the drop in air fares coincided with a switch in business models, there are also other examples of where competition between privatized firms led to an increase in prices. The privatization of telecommunications, for example, coincided with important technological changes which opened the possibility of general price reductions. In Ireland, however, the potential benefits of this technology were hijacked by privatized firms to boost their profits.

The most extraordinary example of this occurred in mobile phone charges. Not long after its privatization, Eircell, the highly profitable mobile subsidiary company of the state owned, Telecom, was sold off to Vodafone. Meanwhile, the licence for a second mobile phone company was sold to Denis O'Brien who, in turn, sold it to BT, who eventually sold it to O2. These two mobile phone companies, Vodafone and 02, dominate the Irish market, controlling over 90 per cent between them. Contrary to the theories about competition reducing prices, they appear to work together to increase prices.

Mobile phone charges are measured in units known as Average Revenue Per User or APRUs. When prices are compared across Europe, it transpires that Ireland has the highest APRU in the EU, with prices 148 per cent above the EU average.[39] Comreg, the regulator for the industry, found that the price discrepancy could not be explained by the rather stereotypical myth that the Irish talk more – it was rather that the Spanish-owned O2 and British-owned Vodaphone charged more. And the most obvious explanation was that they wanted higher profits. Table 9.1 indicates the average rate of return on capital employed for the two mobile operators in Ireland. It shows a tendency to increase the rate of return on capital the more they consolidated their grip on the market. By 2003, both companies were gaining a huge 38 to 39 per cent return on capital invested. This extraordinary level of profit may be compared to Britain where companies had an average return of 12 per cent in this period.[40]

Comreg attempted to tackle the two mobile giants on their

TABLE 9.1
RATE OF RETURN ON CAPITAL EMPLOYED BY VODAFONE AND O2

	1999	2000	2001	2002	2003
Vodafone	26%	35%	32%	31%	39%
02	-16%	-18%	8%	24%	38%

Source: Comreg, Market Analysis – Wholesale voice call termination on individual mobile.

pricing structure because that, after all, is what regulators of privatized industry are supposed to do. They issued a ruling against the companies, but this was then appealed to a new Electronic Communications Appeals Panel. The main purpose of this rather obscure agency, it would appear, is to regulate the activity of the regulator. Rather bizarrely, Comreg initially tried to resist attempts to overturn its ruling, but then settled the case within two days and agreed to pick up a €5 million bill.[41] Meanwhile, the two privatized concerns continued on their merry way.

The privatization of telecommunications did not just lead to higher prices but also brought the plunder of basic infrastructure. The new owners sold off property in prime locations and then failed to invest in areas of the country where they felt there was not a sufficient return. The asset stripping of Eircom has now caused major problems in the provision of services. Broadband provision is so bad that even business elements have begun calling for government investment to undo the damage. The OECD has calculated that Ireland's broadband penetration is only 6.7 per cent compared to an average of 11.7 per cent for the OECD as a whole. The reason for the plunder is that few investors had the money to buy a massive company like Eircom outright and, therefore, used the tactic of leveraged buy-outs. This means that they borrowed heavily against the assets of their future purchase and saddled the company with debt. This left them with little provision for long term investment which could bring better quality services. O'Reilly's consortium which took over Eircom used their control to bolster their own dividend payments, but there is no reason to think that the new owners, Babcock and Brown, will not follow a similar pattern.

The ESB case demonstrates an even more striking example of how privatization leads to an increase in prices for consumers and a deterioration in service. The deregulation of the electricity is an extraordinary complex process that initially involved the break up of the ESB into a number of constituent parts. These are ESB Power Generation, which operates nineteen power stations; ESB Networks, which maintains the transmission system; and ESB Customer Supply, which 'buys' electricity, and then sells it to customers. The ultimate aim of this break-up is to prepare the way for outright privatization.

However, there is a major problem with attempts to privatize electricity because it has certain unique features as a commodity. It cannot be bought and sold like a can of beans. Electricity cannot be stored in a way that would allow a consumer to buy when it is cheap and use when it is dearer. Once electricity is produced by suppliers, it has to be used on the grid immediately and cannot be left around for dealers to haggle over the price. It is a totally standard product, and no matter how many times a consumer switches suppliers, they still get the exact same product. People in modern society are also totally dependent on electricity and cannot avoid taking the prices which suppliers offer.

The neo-liberal answer to this conundrum is to create 'virtual markets', where electricity is sent to an imaginary 'pool' where rival suppliers and bidders interact. Hour or half hour slots of electricity for particular time periods are supposed to be traded within these pools by buyers and sellers. The different suppliers are then supposed to rent periods on the grid and offer electricity to consumers at 'competitive prices'. If you think there is something faintly mad about buyers haggling over imaginary amounts of electricity on a centralized grid, you might very well be right. But the purpose of these Byzantine arrangements was supposed to be to reduce electricity prices.

To implement the theory, a new Commission on Energy Regulation was set up to ensure that ESB 'dominance' was reduced and to create a space for rivals. Even after the disaster that befell the privatization of electricity in California, when prices soared and blackouts occurred more frequently, there was no shaking belief in some quarters in deregulation. Isolde Goggin, the director of Regulated Markets at the Competition Authority argued that California showed that more, rather than less, deregulation was needed. She told an IBEC conference that 'Events in California should not obscure the fact that regulatory reform, when undertaken properly, can yield greater efficiency, lower prices and more choice for the consumers'.[42] This claim was made in 2001, but more than five years later there is no evidence to support it.

Far from bringing lower prices, prices for domestic consumers have shot up dramatically since the deregulation process began in 1999, and by 2006 electricity prices were 52.7 per cent higher. One of the reasons for the sharp rises has been Ireland's greater dependence on oil and gas, but this is by no means the sole reason. Rising energy prices alone cannot fully explain why Ireland's position on electricity prices has changed relative to other countries. There has also been a clear deregulation effect as Ireland has moved from being a country with comparatively low electricity prices for domestic consumers to being in the higher price range. In 1999, for example, a survey by the UK Electricity Association found that only customers in Greece and Finland paid lower tariffs than Irish consumers.[43] By 2005, however, figures from the International Energy Association ranked Ireland in fifth place out of thirty for higher prices.[44]

Deregulation has impacted on electricity prices in a number of different ways.

Firstly, extra costly administrative and regulatory structures were needed to facilitate deregulation and the prices for these have been offloaded onto consumers. The ESB had to pay out €120 million to put in a new billing and meter system to facilitate competition between suppliers – even though no domestic consumers have switched suppliers![45] The energy regulator itself spent an extra €8 million on external consultants over two years but, rather oddly, would not reveal who these consultants were.[46] The overall costs of the regulator have to be borne by the ESB and Bord Gais principally. In the longer term, deregulation will create an even greater bonanza for software companies, as they develop exquisite computer programmes to allow electricity to move from different suppliers in the virtual market to the individual consumer. In Britain, for example, the bill for software development cost £2 billion and took five years to develop.[47] The cost was borne by consumers.

Second, to encourage competition, the ESB had to offer a 10 per cent discount on the electricity supplied to the 'virtual market', but this again helped raise costs elsewhere. The ESB was also forced to spend €1.5 billion on contracts to buy electricity from two rival suppliers, Tynagh Energy and Aughinish Alumina. The largest contract went to Tyangh Energy, owned by the Mountside property company which was associated with a relatively unknown Navan beef processor, Martin Blake, and the Gama construction company. The contract allowed Tynagh to earn about €120 million a year because the ESB had to buy its electricity at premium prices instead of sourcing it from its own supplies. It was, as one journalist put it, a 'licence to print money'[48] but it was paid for by ESB consumers.

Third, deregulation only brought 'choice' to the industrial sector, which can now source electricity from a number of agents. There is no choice for domestic consumers because their relatively small bills do not create a sufficient incentive for companies to enter the market. The director of corporate affairs at Viridian, Robert Greer, explained that 'the customer would end up paying for switching supplier and, of course, you are talking about such a small amount of electricity there would be no profit margin for the supplier'.[49]

However, as large customers now can switch suppliers, this puts pressure on the ESB to reduce their costs in this sector of the market. The result is that the ESB was forced to 'rebalance' charges to help industrial consumers rather than domestic consumers.

Fourth, the ESB has begun paying 'high dividend payments' to the government to mimic the arrangements that would prevail if it were privatized. These dividend payments have risen to €67 million in 2003, and to €80 million in 2004, and these have placed an added pressure on prices. The company has also borrowed €1.2 billion from a consortium of Irish and international banks to upgrade its electricity network.[50] Like in other state companies that are being readied for privatization, the investment is being undertaken now to make it a more attractive proposition for private investors later. But once again the cost of borrowing is being put onto consumers.

If low prices are one myth, then Goggin's claim that privatization brings a more efficient service is another. One of the unusual aspects to the deregulation of electricity across the world has been the more frequent occurrence of black-outs. In 2003, for example, millions of people in North America and Italy were left in darkness as electricity supply ceased. Electricity, by its very nature, needs to be organized on a central system and a surplus capacity must be maintained in case of sudden rises in usage. Deregulation, however, is based on the idea of competition between suppliers and pressure to sell every item of electricity produced. It puts a premium on companies to maintain the lowest possible spare capacity lest they be economically disadvantaged against rival suppliers. Moreover, in a market system, the more limited the supply, the higher the prices they will receive.

The ESB National Grid has already warned of significant shortages in generation plants over the next seven years.[51] The number of 'amber alerts' has also doubled[52] and there have been some unpublicized 'outages' in local areas. The reason for this extraordinary state of affairs is that the Commission on Energy Regulation originally barred the ESB from building new stations and the company has been asked to decommission plants such as the one in Tarbert. This means that the company is more reliant on older, less efficient plants just when electricity consumption in Ireland is growing by about 3 per cent a year.

The Commission finally gave permission to the ESB to build a new power station at Aghada, but only on condition that it sold off 30 per cent of its generational capacity to private operators. This will amount to another form of subsidy as they get 'generation ready sites' at relatively cheap prices. The reality is that the Irish electricity market is quite small and will not increase significantly even with the development of an all-island grid and an inter connector to Britain. The assumption, therefore, that there will be a significant number of suppliers willing to risk high capital costs and long lead- in times to supply an abundance of electricity, just does not pertain. A relatively efficient state-owned firm like the ESB should clearly be allowed to develop its capacity, but a dogma designed to benefit corporate interests is standing in the way.

NOTES

1. ICTU, *Annual Report and Conference Proceedings* (Dublin: ICTU, 1987), p.209.
2. F. O'Toole, *After the Ball* (Dublin: New Island, 2003), p.137.
3. US Chemical Safety and Hazard Investigation Board, *Tosco Avon Refinery Fire* (CSB: Washington, 1999).
4. SIPTU official Michael Halpenny speaking at Joint Committee on Transport hearing on Aer Lingus Privatization, Dáil Debates, 8 April 2006.
5. ICTU, *Public Enterprise and Economic Development* (Dublin: ICTU, n.d.), p.3.
6. CWU, *The Case for Keeping Telecom in Public Ownership* (Dublin: CWU, 1992).
7. D. Begg, *Employee Ownership: An Idea whose time has come* (Dublin: CWU, 1996), p.3.
8. S. Harrell, 'The ESOP Option'. *Multinational Monitor*, 6, 17 (30 November 1985), pp.36–7.
9. L. Kelso, *The Capitalist Manifesto* (Westport, CT: Greenwood, 1975 reprint).
10. M. Miah and B. Sheppard, 'Illusions about Employee Ownership being Shattered at United Airlines'. *Labour Notes*, September 2000.
11. CWU, *Employees Ownership: An Ideas whose Time has come* (Dublin: CWU, 1996).
12. P. Sweeney, *Selling Out* (Dublin: TASC, 2004), p.71.
13. Ibid., p.66.
14. Ibid., p.79.
15. Ibid.
16. J. McManus and U. McCaffrey, 'Four Executive Directors have earned €29 million'. *Irish Times*, 5 March 2004.
17. Dáil Debates, Vol.616, 7 March 2006.
18. D. Gerkin, 'Pension Reserve Fund is back under the Spotlight'. *Sunday Business Post*, 12 March 2006.
19. Sinn Fein submission to Join Oireachtas Committee on Transport regarding the proposed privatization of Aer Lingus.
20. Sweeney, *Selling Out*, p.10.
21. War on Want, *Profiting from Poverty: Privatisation Consultants, DFID and Public Services* (London: War on Want, no date), p.7.
22. UNISON, 'How The Big Five Accountancy firms Influence and Profit from Privatisation Policy (London: UNISON, 2002), p.4.

23. Centre for Public Services, *Management Consultants* (Sheffield: Centre for Public Services, 1999), p.33.
24. War on Want, *Profiting from Poverty*, p.7.
25. Goldman Sachs International, *Report to the Department of Transport of Ireland: Evaluation of Ownership Options Regarding Aer Lingus Group* (Goldman Sachs International, 2004), p.6.
26. Sweeney, *Selling Out*, p.79.
27. United States District Court, Southern District of New York, Civil Action No.03 Civ.2944 (WHP).
28. P. Gumbel, 'How it all went sour'. *Time Europe*, 29 November 2004.
29. Deloitte, *The Effects of Politics on Energy M&A: Central Europe and CIS Regions*, Deloitte energy and resources paper, January 2006.
30. SIPTU, *A New Flight Path for Aer Lingus* (Dublin: SIPTU, 2005), p.4.
31. D. Thomas, 'Aer Lingus Staff under Pressure to Quit'. Personneltoday.com, 20 July 2005.
32. D. Quinn, 'Why Ryanair's O'Leary is a true Home Grown Hero'. *Sunday Independent*, 19 February 2004.
33. R. Curran, 'Skies the Limit for Power-brokers'. *Irish Independent*, 5 June 2002.
34. S. Creaton, *Ryanair: How a Small Irish Airline conquered Europe* (London: Aurum, 2004), p.44.
35. Ibid., p.49.
36. Ibid., p.156.
37. See the Ryan-Be-Fair website www.ryan-be-fair.org.
38. S. McInerney. 'There is no such thing as a Free Flight and Lunch will be €14'. *Sunday Tribune*, 28 May 2006.
39. Commission for Communications Regulation, *Market Analysis –Wholesale Mobile Access and Call Origination: Consultation Paper* (Dublin: Comreg, 2004), p.43.
40. Ibid., p.43.
41. J.Mcmanus, 'Comreg's Efforts no match for Mobile Giant'. *Irish Times*, 23 January 2006.
42. I. Goggin, 'Market Liberalisation and Regulatory Reform – The lessons of California for the Irish Energy Market'. Paper to IBEC Energy Conference, 10 May 2001.
43. E. Oliver, 'Republic's Domestic Electricity Prices third lowest in Europe'. *Irish Times*, 21 June 1999.
44. International Energy Association, *Key Energy Statistics 2006* (Paris: IEA, 2006), p.44–5.
45. E. Oliver, 'Home Electricity market opening costs €120 million'. *Irish Times*, 5 April 2005.
46. I. Guider, 'CER spends €8 million on Consultants'. *Irish Examiner*, 4 July 2005.
47. S. Thomas, *Electricity Liberalisation: The End of the Beginning* (PSIRU, London, 2004) p.8.
48. J. McManus, 'Power Plant Proves to be a Goldmine'. *Irish Times*, 31 October 2005.
49. N. Connolly, 'No Power to the People in new Electricity Market'. *Sunday Business Post*, 6 February 2005.
50. I. Guider, 'ESB to pay State Record €80 million'. *Irish Examiner*, 6 July 2005.
51. E. Oliver, 'National Grid warns of Plant Shortage'. *Irish Times*, 11 December 2004.
52. E. Oliver, 'Surge in 'amber alerts' hits Electricity System'. *Irish Times*, 8 December 2005.

Chapter Ten

People Before Profit

In the north-west corner of Mayo just above Rossport in the town land of Ceathru Thaidhg, there is a large expanse of land that overlooks a roaring sea. A dense carpet of grass covers a blanket bog that stretches far into the distance. There are no walls, fences or signs of ownership as the land is a commonage. A number of designated families from the surrounding area own the ground and no one can claim a right to private possession. It is a quaint survival of a long distant past when individual ownership was regarded as something of an oddity. Throughout history, elites have eyed and sized up common land until they fenced it off and called it their own. Each time they did, though, it called forth a great resistance.

In the Roman empire, there were publicly owned lands, known as the *ager publicus*, which had been farmed for generations by the free labour of smallholder collectives. The rich had to accept them but, 'after a time', Plutarch records, 'the wealthy men, by using the names of fictitious tenants, contrived to transfer many of these holdings to themselves, and finally they openly took possession of the greater part of the land under their own name'.[1] By the second century BC, the rich had carved great estates out of this public land and developed further as a patrician class. Yet decades later the Roman poor gave their enthusiastic backing to the Gracchi brothers, Tiberius and Gaius, as they sought to undo the conquest before being finally cut down.

In pre-modern Europe, the nobility continually encroached on common land, 'waste' land, forests, in the hope of increasing rent. With the rise of the money economy, the enclosure of the commons accelerated as peasants were pushed out to make way for sheep or cattle. The land grabbers covered their crimes in a cloak of respectability and insisted that their names be prefaced with Lord or Sir. Once again, it called forth bitter resistance as movements like the Anabaptists in Germany proclaimed that 'God had made all things in common as today we enjoy air, fire, rain and sun in common, and whatever else some thieving, tyrannical man cannot get hold of and keep for himself'.[2] Their sentiments were echoed two hundred years later in a popular song in Britain,

> The law locks up the man or woman
> Who steals the goose from off the common
> But leaves the greater villain loose
> Who steals the common from the goose.

The tragedy of movements to defend the commons was that they could not propose a way of taking society forward. The expropriation of land by elites was double edged – it brought a great inequality but it also allowed some resources to be used to develop technology and dynamic forms of social organization. Sharing and cultivating land in common in the seventeenth or eighteenth century would have preserved greater equality, but would also have condemned humanity to back-breaking toil.

Today a modern enclosure movement is underway, but it is not about land but the very fabric of society itself. It also occurs at a time when the present socio-economic system has exhausted itself. Far from offering social advances that might alleviate human suffering, it promises only regression and greater misery. The inequalities of early capitalism produced huge social movements that forced it to accept the concept of public utilities, social welfare provision and public institutions. The modern enclosure movement seeks to break up this 'social wage' that gave the majority in the western world some degree of security from the ravages of the market.

The devastating effects of the new attack on the commons are to be seen everywhere. The Victorians could build modern sewerage and water systems to distribute water free to its citizens – modern capitalism sells bottled water and puts in meters. In the conformist decades of the 1950s, most western societies accepted bland ideas about free education or a healthcare system that treated people according to human need. Today, the corporations subvert the free inquiry at the heart of education, and openly advocate a new apartheid in medical treatment between the rich and the poor. In the past, many white-collar employees expected to retire on a fixed percentage of their salary, paid for by an occupational pension scheme that their company subsidized. But in 2006, Bank of Ireland, which made €1.03 billion in profit the previous year, sent a memo to new staff saying they could no longer join such schemes.[3] Ireland, which is supposed to be one of the great success stories of contemporary capitalism, has also the lowest pension wealth.[4]

The new attacks on the commons are designed to cut charges on capital, to commodify the social world and to raise new forms of tribute. Led by the world's finance houses, the large corporations have broken away from the social compromises that grew up in the post-war era, and refuse to pay taxes to fund social rights. In 1965, US corporate taxes made up 4 per cent of gross domestic product, but in 2002, after these same corporations grew enormously, their taxes amounted to only 1.5 per cent of GDP.[5] This has caused the public services to shrink because of the drying up of funding. As a result, the state itself no longer provides adequate services to its citizens, but contracts out many areas from water treatment plants to hospitals. On top of all this, corporations are demanding extra tribute from society. The two key mechanisms are bio-piracy, where they take out patents on living cells and raid the world's genetic stockpile, and intellectual property, where charges are levied on everything from music to scientific discoveries. These trends, as we have seen, are particularly evident in Ireland.

The enclosure of the commons is linked to another important trend in late capitalism – the attempt to increase the rate of exploitation of workers. The term exploitation has, of course, a harsh ring to it, and few employers will say that they want more of it. It is far more likely that certain platitudes will be used about 'flexibility' to meet 'customer requirements'. 'Flexibility' is one of those nebulous terms that has close parallels with the way in which words like 'globalization' are used. It purports to describe a new spirit of the age driven by technological imperatives and cultural changes such as 'individualization'. But just as we saw with 'globalization', it cannot be analyzed without reference to the growth of corporate power. When looked at from this background, it appears as another rhetorical device to remove barriers to capital.

In the past, many workers had definite expectations about how work was regulated. There were certain 'inflexible' rules such as job descriptions, weekends off, overtime payments for after-hours work and, crucially, a sharp distinction between work and leisure. Early capitalism favoured the latter distinction as they sought to infuse the workforce with a new industrial discipline.[6] Waged work took place in the employers' time and so manual workers had to clock in and clock out. If they wanted to show creativity or enjoy social interaction, they were to do that 'in their own time'. In late capitalism, however, these rules are seen as a hindrance to using workers just when and where their corporation needs them. As Madeleine Bunting puts it,

> The traditional patterns of working time and individuals private lives, which provided boundaries between work and rest, have been erased. This 'timelessness' is one of the characteristics required of a flexible labour force. It takes on different characteristics in different jobs: shift systems which start early or late; on call requirements; weekend working; an increase in night shifts. Work intrudes into a million bedrooms with pagers, bleepers, and alarms to interrupt your rest.[7]

Once at work, the modern employee is expected to show 'functional flexibility', willing to go beyond their contract to do different forms of work and ready to be redeployed wherever they are needed. This means a change of mind-set so that the employee puts their body and soul into the job. The great irony is that although corporations repeatedly stress that everything is reducible to the cash nexus, workers are expected to show commitment and emotional involvement with their brand. As consultants with the Hay group put it,

> It is about striking a new contract in which the organisation invests *emotionally* in its workforce. In exchange, employees make a similar emotional investment, pouring their

'discretionary effort' into their work and delivering superior performance. The new contract says, 'We'll make your job (and life) more meaningful. You give us your hearts and minds'.[8]

The demands for greater flexibility and emotional subservience to corporate banalities is certainly at odds with the rhetoric about a 'knowledge society' where each can enjoy 'empowerment' and 'autonomy'. It is sometimes assumed that those with higher educational qualifications are likely to experience greater job satisfaction because they have 'cultural capital'. Some sociologists who think we have entered a post-industrial society often repeat this image of a 'polarized' labour force with middle-class winners and unskilled manual victims. Thus, O'Riain has argued that Ireland has a 'post-industrial professionalized labour force'[9] composed of a mainly male workforce in high tech business and finance, and a mainly female, public sector, social-services grouping. Both, it is claimed, are buffered from job insecurity and have opened a growing distance between themselves and the rest of the labour force.

This notion of a 'polarized' labour force misses the way in which white-collar work is undergoing major change. These changes mean that differences within the labour force are relatively minor when compared to the polarization that has opened up between most workers, white collar and blue collar, and the neo-liberal elite. Computers and satellite technology may make it easier to transmit information, but they do not change the social relations under which an economy is organized. Claims that we have moved to a 'knowledge' or 'post-industrial society' are quite abstract categories because they ignore the concentration of economic power in corporations and neglect to focus on their new drive to intensify work effort. Ironically, given all rhetoric about knowledge society, it is white-collar employees who currently face the most pressure to conform to the new demands. Studies in Ireland are limited in this area, so we need to look elsewhere to establish patterns.

One of the key researchers in this area is Francis Green, who has argued that many of the technical changes which have reshaped white-collar work tend to enhance the ability of management to deliver work more quickly to specific, targeted individuals. The email and the laptop, for example, means that work can be brought directly to a mobile staff and the distinction between work and leisure time can be blurred. This effort-biased technology has reduced 'job discretion' and increased 'work strain'. Whereas manual workers were the principal targets of job insecurity and intensification of work in the 1980s, white-collar employees have experienced this in the 1990s. He notes,

> The rise of job strain is associated with work intensifica-
> tion, while the fall in job satisfaction is associated partly
> with work intensification but also with the falling extent of
> discretion that workers have in their daily task ... that dis-
> cretion fell across all occupations and industries, but espe-
> cially for professional workers.[10]

The growth in work intensity is confirmed by the European surveys on working conditions. 56 per cent of respondents now say
they are working at very high speed, and 60 per cent contend
with tight deadlines at least one quarter of their time.[11] Job insecurity and work intensification is associated with poor general
health and tense family relationships.[12] In the US, studies of
more routine white-collar work found a similar pattern,

> From the automated check-out counter in retail to Global
> Positioning Systems in transportation to electronic medical
> records, new technologies are being implemented in forms
> that management can easily manipulate and control, and
> then in turn used to control the work process and the
> workers therein.[13]

No matter how much information management possess,
however, they are never fully in control and so it would be
wrong to assume that workers are powerless. However, the
point is that in the Orwellian world of late capitalism, the rhetoric about information technology and the knowledge economy
is often a cover for greater managerial control over the work
process. This change is often recognized in casual conversation.
Whereas in the past, people often answered the question 'How's
it going?' with the cursory response of 'fine', now it is not
uncommon to hear answers such as 'busy' or even 'frantic'.

On two central fronts, therefore, corporations are seeking their full liberation. They will not accept any corporate free zones that protect areas of the social world from commodification and profit. And there are to be no barriers to the intensification of work and raising the rate of exploitation. It is truly an extraordinary transformation – but why did it occur?

The most plausible explanation is that something profound has occurred within the functioning of the wider economic system. Dumenil and Levy have charted how capitalism has faced a number of 'structural crises' over the past hundred years that have been resolved in different ways.[14] In the late 1930s, the structural crisis was resolved though greater state intervention, the suppression of financial speculation and the growth of a new managerial autonomy that allowed for compromise with the workforce. In the 1970s, modern capitalism again entered a structural crisis and neo-liberalism was offered as a solution. It was based on a strong utopian element that sought a return to 'pure markets', but in reality it also represented an important shift within the ruling elite. Instead of the social compromises of the past, it offered a new mechanism of rule, namely 'a mode of domination based on the institution of insecurity, domination through precariousness: a deregulated financial market that fosters a deregulated labour market and thereby the casualisation of labour that cows workers into submission'.[15]

The aim was to reverse the decline in rates of profitability through an aggressive assertion of 'shareholder value' where high dividends were demanded within each corporation. Inside the workplace that meant more pressure on staff – outside, it meant new demands to cut costs and plunder parts of the public realm.

This neo-liberal project grew within a particular political context – a weakening US economy and a re-assertion of its military power. Overall, the US share of world manufacturing production sank from over 50 per cent in 1945 to 31 per cent in 1980, and is now about 25 per cent.[16] Nothing underlines the slide more than a shift from being the world's largest creditor nation to becoming the world largest debtor nation. The US is still the largest economy and retains important advantages over both its European and Chinese rivals. In a competitive world, however, elites do not worry just about absolutes but about how they are doing relative to their rivals.

The neo-liberal project arose in the late 1970s as a US domestic response to this decline. US 'runaway' corporations found that by shifting production to countries like South Korea they could undercut their rivals. At home, Reagan's destruction of the air traffic controllers' union, PATCO, inspired an employers' offensive that reduced real wages for nearly twenty years. More broadly, the US used deregulation to become the centre of the global financial system. As Harvey put it, 'Threatened in the realm of production, the US countered by asserting its hegemony through finance'.[17] Through the medium of the financial institutions and global governance structures such as the WTO, where the US had an inordinate influence, the neo-liberal project was spread throughout the world.

Neo-liberalism was also inextricably coupled with its twin brother of war and militarism. The vast discrepancy between the relative decline of the US's economic weight and its overwhelming military prowess was simply too tempting for its elite. They quickly understood that by controlling oil supplies and reminding economic rivals such as Japan or Europe of their dependence on its security umbrella, the US could gain significant leverage. Sometimes that leverage came with the hidden transfer of financial resources to the Dollar-Wall Street regime. At other times it allowed the US to exert extra pressure to open markets to products such as GM food where it had taken a lead. The sheer military power was also the ultimate protection for the neo-liberal project of plundering the global commons.

The connection between neo-liberalism and support for the US imperial project is by no means absolute. There are many ruling elites who admire the recipe of neo-liberalism, but feel threatened by the ambitions of the neo-cons who have seized control in Washington. There are also a minority within some elites who are comfortable with US hegemony but worry about the social tensions generated by the neo-liberal model. However, within the Irish elite, the connections are close and tight.

The Irish political elite, have embraced neo-liberalism on a grand scale and have offered themselves as a bridgehead for US influence in Europe. The most tangible token of their loyalty is manifested in the way the second largest airport at Shannon has been turned into a US war-port. But on a broader level, the Irish elite has thoroughly embraced the new robbery of the commons, and has rewarded tribute from intellectual property and bio-piracy by removing tax on patents. Their enthusiasm to help Microsoft and the US-led pharmaceutical industry knows no bounds. Despite rhetorical flourishes about social solidarity, they thoroughly support the Boston model of privatization and deregulation. Thomas Friedman, *New York Times* columnist who rivals Kevin Myers in his tooth and claw embrace of the present world order, has attributed the growth of the Celtic Tiger to an 'Anglo-Saxon' model of flexible labour markets and suggested that

The Germans and French may want to take a few tips from the Celtic Tiger. One of the first reforms Ireland instituted was to make it easier to fire people, without having to pay years of severance. Sounds brutal, I know. But the easier it is to fire people, the more willing companies are to hire.[18]

Although Friedman is wrong to claim that sackings bring an economic boom, his more interesting point is made implicitly: Ireland is viewed as very much part of the Anglo-American camp.

The corporate take-over of twenty-first-century Ireland is therefore evident in the three central dimensions. There is a concerted attempt to subjugate schools, universities, hospitals, waste collection and public utilities to a corporate model, and in some cases privatize them completely. There is a strategy to weaken the unions at ground level to give management a free hand to intensify work. There is a close alignment of Irish foreign policy with the needs of the US empire. But on each of these dimensions there is resistance.

PEOPLE POWER

The resistance takes many forms and is closely related to levels of confidence and organization. It arises because the hegemony of the ruling elite has been weakened by the neo-liberal project. 'Hegemony' was a term that the Italian Marxist, Gramsci, developed to explain how the outlook of a society's rulers is embraced by the wider population.[19] This occurs because a middle layer of teachers, priests or local dignitaries function as a conveyor belt to win the loyalty of those below them. Today, however, this hegemony is weaker because while many will sullenly accept the present order of society, they do so with a growing distrust and cynicism. The majority of people in the Western world, for example, view the US President as a dangerous extremist. They dislike the fanatical zeal of business leaders like Michael O'Leary. There is a deep and profound cynicism about absurd forms of business-speak that pervade everyday discourse.

Cynicism, however, is a double-edged sword – it implies a withdrawal of faith in an elite, but it also mingles with a sense of powerlessness. This fatalism has become one of the most important weapons in the armoury of the elite who trade on a myth of their invincibility. As long as they can convince their opponents that they will always be divided and will never gain victories, they are secure. This is one reason why our rulers encourage the idea of a 'dog eat dog' world where everyone only looks out for themselves and where no sustained collective action is possible. This viewpoint can, unfortunately, receive an echo from activists who have been burnt by past defeats and who harbour a bitterness about the way their fellow workers or neighbours did not support them. In fact, however, there have always been large social movements that can inflict defeats on those above them.

Every weekend in summer, thousands stroll on the beautiful seafront of Dun Laoghaire to enjoy a view of an expansive sea. Yet developers once eyed this particular commons and made plans to build hundreds of upper-class apartments right on the seafront. An abject local council who felt they were short of funds was willing to destroy a historic building which once housed the local baths in return for a PPP scheme to gain extra money. However, local activists established a Save our Seafront Campaign and planned resistance. 'We were called lunatics by a local Labour Party councillor for daring to oppose the plans', explained Richard Boyd Barrett, the chairperson of the campaign 'but we knew that if we mobilized the majority we would win through "people power".[20] Soon protests grew from hundreds to thousands, and politicians scrambled for a space on platforms. At one point, the legendary singers Christy Moore and Ronnie Drew sung to an audience of thousands to stir up spirits. And Boyd Barrett was right – there are no apartments on Dun Laoghaire's seafront today because the local campaign won.

Neither is there a nuclear power plant in Carnsore Point despite the best efforts of the government to build one. Twenty years ago, tens of thousands made their way 'to the point' to say it would never happen. A vibrant anti-nuclear campaign educated hundreds about the danger of nuclear power stations and they, in turn, were able to convince the majority of their fellow citizens to mobilize against the government.

Neither do Irish people pay water charges because of another mass movement which defeated the rulers. In the mid-1990s, all the political establishment from Labour to Fianna Fail argued that since the EU had decreed there must be water charges, 'resistance was futile'. At the countless local meetings, people also heard the argument that although their local politician was 'totally opposed' to the charges, there was no option but to abide by the law and pay up. However, good sense prevailed when people decided they would not obey unjust laws and refused to pay. When contractors were sent to the Hillview estate in Waterford to disconnect the water supply of non-payers, they were surrounded by hundreds of local residents who forced them to leave. When similar contractors went into other areas and turned off the water, teams of plumbers who were linked to the anti-water charges campaign reconnected the supply. Once again, 'people power' succeeded, and today the Irish are unique in Europe in not paying for water.

The weakest area of resistance over the last two decades has been organized labour, as social partnership has damaged the movement. However, the unions are not a monolith and are subject to pressure from below. When Irish Ferries tried to make its staff redundant, shop stewards came to the SIPTU conference and asked their fellow delegates for support. The response was electric and activists left the conference determined to build solidarity. All the legal armoury which had been so carefully constructed to weaken unions was simply brushed aside as thousands joined a solidarity strike. Employers who toyed with the idea that Eamonn Rothwell, the owner of Irish Ferries, might be their new William Martin Murphy, became alarmed. The Bank of Ireland even distanced itself from comments made about the dispute by its chief economist, Dan McLoughlin. The movement forced Irish Ferries to retreat and pay a minimum wage. More could have been won if the union leaders had not lost their nerve and settled for a weaker compromise than was necessary. But the message was still out: people power gets results.

Not always, of course, and the frustrating thing for many people is the dawning recognition of just how high the stakes can be. On 15 February 2003, over 100,000 people marched against Bush's threatened war on Iraq. It was part of a global day of action that saw millions demonstrate around the world. The Taoiseach, Bertie Ahern, responded with some buffoonery about how the march was really supporting his foreign policies, and then increased support for Bush. Behind the scenes, a more repressive response was put in place as posters were removed from the streets of Dublin and advertisements for an anti-war concert with Christy Moore were banned from RTE. The majority of people who marched on 15 February 2003 thought that if the people of the world displayed their opposition to war, then surely their governments would listen. When this did not happen, many drew the conclusion that marching does not achieve anything. A minority, however, understood that the Irish government is not answerable to its own people, but to the military-industrial complex that dominates the US. Their conclusion was that the movement had to go beyond marching to mass civil disobedience.

Two great forces, therefore, will shape the direction of twenty-first-century Ireland. On the one hand are the corporations, the political elite and those they have convinced of the neo-liberal way. On the other hand, are networks of resistance that straddle the social movements and organized labour. Success for the anti-corporate forces depends on linking these different strands of their movement together and developing an alternative political vision.

ANOTHER IRELAND IS POSSIBLE

When Noam Chomsky visited Ireland, thousands queued up to hear him at every meeting where he spoke. There were many more who identify with the sentiments of a broader anti-capitalist movement that has swept the world since the huge protests in Seattle in 1999. This ferment of radical ideas does not often feature in the conventional media, but it sustains many of the protest movements that have developed recently. The activists who have developed in these networks have the energy and enthusiasm to offer an alternative vision of Ireland to the picture I have painted in this book.

But they will not do so if they cut themselves off and adopt a moralistic attitude to the majority of the population because any strategy that seeks to bring change through an enlightened minority is doomed. The sheer resources that corporations now possess mean that small activist networks will become either marginalized or co-opted. The only way to win the world back from the corporations is to wield together a movement that has greater power than them. That can only come from the fusion of the energy that has developed in activist networks with the potential power of organized labour.

Organized labour has been in a Rip Van Winkle style sleep for two decades. While it was slumbering under the beguiling canopy of social partnership, the neo-liberals changed the country. Those changes have in turn bred a certain defeatism in its ranks. Shop stewards, for example, often want to stand up to aggressive employers, but are unsure of how to resist because their leadership keep referring to 'proper procedures' which diffuse their power. However, the energy and experience that come from the large scale protests outside the channels of organized labour can help to lift this defeatism.

This broad movement that relies on protest, direct action and people power receives little real support from the official left composed of Labour, Sinn Fein and the Greens. The parties of the old left aim to get into government, and movements from below are seen principally as a stepping stone on the way. The old left associate themselves with the anti-war rallies and offer to speak on the platforms of local protests, but do not see 'people power' as the new way of doing politics. Instead the old left keeps its options for government open and, incredibly, none will rule out the possibility of entering a coalition with Fianna Fail or Fine Gael. This supposedly 'realistic' strategy only stores up a disillusioned cynicism that will flower in future if there is not a better alternative.

What Ireland needs, therefore, is a new left party that will look to 'people power' to defeat the influence that corporations currently hold over society. Such a party should not be afraid to acknowledge that it is formed from diverse backgrounds and is open to debate on the best way to end corporate power. Some may come to a new Left party from many years of working in parties like Labour, and will not drop their belief in the need for fundamental reforms. Others will argue that the system itself is fundamentally flawed and will advocate a more revolutionary road. But what they have in common is that they base themselves on social movements and 'people power' to defeat neo-liberalism.

Is such a new left party possible in Ireland? It is certainly happening elsewhere and is indeed the main hope for the international left. In Germany, a new left party has come together under the leadership of Oscar Lafontaine, and includes a mixture of revolutionaries, ex-communists and old labour trade unionists. In Portugal, a Left Bloc has arisen from a series of social movements and offers the main radical alternative. In Britain, new left parties have emerged in the form of Solidarity in Scotland and Respect in England and Wales. In France, there is an intense debate underway about constructing such a formation after the defeat of the Nice treaty, and government plans to make it easier to dismiss younger workers. Throughout Latin America many are inspired by the example of Venezuela and Bolivia to seek a different way of doing politics. There seems no reason, therefore, why a new left party is not possible in Ireland.

One of the great myths that came out of the US think tanks was the 'end of history' thesis where it was claimed that there was no longer any alternative to capitalism.[21] Many, however, reject this myth and the anti-corporate movement has emerged on the global stage with the simple slogan, 'Another world is possible'. The slogan encapsulates both the diversity of the movement and a new confidence that history has indeed not ended. But it also raises a question: what exactly is the alternative that is offered? The dilemma that confronts any advocate of change is that, if they outline a detailed blueprint, they appear as messianic and impractical whereas, if they do not offer anything, they appear as if they are only negative. This dilemma can only be resolved if we see an alternative Ireland being based on three broad principles.

First, the vast concentration of economic power that corporations now posses must be broken up and their resources taken into public ownership. The huge corporations that dominate our lives are pre-eminently social institutions. They coordinate the labour of tens of thousands of people but do so in a way that subordinates their needs and that of the wider society to privileged people who sit on the boards of directors. But, it may be asked, what possible social function do these boards perform? Their primary purpose appears to be to extract shareholder value in the form of dividend payments to the already rich. Why could the actual work that is performed by corporations not be controlled by the representatives of society itself rather than a handful of directors? In this way, society gets a say in how its resources are deployed and democracy becomes more meaningful. Public ownership of the commanding heights of the economy makes more sense now than at any time since the idea was first promulgated. The commanding heights, it should be stressed, do not include chip shops, bicycle shops and most petty enterprises that consume the energies of their owners. Therefore, a proposal to take the large corporations into public ownership is only against the interests of a tiny minority.

Second, decisions about the economy cannot be left to a mystical force known as 'the invisible hand' of the market. For hundreds of years, it was argued that the mass of the people could not have a say in the running of their society and they had to leave decision-making to a king or queen who was God's appointee on earth. In a similar fashion, it is often asserted today that most people can have no input into running an economy because it is 'too complex'. But this is a fundamentally undemocratic assumption. There is no good reason why society cannot develop institutions which make decisions on how economic resources can be deployed in a cooperative fashion. Our planet faces major threats in the coming decades from global warming and only a high level of cooperation and planning could possibly rectify this. We can no longer afford absurd forms of competition whereby countries and corporations compete to buy pollution slots for their CO_2 emissions. We need instead to share the technology which can reduce those emissions and plan together how we will undo past damage. If that principle applies to the survival of the planet itself, it equally must apply to other areas of human need. Instead of boards of directors dictating which pharmaceuticals will be produced, or how much money will be wasted on advertising, society as a whole should democratically plan what needs to be produced.

Third, the key issue, therefore, is the limits or scope of democracy itself. Universal suffrage was an historical achievement that was won through the struggle of previous generations. But today parliamentary rule is being hollowed out from the inside by the rise of corporate power. Far from governments representing the will of the people, we have moved to a 'managed-democracy' where periodic elections are used to legitimate decisions already made. This is covered over by vacuous forms of 'stakeholder consultation' which replace anything resembling an active citizenry that has an input into decisions.

This can only be reversed if democracy is not simply understood as a purely political phenomenon, but has important economic dimensions as well. There is a strange paradox in rhetorically asserting that all have a right to vote in general elections to determine how the country will be run, and then claiming that in their daily working lives, these same people must do exactly as they are told. Democracy cannot just be about 'running the country' but it must also be about having a say on how the local workplace is organized. The absurd notion that some must function as permanent 'managers' while others are not 'paid to think' is surely a relic of past ages that has no more validity than the notion that aristocrats are born to rule. An alternative Ireland must therefore embody a form of economic democracy which starts to end the distinction between mental and manual labour, and the division between conception and execution, which are the core principles around which work is presently organized. Only by using the combined energies of all can we generate better productivity and efficiencies.

It is not necessary to sketch how these principles might apply in precise detail. Indeed, it would be faintly absurd to do so. They are merely pointers to suggest that another Ireland, which is free from corporate domination, is possible. The real challenge is to make it happen.

NOTES

1. Quoted in M. Parenti, *The Assassination of Julius Caesar: A People's History of Ancient Rome* (New York/London: New Press, 2003), p.48.
2. N. Cohn, *The Pursuit of the Millennium: Revolutionary Millenarians and Mystical Anarchists of the Middle Ages* (London: Pimlico, 2004), p.258.
3. 'Bank of Ireland at War with Unions over Pensions'. *Finance Week*, 30 May 2006.
4. OECD, *Pensions at a Glance: Public Policies across OECD Countries* (Paris: OECD, 2005), p.3.
5. 'The Corporate Tax Game' *Business Week*, 31 March 2003.
6. E.P. Thompson, 'Time, Work Discipline and Industrial Capitalism', in *Customs in Common* (London: Merlin, 1991).
7. Bunting, *Willing Slaves: How the Overwork Culture is Ruling our Lives* (London: Harper Collins, 2004), p.16.
8. Ibid., p.110.
9. S. O'Riain, *The Politics of High Tech Growth: Developmental Network States in the Global Economy* (Cambridge: Cambridge University Press, 2005), p.140.
10. F. Green, 'Work Intensification, Discretion and Decline in Well Being at Work'. *Eastern Economic Journal*, 30, 4 (2004), pp.615–25.
11. P. Paoli and D. Merllie, *Third European Survey on Working Conditions 2000* (Dublin: European Foundation, 2001), p.14.
12. ESCR Centre for Business Research, *Job Insecurity and Work Intensification: Flexibility and the Boundaries of Work* (London: Rowntree Foundation, 1999).
13. C. Richardson and N. Lessin, 'Call Centres and the Postal Service: Looking at the Future of Work', in T. Juravich, *The Future of Work in Massachusetts* (Amherst, MA: University of Massachusetts, 2005), p.25.
14. G. Dumenil and D. Levy, *The Nature and Contradictions of Neo-Liberalism* (Paris: CEPREMAP-ENS, 2004).
15. P. Bourdieu, *Firing Back: Against the Tyranny of the Market* (London: Verso, 2005), p.29.
16. J. Rees, *Imperialism and Resistance* (London: Routledge, 2006), p.43.
17. D. Harvey, *The New Imperialism* (Oxford: Oxford University Press, 2003), p.62.
18. T. Friedman, 'Follow the Leapin' Leprechaun'. *New York Times*, 1 July 2005.
19. Perry Anderson, 'The Antimonies of Antonio Gramsci'. *New Left Review*, 100 (Nov. 1976–Jan. 1977), pp.5–78.
20. Interview with author.
21. F. Fukuyama, *The End of History and the Last Man* (Harmondsworth: Penguin, 1992).

Select Bibliography

Abramson, J., *Overdosed America* (New York: Harper Perennial, 2004).

Acuff, D., *What Kids Buy and Why* (New York: The Free Press, 1997).

Allen, K., *Fianna Fail and Irish Labour: 1926 to the Present* (London: Pluto Press, 1997).

——, 'Double Speak: Command and Control Models in a Neo-Liberal Economy', in B. Fanning (ed.), *Immigration and Social Change in the Republic of Ireland* (Manchester: Manchester University Press, 2006), pp.96–113.

Allen, R., *No Global: The People of Ireland Versus the Multinationals* (London: Pluto Press, 2004).

Anderson, Perry, 'The Antimonies of Antonio Gramsci'. *New Left Review*, 100 (Nov. 1976–Jan. 1977), pp.5–78.

Anderson S. and J. Cavanagh, *Field Guide to the Global Economy* (New York: Norton, 2005).

Angell, M., *The Truth about Drug Companies* (New York: Random House, 2004).

Aries, P., *Centuries of Childhood* (London: Pimlico, 1996).

Bakan, J., *The Corporation: The Pathological Pursuit of Profit and Power* (London: Constable, 2004).

Barlow M. and T. Clake, *Blue Gold: The Battle Against Corporate Theft of the World's Water* (London: Earthscan, 2002).

Bellamy Foster, J., *Marx's Ecology* (New York: Monthly Review Press, 2000).

Bell, D., *The Coming of the Post Industrial Society* (New York: Basic Books, 1973).

Bew P. and H. Patterson, *Sean Lemass* (Dublin: Gill and MacMillan, 1982).

Blundel, J., *Waging the War of Ideas* (London: Institute of Economic Affairs, 2001).

Bollier, D., *Public Assets, Private Profits: Reclaiming the American Commons in an Age of Market Enclosure* (Washington: New America Foundation, 2001).

Bosanquet, N., *After The New Right* (Aldershot: Heinemann, 1984).

Bourdieu, P., *Firing Back: Against the Tyranny of the Market* (London: Verso, 2005).

Bowen, J., *A History of Western Education Vol.2* (London: Methuen, 1975).

Boyle, M., 'Cleaning up after the Celtic Tiger: Scalar "fixes" in the Political Ecology of Tiger Economies'. *Transactions of the Institute of British Geographers*, 27, 2 (2002), pp.172–94.

Braithwaite, J., 'Regulating Nursing Homes: The Challenge of Regulating Care for Older People in Australia'. *British Journal of Medicine*, 323, 7310 (25 August 2001), pp.443–6.

Brenner, R., *The Economics of Global Turbulence*. Special issue of *New Left Review*, 229 (1998).

Brenner, R., 'Towards the Precipice'. *London Review of Books*, 25, 3 (6 February 2003).

Bunting, M., *Willing Slaves: How Overwork Culture is Ruining our Lives* (London: Harper Collins, 2004).

Cahill D. and S. Beder, 'Regulating the Power Shift: The State, Capital and Electricity Privatisation in Australia'. *Journal of Australian Political Economy*, 55 (June 2005).

California Global Corporate Accountability Project, *Dodging Dilemmas? Environmental and Social Accountability in Global Operations of California-Based High Tech Companies* (San Francisco: California Global Accountability Project, 2002), pp.5–22.

Centre for Public Inquiry, *The Great Corrib Gas Controversy* (Dublin: CPI, 2005).

Chambers, D., *Protection or Pollution: An Evaluation of the Environmental Protection Agency* (Cork: Cork Environmental Alliance, no date).

Clancy, P. and G. Murphy, *Outsourcing Government: Public Bodies and Accountability* (Dublin: Tasc/New Island, 2000).

Cohn, N., *The Pursuit of the Millennium: Revolutionary Millenarians and Mystical Anarchists of the Middle Ages* (London: Pimlico, 2004).

Collins, S., *The Race to Commercialize BioTechnology: Molecules, Markets and the State in the United States and Japan* (London: Routledge, 2004).

Combat Poverty Agency, *Waste Collection Charges and Low Income Households* (Dublin: CPA, 2003).

Conroy, P. and M. Pierce, *Temporary Agency Work: National Reports Ireland* (Dublin: European Foundation for Improvement of Living and Working Conditions, 2002).

Constable, P. and A. Valenzuela, *A Nation of Enemies: Chile Under Pinochet* (New York: Norton, 1973).

Corporate Europe Observatory, *Power Struggle over Biotech in Brussels* (Brussels: CEO, 2004).

Corrigan, C., *OECD Thematic Review of Early Childhood Education and Care: Background Report, Ireland* (Paris: OECD, 2005).

Creaton, S., *Ryanair: How a Small Irish Airline Conquered Europe* (London: Aurum, 2004).

Crowley, D., A. Staines, C. Collins, J. Bracken, M. Bruen, J. Fry, V. Hrymak, D. Malone, B. Magette, M. Ryan and C. Thunhurst, *Health and Environmental Effects of Landfilling and Incineration of Waste – A Literature Review* (Dublin: Health Research Board, 2003).

CSO, *Quarterly National Household Survey: Travel to Work Module Q1 2000* (Dublin: CSO, 2000).

——, *Environmental Accounts for Ireland 1997–2004* (Dublin: CSO, 2006).

Cullen, P., *With a Little Help from my Friends: Planning Corruption in Ireland* (Dublin: Gill and Macmillan, 2002).

Cummins, I. and J. Beasant, *Shell Shock: The Secrets and Spin of an Oil Giant* (London: Mainstream Publishing, 2005).

Dale Tussing, A. and M. Wren, *How Ireland Cares: The Case for Health Care Reform* (Dublin: New Island, 2006).

Dore, R. *Stock Market Capitalism: Welfare Capitalism* (Oxford: Oxford University Press, 2000).

Devereaux, P.J., P. Choi, C. Lacchetti, B. Weaver, H. Schunemann, T. Haines, J. Lavis, B. Grant, D. Haslam, M. Bhandari, T. Sullivan, D. Cook, S. Walyer, M. Meade, H.

Khan, N. Bhatnagar and G. Guyatt, 'A Systematic Review and Meta-analysis of Studies Comparing Mortality Rates of Private for Profit and Private not for Profit Hospitals'. *Canadian Medical Association Journal*, 166, 11 (28 May 2002), pp.1399–1406.

Draekord, M., *Privatisation and Social Policy* (Harlow: Longman, 2000).

Dring, C. and A. Hope, *The Impact of Alcohol Advertising on Teenagers in Ireland* (Dublin: Health Promotion Unit, Department of Health and Children, 2001).

Dumenil, G. and D. Levy, *The Nature and Contradictions of Neo-Liberalism* (Paris: CEPREMAP-ENS, 2004).

Ebenstein, A., *Friedrich Hayek* (New York: Palgrave, 2001).

——, *Hayek's Journey: The Mind of Frederich Hayek* (Basingstoke: Palgrave, 2003).

Elliot, L. and D. Atkinson, *The Age of Insecurity* (London: Verso, 1998).

Enterprise Strategy Group, *Ahead of the Curve: Ireland's Place in the Global Economy* (Dublin: Forfas, 2004).

EPA, *The Nature and Extent of Unauthorised Waste Activity in Ireland* (Dublin: EPA, 2005).

——, *National Waste Report 2004* (Dublin: EPA, 2005).

——, *Municipal Solid Waste Incineration as part of Ireland's Integrated Waste Management Strategy* (Dublin: EPA, no date).

ESCR Centre for Business Research, *Job Insecurity and Work Intensification: Flexibility and the Boundaries of Work* (London: Rowntree Foundation, 1999).

European Environment Agency, *Environment in the European Union at the turn of the Century* (Brussels: EEA, 1999).

——, *Effectiveness of Packaging Waste Management Systems in Selected Countries: An EEA Pilot Study* (Brussels: EEA, 2005).

——, *The European Environment: State and Outlook 2005* (Brussels: EEA, 2005)

Florio, M., *The Great Divesture* (Cambridge, MA: MIT Press 2004).

Forfas, *Waste Management Benchmarking Study* (Dublin: Forfas, 2006).

Frank, Thomas, *One Market under God* (New York: Random House, 2000)

Friedman, M., *There is No Such Thing as a Free Lunch* (LaSalle, IL: Open Court, 1975).

——, *Capitalism and Freedom* (Chicago: University of Chicago Press, 1982).

Frieberg, M., B. Saffran, T. Stinson, W. Nelson and C. Bennett, 'Evaluation of Conflict of Interest in Economic Analysis on New Drugs in Oncology'. *Journal of American Medical Association*, 282, 15 (20 October 1999), pp.1453–7.

Fukuyama, F., *The End of History and the Last man* (Harmondsworth: Penguin, 1992

Geiger, R., *Knowledge and Money: Research Universities and the Paradox of the Marketplace* (Palo Alto, CA: Stanford University Press, 2004).

Gelinas, J., *Juggernaut Politics: Understanding Predatory Globalisation* (London and New York: Zed Books, 2003).

Giddens, A., *Beyond Left and Right* (Cambridge: Polity, 1994).

Giroux, H., *Stealing Innocence: Corporate Culture's War on Children* (New York: Palgave, 2000).

Giroux, H. and S. Giroux, *Take Back Higher Education* (New York: Palgrave Macmillan, 2006).

Goodbody Consultants, *Review of Area-Based Tax Incentive Renewal Schemes: Final Report* (Dublin: Government Publications, 2005).

Goozner, M., *The $800 Million Pill* (Berkeley, CA: University of California Press, 2004).

Gould, E. and C. Joy, *In Whose Service* (London: World Development Movement, 2000).

Gramsci, A., *Selections from Prison Note Books* (London: Lawrence and Wishart, 1971).

Green, F., 'Work Intensification, Discretion and Decline in Well Being at Work'. *Eastern Economic Journal*, 30, 4 (2004), pp.615–25.

Greenberg, D., *Science, Money and Politics* (Chicago, IL: University of Chicago Press, 2001).

Grossman, R. and F. Adams, *Taking Care of Business: Citizenship and the Charter of Incorporation* (Yarmouth, MA: Charter Ink, 1993).

Hall, D., 'Privatisation, Multi-nationals and Corruption'. *Development in Practice*, 9, 5 (November 1999), pp.539–56.

Hardin, G., 'The Tragedy of the Commons'. *Science*, 162 (13

December 1968), pp.1243–8.

Harrington, C., 'Residential Nursing Facilities in the United States'. *British Journal of Medicine*, 323, 7311 (1 September 2001), pp.507–10.

Harrington, C., C. Kovner, M. Mezey, J. Kayser-Jones, S. Burger and M. Mohler, 'Experts Recommend Minimum Nurse Staffing Standards for Nursing Facilities in the United States'. *Gerontologist*, 40, 1 (2000), pp.5–16.

Harrington, C., S. Woolhandler, J. Mullan, H. Carrillo and D. Himmelstein, 'Does Investor-Ownership of Nursing Homes Compromise the Quality of Care'. *International Journal of Health Sciences*, 32, 2 (2002) pp.315–25.

Harvey, D., *The New Imperialism* (Oxford: Oxford University Press, 2003).

Hastings, G., M. Stead, L. McDermott, A. Forsyth, A. MacKintosh, M. Rayner, C. Godfrey, M. Caraher and K. Angus, *Review of Research on The effects of Food Promotion to Children* (Glasgow: University of Strathclyde, Centre for Social Marketing, 2003).

Hayek, F., *Law, Legislation and Liberty: Vol.1, Rules and Order* (London: Routledge, 1973).

——, *The Constitution of Liberty* (London, New York: Routledge, 1993).

——, *The Road to Serfdom* (London: Routledge, 1997).

Henwood, D., *Wall St* (London: Verso, 1999).

Hibell, B., B. Andersson, S. Ahlstrom, O. Balakiereva, T. Bjarnason, A. Kokkevi and M. Morgan, *The 1999 European School Survey Project on Alcohol and Other Drugs Report: Alcohol and other drug use among students in 30 European countries* (Stockholm: The Swedish Council for Information on Alcohol and other Drugs, 2000).

Himmelstein, D., S. Wollhandler, I. Hellander and S. Wolfe, 'Quality of Care in Investor-Owned vs Not-for-Profit HMOs'. *Journal of American Medical Association*, 282, 2 (14 July 1999), pp.59–163.

Holborow, M., 'Language and Ideology: Interconnections between English and NeoLiberalism', in J. Edge (ed.), *ReLocating TESOL in the Age of Empire* (London: Palgrave, 2006), pp.96–7.

Indecon, *Review of Property based Tax Incentive Scheme: Report for Department of Finance* (Dublin: Government Publications, 2006).

Juravich, T., *The Future of Work in Massachusetts* (Amherst, MA: University of Massachusetts, 2005).

Keynes, J.M., *The General Theory of Employment, Interest and Money* (London: Macmillan, 1973).

Kirp, D., *Shakespeare, Einstein and the Bottom Line* (Harvard: Harvard University Press, 2003)

Klaehn, J., 'A Critical Review of Herman and Chomsky's "Propaganda Model"'. *European Journal of Communications*, 17, 2 (2002), pp.147–82.

Kleinert, J., *The Role of Multinational Enterprises in Globalization* (Kiel: Springer, 2004).

Krimsky, S., 'The Temptations of Corporate Funding'. *Trusteeship: Journal of Association of Governing Boards of Universities and Colleges*, (March/April 2004), pp.18–23.

——, 'The Profit of Scientific Discovery and Its Normative Effects'. *Chicago-Kent Law Review*, 75, 1, (1999), pp.15–39.

Krugman, P., *Peddling Prosperity: Economic Sense and Nonsense in an age of Diminished Expectation* (New York and London: Norton, 1994).

Krugman, P. and R. Wells, 'The Health Care Crisis and What to do About It'. *New York Review of Books*, 53, 5 (23 March 2006).

Labour Relations Commission, *Migrant Workers and Access to the Statutory Dispute Resolution Agencies* (Dublin: LRC, 2005).

Lang, T. and M. Headsman, *Food Wars* (London: Earthscan, 2004).

Lapavitas, C., 'Mainstream Economics in the Neoliberal Era', in A. Saad-Filho and D. Johnston (Eds), *Neoliberalism: A Critical Reader* (London: Pluto Press, 2005), pp.30–41.

Leonard, H.J., *Pollution and the Struggle for World Product: Multinational Corporations, Environment and International Comparative Advantage* (Cambridge: Cambridge University Press, 1988).

Levidow, L., 'Marketing Higher Education: Neo-liberal Strategies and Counter Strategies'. *Education and Social Justice*, 3, 2 (2001), pp.12–21.

Lexchin, J., 'Doctors and Dealers: Therapeutic Education of

Pharmaceutical Promotion'. *International Journal of Health Services*, 19, 4 (1989), pp.663–79.

Leys, C., *Market Driven Politics* (London: Verso, 2001).

McDowell, A., 'How Ireland Can Help to Complete the Trans Atlantic Marketplace', in J. Carroll and J. Travers (Eds), Institute of European Affairs, *An Indispensable Partnership: EU-US Relations from an Irish Perspective* (Dublin: IEA, 2004), pp.47–60.

McNeal, J., *Kids as Consumers: A Handbook of Marketing to Children* (New York: Lexington Books, 1992).

Mangan, I., *Older People in Long Stay Care* (Dublin: Irish Human Right Commission, 2003).

Marquand, D., *Decline of the Public: the Hallowing Out of Citizenship* (Cambridge: Polity, 2004).

Marshall, T.H., *Citizenship and Social Class* (Cambridge: Cambridge University Press, 1950).

Martin, S. and D. Parker, *The Impact of Privatisation: Ownership and Corporate Performance in the UK* (London: Routledge, 1997).

Mayo, E., *The Shopping Generation* (London: National Consumer Council, 2005).

Meagher, E., 'Compliance of Intel with Integration Pollution Prevention Control licence'. (MA Thesis, Department of Geography, National University of Ireland, Maynooth, 2005).

Merton, R., 'The Normative Structure of Science', in R. Merton, *The Sociology of Science* (Chicago, IL: University of Chicago Press, 1973), pp.267–78.

Moody, K., *Workers in a Lean World* (London: Verso, 1997).

Morgenroth, E., 'Waste Collection, Double Taxation and Local Finance', in T. Callan and A. Doris (eds), *Budget Perspective 2006* (Dublin: ESRI, 2005), pp.61–74.

Moynihan, R. and A. Cassels, *Selling Sickness: How Drug Companies are Turning us all into Patients* (Crows Nest, New South Wales: Allen and Unwin, 2005).

Mueller, F., *No Lobbyists as Such: The War over Software Patents in the European Union* (Starnberg, Germany: SWM Software Market, no date).

National Economic Social Forum, *Early Childhood Care and Education, Report 31* (Dublin: NESF, 2005).

National Women's Council of Ireland, *An Accessible Childcare Model* (Dublin: NWCI, 2006).

Noble, D., *Digital Diploma Mills: The Automation of Higher Education* (New York: Monthly Review Press, 2002).

O'Grady, P., *Why is the Irish Health Service in Crisis?* (Dublin: Bookmarks, 2005).

O'Riain, S., *The Politics of High Tech Growth: Developmental Network States in the Global Economy* (Cambridge: Cambridge University Press, 2005).

O'Toole, F., *After the Ball* (Dublin: New Island, 2003).

OECD, *Pensions at a Glance: Public Policies across OECD Countries* (Paris: OECD, 2005).

Ohmae, K., 'The End of the Nation State', in F. Lechner and J. Boli (Eds), *The Globalization Reader* (Oxford: Blackwell, 2003), pp.214–18.

Osborne, D. and T. Gaebler, *Reinventing Government* (Boston: Addison-Wesley, 1992).

Paoli, P. and D. Merllie, *Third European Survey on Working Conditions 2000* (Dublin: European Foundation, 2001).

Parenti, M., *The Assassination of Julius Caesar: a People's History of Ancient Rome* (New York/London: New Press, 2003).

Pattison, R. and H. Katz, 'Investor Owned and Not-For Profit Hospitals'. *New England Journal of Medicine*, 309, 6 (1983), pp.347–53.

Pollin, R., *Contours of Descent* (London: Verso, 2003).

Polanyi, K., *The Great Transformation* (Boston: Beacon Hill, 1957).

——, 'The Republic of Science', in P. Mirowski and E. Mirjam Sent (Eds), *Science: Bought and Sold* (Chicago: University of Chicago Press, 2002), pp.465–85.

Prashad, V., *Fat Cats and Running Dogs: The Enron Stage of Capitalism* (London: Zed Books, 2002).

Quart, A., *Branded: The Buying and Selling of Teenagers* (London: Arrow, 2003).

Quinn, B., *Maverick* (Dingle: Brandon, 2001).

Readings, B., *The University in Ruins* (Harvard: Harvard University Press, 1996).

Rees, J., *Imperialism and Resistance* (London: Routledge, 2006).

Richardson, C. and N. Lessin, 'Call Centres and the Postal Service: Looking at the Future of Work', in J. Rutherford,

'Cultural Studies in the Corporate University', in *Cultural Studies*, 19, 3 (May 2005), pp.297–317.

Schor, J., *Born to Buy* (New York: Scribner, 2004).

Shipan, C., *Independence and the Irish Environmental Agency: A Comparative Assessment* (Dublin: Policy Institute, TCD, 2003).

Shorter, E., *The Making of the Modern Family* (London, Collins, 1976).

Sidelsky, R., *John Maynard Keynes: The Economist as Saviour* (London: Penguin, 1992).

Silverman, E., J. Skinner and E. Fisher, 'The Association between for profit Hospital Ownership and Increased Medicare Spending'. *New England Journal of Medicine*, 341, 6 (August 1999), pp.420–5.

Slaughter, S. and G. Roades, 'The Emergence of a Competitiveness Research and Development Policy Coalition and the Commercialization of Academic Science and Technology', in P. Mirowski and E. Mirjam Sent (Eds), *Science: Bought and Sold* (Chicago: University of Chicago Press, 2002), pp.69–108.

Soros, G., *The Crisis of Global Capitalism* (London: Little Brown, 1998).

Stelfox, H., G. Chua, K. O Rourke and A. Detsky, 'Conflict of Interest in the Debate Over Calcium Channel Antagonists'. *New England Journal of Medicine*, 338, 2 (8 January 1998), pp.101–6.

Stigler, G., 'Director's Law of Public Income Redistribution'. *Journal of Law and Economics*,13, 1 (1970), pp.1–10.

Stiglitz, J., *The Roaring Nineties: A New History of the World's Most Prosperous Decade* (New York: Norton, 2003).

——, *Globalization and Its Discontents* (New York and London: Norton, 2002).

Strategic Task Force Report on Alcohol, *Interim Report* (Dublin: Government Publications, 2002).

——, *Second Report* (Dublin: Government Publications, 2004).

Sulston, J. and G. Ferry, *The Common Thread* (London: Bantham Press, 2002).

Sweeney, P., *Selling Out* (Dublin: TASC, 2004).

Taylor, G., *Conserving the Emerald Tiger* (Galway: Arlen House, 2001).

Thomas, S., *Electricity Liberalisation: The End of the Beginning* (London: PSIRU, 2004).

Thompson, E.P., 'Time, Work Discipline and Industrial Capitalism', in *Customs in Common* (London: Merlin, 1991), pp.352–401.

Thompson, J., P. Baird and J. Downie, *Report of the Committee of Inquiry on the case involving Dr Nancy Olivieri, the Hospital for Sick Children, the University of Toronto and Apotex Inc* (Ottawa: Canadian Association of University Teachers, 2001).

Trouiller, P., O. Piero, E. Torreele, J. Orbinski, R. Laing and N. Ford, 'Drug Development for Neglected Diseases: A Deficient Market and a Public Health Failure'. *The Lancet*, 359, 9324 (22 June 2002), pp.2188–94.

Turrell, A., 'Nursing Homes: A Suitable Alternative to Hospital Care for Older People in the UK'. *Age and Aging*, 30, S3, (2001), pp.24–32.

Valdes, J., *Pinochet's Economists: The Chicago School in Chile* (Cambridge and New York: Cambridge University Press, 1995).

Washburn, J., *University Inc: The Corporate Corruption of American Higher Education* (New York: Basic Books, 2005).

Waters, L., *Enemies of Promise: Publishing, Perishing and the Eclipse of Scholarship* (Chicago: Prickly Paradigm Press, 2004).

Watt, J.M., R. Derzon, S. Renn, C. Schram, J. Hahn and G. Pillari, 'The Comparative Economic Performance of Investor Owned Chain and Non-For Profit Hospitals'. *New England Journal of Medicine*, 314, 2 (1986), pp.89–96.

Whittington, G.J., T. Kendall, P. Fonagy, D. Cottrell, A. Cotgrove and E. Boddington, 'Selective Serotin Re-uptake Inhibitors in Childhood Depression: Systematic Review of Published Versus Unpublished Data'. *The Lancet*, 363, 9418 (24 April 2004), pp.1341–5.

World Bank, *World Development Report: Knowledge for Development* (New York: Oxford University Press, 1999).

Wren, M., *Unhealthy State* (Dublin: New Island, 2003).

Wren, M., 'Health Spending and the Black Hole'. *ESRI Quarterly Economic Commentary*, (Autumn 2004), pp.1–23.

Zerzan, J., S. Stearns and L. Hanson, 'Access to Palliative Care and Hospice in Nursing Homes'. *Journal of American Medical Association*, 284,19 (15 November 2000), pp.2489–94.

Zucker, L.G., M.R. Darby and M.B. Brewer, 'Intellectual Human Capital and the Birth of US Biotechnology Enterprises'. *American Economic Review*, 88, 1 (March 1998), pp.290–306.

Index

An Ambition for Equality

Niall Crowley

An Ambition for Equality identifies and explores the different means by which we promote equality and combat discrimination. These means include equality legislation, equality institutions, equality mainstreaming and positive action measures. These elements make up what is referred to as a strategic framework for action on equality. The concept of equality is examined. Different levels of ambition for equality are identified in terms of liberal approaches to achieving equality and in terms of the pursuit of an equality of condition. A range of equality objectives are discussed as a necessary focus for a strategic framework for action on equality. Irish equality legislation includes the Employment Equality Acts and the Equal Status Acts. This book explores the casework under the legislation and casts a critical eye on the provisions in that legislation. The role and mandate of the Equality Authority under this equality legislation is also examined. As Chief Executive Officer of the Equality Authority, the author's work and experience provides the focus around which the implementation of Irish equality legislation and approaches to mainstreaming and targeting are examined. *An Ambition for Equality* mixes practical experience in the promotion of equality with an academic perspective on the core concepts in the field, developing a critical analysis of the progress seen in Ireland in the effective promotion of equality.

Justice in Controversy Series

2005   232 pages, tables
978 0 7165 3381 8   cloth   €65.00/£45.00/$79.50
978 0 7165 3382 5   paper   €25.00/£18.50/$29.50

Youth Justice in Ireland
Tough Lives, Rough Justice

Ursula Kilkelly
Foreword by **Fr Peter McVerry S.J.**

Juvenile justice in Ireland is in crisis. Kilkelly draws a picture of the juvenile offender in Ireland, aiming to: highlight the circumstances of offending children and their families, show the type and number of offences committed, identify and explore trends in juvenile offending, and consider the complexity of problems that such children face. The book sets out a comprehensive and critical analysis of the legislative and policy framework currently governing the operation of the juvenile justice system. This includes evaluating the continued use of the Children Act, 1908 and examining the extent to which the Children Act, 2001 has been implemented.

It critically evaluates the response of the legal system to juvenile offending in the light of the modern legislative framework and international best practice. In this context, the book adopts a critical approach to the operation of the juvenile justice system looking at the following elements: the Garda Diversion Scheme; the operation of the Children Court; custodial and non-custodial sanctions imposed on children, and the detention of children. In addition, the book considers the complex problems that such children present to the legal system. It compares cases of offending and non-offending children and examines the overlap between, and different approaches of the care and justice systems in this area. In this regard, it considers the approach taken by many children who have been forced to take High Court proceedings to have their needs met, and it contrasts this with the route most children take through the (criminal) Children Court. Throughout, the approach is one which challenges certain perceptions about juvenile offending and crime in Ireland, and the justice system's response to it.

Justice in Controversy Series

2006   304 pages
978 0 7165 2836 4   cloth   €55.00/£37.50/$65.00
978 0 7165 3348 1   paper   €27.50/£20.00/$30.00

The Blame Game
Rethinking Ireland's Sustainable Development and Environmental Performance

Brendan Flynn

It examines the evolution of Irish environmental policy over the so-called 'Celtic Tiger' years of Ireland's economic boom while looking to the future as well. It considers why Ireland's environmental performance has been so lacklustre during this period, and what scope exists for improvement. The emphasis is placed primarily on institutional aspects of Irish environmental policy. In particular, this book offers a strong critique of the current Irish style of reaching environmental decisions, an excessive dependence on legal instruments, and a weak Irish local government system. The author further argues that Ireland has developed an institutional style of policy-making that urgently needs reform. He suggests a number of discreet but related problems that need to be understood and addressed. These include an excessive adversarial style of interaction between environmentalists, the Irish state, and business–the 'blame game' described in the title. Also fatal is a complacency among the Irish policy elite, who have chosen to downplay environmental problems and continue to think of environmental policy as merely about corrective regulation, rather than adopting the wider and more ambitious vision of sustainable development.

Individual chapters cover a range of topics, and the book will appeal to readers interested in comparative environmental policy and politics, the role of institutions in environmental policy-making, or indeed anyone keen to understand the post 'Celtic Tiger' politics and society of an Ireland in transition.

Justice in Controversy Series

2006   256 pages
978 0 7165 2839 5   cloth   €60.00/£37.50/$75.00
978 0 7165 3351 1   paper   €27.50/£19.50/$30.00

The Presumption of Innocence and Irish Criminal Law

Whittling the 'Golden Thread'

Claire Hamilton

Foreword by **Hon. Justice Adrian Hardiman**

The right to be presumed innocent until proven guilty has been described as the 'golden thread' running through the web of English criminal law and a 'fundamental postulate' of Irish criminal law which enjoys constitutional protection. Reflecting on the bail laws in the O'Callaghan case, Walsh J. described the presumption as a 'very real thing and not simply a procedural rule taking effect only at the trial'. The purpose of this book is to consider whether the reality matches the rhetoric surrounding this central precept of our criminal law and to consider its efficacy in the light of recent or proposed legislative innovations. Considerable space is devoted to the anti-crime package introduced by the government in the period of heightened concern about crime which followed the murder of journalist Veronica Guerin. Described by the Bar Council as 'the most radical single package of alterations to Irish criminal law and procedure ever put together', the effect of the package was an amendment of the bail laws and the introduction of preventative detention; a curtailment of the right to silence for those charged with serious drugs offences and the introduction of a novel civil forfeiture process to facilitate the seizure of the proceeds of crime, a development which arguably circumvents the presumption. Given these developments, the question posed in the book is whether we can lay claim to a presumption that is more than merely theoretical or illusory.

Justice in Controversy Series

2007   256 pages   illus
978 0 7165 3407 5   cloth   €60.00/£37.50/$65.00
978 0 7165 3408 2   paper €27.50/£20.00/$30.00

Single Europe, Single Ireland?
Uneven Development in Process

James Goodman

The national conflict in Ireland has created, and feeds off, sharply uneven development between the island's north and south. This is reflected in a history of diverging socio-economic interests, conflicting ideological positions and divided institutions, which date back to the mid-nineteenth century. Since the 1950s this unevenness has been reversed, first through economic convergence, and with increasing intensity, through ideological and institutional reorientations. Integration in the European Union's 'Single Market' has greatly accelerated this process, to the extent that the need for stronger north–south linkages has almost reached the status of conventional wisdom, north and south.

Single Europe, Single Ireland? outlines this process of reversing uneven development providing a historical account of the conflict, emphasising its north–south dimensions. This gives an essential backdrop to discussions of socio-economic interests, party-political positions and state policies, north and south. Across these issue areas, the process of EU integration is linked to the wider process of convergence in Ireland. This is set against on-going divisions and divergences, leading to the conclusion in the book that north–south linkages require concerted state action and guidance.

2000   208 pages
978 0 7165 2646 9   cloth   €47.50/£37.50/$52.50
978 0 7165 2647 6   paper   €25.00/£18.50/$27.50

Ireland's Shannon Story

Leaders, Visions and Networks:
A Case Study in Local and Regional Development

Brian Callanan

This book covers one of Ireland's most significant single development efforts in the twentieth century. Beginning with the early era in the 1940s the book explains how the Shannon Airport experiment originated through local effort spurred by sympathetic political leaders. It developed into a multi-million pound enterprise in what was a remote location in the west of Ireland.

Callanan examines the early 1960s initiatives which were typified by experimentation, trial and error; they led to the growth of an industrial estate, a new town, and emerging tourist attractions. Many of these projects were first viewed with suspicion and hostility; stoic bureaucracy had to be overcome. These barriers were overcome by a strong local leadership, closely associated with national policy makers, together with a clear vision of what could be achieved and supported by personal contacts and networks between decision-makers.

The work draws out lessons that were learned by the inexperienced leaders from mistakes they made. General international conclusions indicate how development can be powered at local and regional level, linking the Shannon story to a wider development theory and practical experiences in other countries.

1999   260 pages
978 0 7165 2710 7   cloth   €65.00/£45.00/$75.00
978 0 7165 2643 8   paper   €27.50/£20.00/$35.00